Three Weeks in Paris

BARBARA TAYLOR BRADFORD

Three Weeks in Paris

LONDON NEW YORK SYDNEY TORONTO

This edition published 2002
by BCA
by arrangement with HarperCollins*Publishers*

CN 102942

This novel is entirely a work of fiction.
The names, characters and incidents portrayed in it are
the work of the author's imagination. Any resemblance to
actual persons, living or dead, events or localities is
entirely coincidental.

Typeset in Sabon by Palimpsest Book Production Limited,
Polmont, Stirlingshire

Printed and bound in Germany by
GGP Media, Pössneck

For Bob, truly a man for all seasons,
with all my love

Contents

PROLOGUE

On the rue Jacob the man shivered and turned up the collar of his overcoat. It was a bitter February day, icy from the wind that swept down from the Russian steppes and across the plains of Europe to hit Paris with a sharp blast.

The sky was a faded blue, the sun watery as it slanted across the rooftops, almost silvery in this cold northern light, and without warmth. But Paris was always beautiful, whatever the weather; even when it rained it had a special quality all of its own.

Spotting a cab he hailed it, and as it slowed to a standstill he got in quickly and asked the driver to take him to the post office. Once he was there he unwrapped the package of stamped envelopes, seventy-one in all, and dropped them, in small batches, into a letter box, then returned to the cab.

The man now gave the driver the address of the FedEx office, settled back against the seat, glancing out of the window from time to time. How happy he was to be back in the City of Light, but, nonetheless, he could not help wishing it were a little warmer today. There was a chill in his bones.

In the FedEx office the man filled in the appropriate labels and handed them over to the clerk along with the white envelopes. All were processed for delivery within the next twenty-four hours, their destinations four cities in distant far-flung corners of the world. Back in the taxi he instructed the driver to take him to the Quai Voltaire. Once there, he alighted and headed towards one of his favourite bistros on the Left Bank.

And as he walked, lost in his thoughts, he had no way of knowing that he had just set in motion a chain of events that would have far-reaching effects. Because of his actions lives were about to be changed irrevocably: and so profoundly they would never be the same again.

PART ONE

Les Girls

CHAPTER ONE

ALEXANDRA

I t was her favourite time of day. *Dusk*. That in-between hour before night descended when everything was softly muted, merging together. The twilight hour.

Her Scottish nanny had called it *the gloaming*. She loved that name, it conjured up so much, and even when she was a little girl she had looked forward to the late afternoon, that period just before supper. As she had walked home from school with her brother Tim, Nanny between them tightly holding on to their hands, she had always felt a twinge of excitement, an expectancy, as if something special awaited her. This feeling had never changed. It had stayed with her over the years, and wherever she was in the world dusk never failed to give her a distinct sense of anticipation.

She stepped away from her drawing table, and went across to the window of her downtown loft, peered out, looking towards the upper reaches of Manhattan. To Alexandra Gordon the sky was absolutely perfect at this precise moment . . . its colour a mixture of plum and violet toned down by a hint of smoky grey bleeding into a faded pink. The colours of antiquity, reminiscent of Byzantium and Florence and ancient Greece. And the towers and spires and skyscrapers of this great modern metropolis were blurred, smudged into a sort of timelessness; seemed of no particular period at this moment, inchoate images cast against that almost-violet sky.

Alexandra smiled. For as far back as she could remember she had believed that this time of day was magical. In the movie business, which she was occasionally a part of these days, dusk was actually *called* 'the Magic Hour'. Wasn't it odd that she herself had named it that when she was only a child?

Staring out across the skyline, fragments of her childhood came rushing back to her. For a moment she fell down into her memories . . . memories of the years spent growing up on the Upper East Side of this city . . . of a childhood filled with love and security and the most wondrous of times. Even though their mother had worked, still worked in fact, she and Tim had never been neglected by her, nor by their father. But it was her mother who was the best part of her, and, in more than one sense, she was the product of her mother. And not a bad product at that, she thought, continuing to stand in front of the picture window, lost in remembrances of times past.

Eventually she roused herself and went back to the drawing board, looked at the panel she had just completed. It was the final one in a series of six, and together they composed a winter landscape in the countryside.

She knew she had captured most effectively the essence of

a cold, snowy evening in the woods, and bending forward she picked up the panel and carried it to the other side of the studio, placed it on a wide viewing shelf where the rest of the panels were aligned. Staring intently at the almost complete set, she envisioned them as a giant-sized backdrop on the stage, which is what they would soon become. As far as she was concerned, the panels were arresting, and depicted exactly what the director had requested.

'I want to experience the cold, Alexa,' Tony Verity had told her at the first production meeting, after he had taken her through the play. 'I want to shiver with cold, crunch down into my overcoat, *feel* the icy night in my bones. Your sets must make me want to rush indoors, to be in front of a roaring fire.'

He *will* feel all that, she told herself, and stepped back, eyeing her latest work from a distance, objectively, her head on one side, thinking of the way she had created the panels in her imagination first. She had envisioned St Petersburg in winter, and then focused on an imaginary forest beyond that city.

In her mind's eye, the scenery had come alive, almost like a reel of film playing in her head . . . bare trees glistening with dripping icicles, drifts of new snow sweeping up between the trees like white dunes. White nights. White sky. White moon. White silence.

That was the mood she sought, had striven for, and wished to convey to the audience. And she believed she had accomplished that with these panels, which would be photographed later this week and then blown up for the stage.

She had not used any other colours except a hint of

grey and black for a few of the skeletal branches. Her final touch, and perhaps her most imaginative, had been a set of lone footprints in the snow. Footprints leading up between the trees, as if heading for a special, perhaps even secret destination. Enigmatic. Mysterious. Even troubling, in a way . . .

The sharp buzzing of the doorbell brought her head up sharply, and her concentration was broken. She went to the intercom on the wall, lifted the phone. 'Hello?'

'It's Jack. I know I'm early. Can I come up?'

'Yes, it's okay.' She pressed the button which released the street door, and then ran downstairs to the floor below in order to let him in.

A few seconds later Jack Wilton, bundled up in a black duffle coat, and carrying a large brown shopping bag, was swinging out of the lift, walking towards her down the corridor, a grin on his keen, intelligent face.

'Sorry if I'm mucking up your working day, but I was around the corner. At the Cromer Gallery with Billy Tomkins. It seems sort of daft to go home and then come back here later. I'll sit in a corner down here and watch CNN until you quit.'

'I just did,' she said, laughing. 'I've actually finished the last panel, Jack.'

'That's great! Congratulations.' As he stepped into the small foyer of her apartment he put down the shopping bag, reached for her, pulled her into his arms, and, stretching out his leg, he pushed the door closed with his booted foot.

He hugged her tightly, brought her closer, and as his lips brushed her cheek, then nuzzled her ear, she felt a tiny frisson, and this shivery feeling ran all the way down to her toes. There was an electricity between them that had been missing for ages. She was startled.

Seemingly, so was he. Jack pulled away, glanced at her quickly and then instantly brought his mouth to hers, kissing her deeply, passionately. After a second, he moved his mouth close to her ear, and murmured, 'Let's go and find a bed.'

She leaned back, looking up into his grey eyes, which were more soulful than ever at this moment. 'Don't be silly.' As she spoke a small, tantalizing smile touched her lips and her sparkling eyes were suddenly inviting.

'Silly? There's nothing silly about going to bed. I think it's a rather serious thing.' Throwing his duffle coat on the floor next to the shopping bag and putting his arm around her, he led her into the bedroom.

He stopped in the middle of the room and taking hold of her shoulders he turned her to face him, stared into her eyes, his own questioning. 'You went missing for a bit,' he said, sounding more English than ever.

She stared back at him, said nothing.

He tilted her chin, leaned down and kissed her lightly on the mouth. 'But I have the distinct feeling you're suddenly back.'

'I think so.'

'I'm glad, Lexi.'

'So am I,' she answered.

He smiled and led her towards the bed without another word. They sat down together side by side, and he began to unbutton her shirt; she tugged at his tweed jacket, and within seconds they were both undressed, stretched out on the bed.

Leaning over her, he asked, 'And where was it that you went?'

'Not sure. Fell into a deep pit with my work, I suppose.'

He nodded, understanding, since he was an artist and tended to do the same at times when he was painting. But he had really missed her, and her withdrawal, her remoteness had worried him. Now he brought his mouth down to her, his kisses tender.

Alexandra felt that frisson once more, and she began to shiver slightly under his touching and kissing. He continued to kiss her as he stroked her thigh, and she experienced a sudden rush of heat, a tingling between her legs.

Unexpectedly, she stiffened. Swiftly, he brought his mouth to her mouth; his tongue sought hers, slid alongside hers, and they shared a moment of complete intimacy.

And all the while he did not stop stroking her inner thigh and the centre of her womanhood, his fingers working gently but expertly. To him it soon seemed as though she was opening like a lush flower bursting forth under a warm sun.

When she began to gasp, he increased his pressure and speed, wanting her to reach a point of ecstasy. He loved this woman, and he wanted to bind her to him, and he wanted to make love to her now, be joined with her.

With great speed, he entered her, thrusting into her so forcefully she cried out. Sliding his hands under her buttocks, he lifted her up, drew her closer to him, calling out her name as he did. 'Come to me again, come with me, come where I'm going, Lexi!' he exclaimed, his voice harsh, rasping.

And so she did as he demanded, wrapped her legs around his back, let her hands rest lightly on his shoulders. Together they soared, and as he began to shudder against her, he told her over and over again how much he loved making love to her.

Afterwards, when they finally lay still, relaxed and depleted, he lifted the duvet up and covered them with it, then took her in his arms. He said against her hair, 'Isn't this as good as it gets?'

When she remained silent, he added, 'You know how good we are together . . .'

'Yes.'

'You're not going to go away from me again, are you?'

'No . . . it *was* the work, the pressure.'

'I'm relieved it wasn't me. That you weren't having second thoughts about me.'

She smiled. 'You're the best, Jack, the very best. Special . . . *unique*, actually.'

'Ah, flattery will get you everywhere.'

'I've just been there, haven't I?'

'Where?'

'*Everywhere*. With you . . . to some wonderful place.'

Pushing himself up on one elbow, he peered down at her in the dim light of the fading day, wondering if she were teasing him. Then he saw the intensity in her light green eyes, and he said softly, 'Let's make it permanent.'

Those lucid green eyes he loved widened. 'Jack . . . I don't know what to say . . .'

'Say yes.'

'Okay. Yes.'

'I'm talking marriage,' he muttered, a sudden edge to his voice. He focused all of his attention on her, his eyes probing.

'I *know* that.'

'Will you?'

'Will I what?' Now she was teasing him and enjoying doing so, as she usually did.

'Will you marry me?'

'Yes, I will.'

A slow, warm smile spread itself across his lean face, and he bent into her, kissed her forehead, her nose, her lips. Resting his head next to hers on the pillow, he continued, 'I'm glad. Really so *bloody* glad, Lexi, that you're going to be mine, all mine. Wow, this is great! And we'll have a baby or two, won't we?'

She laughed, happy that he was so obviously delirious with joy. 'Of course. You know what, maybe we just made one.'

'It's a possibility. But to be really sure, shall we try again?'

'You mean right now?'

'I do.'

'Can you?'

'Don't be so ridiculous, of course I can. Feel this.' Taking hold of her hand, he put it on him under the duvet. 'See what you do to me. And I'll always be ready to make babies with you, darling.'

'Then stop boasting and let's do it!' she exclaimed, sliding a leg over him, kissing him on the mouth. 'Let's do it all night, in fact. It's one of the things I love to do with you, Jack.'

'Don't you want dinner?' He raised a brow.

'Oh, who cares about food when we've something so important and crucial to do.'

He started to laugh. 'I care. But we don't have to venture out, my sweet. I brought dinner with me. In the shopping bag.'

'Oh, so you planned all this, did you? Very devious, you are, Jack Wilton. You wicked, sexy man. I might have known you came here to seduce me. To impregnate me.'

'Seduce you! What a bloody cheek! You've just displayed the most incredible example of splendid cooperation I've ever come across. As for impregnating you, you can bet your sweet ass I'm going to do that.'

They began to roar with laughter, hugging each other and rolling around on the bed, filled with hilarity and pleasure in each other, and the sheer happiness of being young and alive. But after a moment or two of this gentle horseplay, Jack's face turned serious, and he held Alexandra still. 'You're not going to change your mind, are you, Lexi?'

''Course not, silly.' She touched his cheek lightly, smiled seductively. 'Shall we get to it then . . . making babies, I mean.'

'Try and stop me –' he began and paused.

The shrilling of the intercom startled Alexandra, and nonplussed she stared at Jack. Then she scrambled off the bed, took a woollen dressing gown out of the wardrobe, and struggled into it as she ran to the foyer. Lifting the intercom phone, she said, 'Hello?'

'FedEx delivery for Ms Gordon.'

'Thanks. I'll buzz you in. I'm on the fourteenth floor.'

* * *

23

The carbon copy of the original label on the front of the FedEx envelope was so faint she could barely make out the name and address of the sender. In fact, the only part she could read was *Paris, France*.

She stood holding the envelope, a small furrow crinkling the bridge of her nose. And then her heart missed a beat.

From the doorway of the bedroom, Jack said, 'Who's it from? You look puzzled.'

'I can't make out the name. Best thing to do is open it, I suppose,' she replied, forcing a laugh.

'That might be a good idea.' Jack's voice was touched with acerbity.

She glanced across at him swiftly, detecting at once a hint of impatience . . . as if it were her fault their lovemaking had been interrupted by the FedEx delivery. But wishing to keep things on an even keel, to placate him, she exclaimed, 'Oh, it can wait!' Dropping the envelope on the small table in the foyer, she added, 'Let's go back to bed.'

'Naw, the mood's gone, ducks. I'm gonna take a quick shower, make a cuppa rosy lee, then start on dinner,' he answered her in a bogus Cockney accent.

She stood staring at him, biting her lip.

Observing the crestfallen expression in her eyes, Jack Wilton instantly regretted his truculent attitude. He softened, pulled her towards him, embraced her. 'I'm sorry, I *was* a bit snotty, Lexi. *Sorry, sorry, sorry*. Okay?' His eyes held hers, a brow lifted quizzically. 'Don't you see, I was put out . . . and you *know* why. I was all ready to make babies.' He grinned, kissed the tip of her nose. 'So . . .' He shrugged nonchalantly. 'Let's go and take a shower together.'

'I guess I ought to open –'

He cut her off. 'It'll wait.' Taking hold of her hand, he led her across to the bathroom and into the shower, turned on the taps, adjusted the temperature, held her close again as the water sluiced over their bodies.

Alexandra leaned against him, closed her eyes, thinking of the envelope she had left on the table. She was beginning to worry about it, anxiety-ridden and tense inside. She could well imagine who it was from. It could be only one person. And the thought terrified her.

But she was wrong.

A short while later, when she finally opened the envelope it was not a letter inside, as she had misguidedly believed, but an invitation. Her relief was enormous and the anxiety instantly dissipated.

She sat on the sofa in her living room, staring at it, and a smile broke through, lighting up her face. Leaping to her feet, she ran across the room to the kitchen, where Jack was cooking. 'Jack, it's an invitation. To a party. In Paris.'

Jack glanced up from the bowl of fresh tomatoes he was stirring, took a sip of his tea, and asked, 'Who's the party for then?'

'Anya. My wonderful Anya Sedgwick.'

'The woman who owns the school you went to . . . what's it called again? Ah yes, the Anya Sedgwick School of Decorative Arts.'

'That's right.'

'And what's the occasion –?'

'Her birthday.' Leaning against the door jamb, she began to read from the engraved invitation. 'The pleasure of your company is requested at a celebration in honour of Anya Sedgwick on the occasion of her eighty-fifth birthday. On Saturday June the second, 2001. At Ledoyen, Carré Champs Elysées, Paris. Cocktails at eight o'clock. Supper at nine o'clock. Dancing from ten o'clock on. Hey, isn't that great, Jack. Oh, how wonderful.'

'Sounds like it's going to be a super bash. Can you take a friend, do you think?'

Alexandra glanced at the invitation again. Her name had been written across the top in the most elegant calligraphy she had ever seen. But it was only *her* name. The words, *and guest*, were missing. 'I don't think I can. It has only my name on it. I'm sure it's just for her family and former pupils . . .' Alexandra's voice trailed off.

He was silent for a moment, concentrating as he finely chopped an onion. When he at last looked up, he asked, 'Are you going to go?'

'I'm not sure. I don't know. It all depends on work, I guess. I've only one small set to finish for *Winter Weekend*, and then that's it. I'll be out of work, if something doesn't pop up.'

'I'm sure it will, Lexi,' he reassured, glancing at her, smiling. 'Now scoot, and let me finish the pasta pomodoro, and before you can say Jack Robinson I'll have dinner for my lady.'

She laughed, said 'Okay,' and went back to the sofa, still holding the invitation in her hand. Seating herself, she stared at it for a moment longer, her mind on Anya Sedgwick, the woman who had been her teacher, mentor and friend. She had not seen her for a year. It would be lovely to be in her company again, to celebrate this important milestone in her life ... Paris in the spring. How truly glorious it would be ...

But Tom Conners was in Paris.

When she thought of him she found it hard to breathe.

CHAPTER TWO

Alexandra awakened with a start, and after a moment she sat up, blinking, adjusting her eyes in the darkness. The room was quiet, bathed in silence, but for a long moment she felt a presence, as if someone stood nearby, hovered close to the bed.

She remained still, breathing deeply, pushing the feeling away, knowing this was all it was . . . just a *feeling*, the sensation that he was with her in the room because her dream had been so very real.

But then it always was, whenever she dreamed it. Everything that happened had a validity to it, was vivid, lifelike; even now, as she rested against the pillows, she could smell him, smell his body, his hair, the cologne he used. Jicky by Guerlain. It seemed to her that even the taste of him lingered on her mouth, as if he had kissed her deeply.

Except that he had not been here tonight . . . only in the

dream, one so extraordinarily alive in her
awakening she had believed he truly was i~
But, of course, she was alone.

Suddenly knowing that sleep would be elus
the moment, Alexa sat up, switched on the bed
slid her long legs out of bed. As she glided across the floor,
she realized she was bathed in sweat, as she usually was after
this recurring dream.

Wrapping herself in her pale blue woollen dressing gown,
she hurried through the small front foyer and went into the
kitchen, snapping on lights as she did.

What she needed was a cup of tea. Camomile tea. It
would soothe her, encourage sleep. After filling the kettle
with water and putting it on the gas ring, she sat down on
the stool, contemplating the dream which she had with such
regularity.

The odd thing was, the dream was always exactly the
same. Nothing ever changed. He was suddenly there with
her, either coming through the door or standing by the bed
looking down at her. And inevitably he slid into bed, made
love to her, cradling her in his arms, telling her he missed
her, wanted her, needed her. And always he reminded her
that she was the love of his life. His one true love.

And the dream was rooted in such uncanny reality she was
invariably shaken; even her body felt as if it had been invaded
by a sensual and virile man. It was, she muttered under her
breath, filling the mug with boiling hot water. At least it was
this afternoon. Jack Wilton made love to me when he arrived
here today . . . in the gloaming he loved me well.

Yes, a small voice said in her head, but in the dream you

...had it was Tom Conners loving you. It's never anybody else but Tom Conners in the dream, and that's your basic problem.

Sighing to herself, Alexa turned on a lamp and sat down in the comfortable, overstuffed chair near the fireplace, sipping the camomile tea, staring into the dying embers of the log fire.

What was wrong with her? The question hovered over her like a black cloud.

She had made love with Jack and enjoyed every moment of it, and there had been this unexpected and wonderful renewal of passion between them, a passion sadly absent for months. To excuse this she had blamed tiredness, work, the pressure and stress of designing sets at top speed for the new play. But in all truthfulness, something else had been at play. Exactly what that was she wasn't sure. She had pulled away from having sex with Jack, had avoided it. There had been a strange reluctance in her to be intimate with him, and she had mentally recoiled. But why? He was appealing, attractive, good-looking in a quiet way, and had a very endearing personality. He was even funny, made her laugh.

So many images invaded her, bounced around in her head, and conflicting thoughts jostled for prominence in her mind. She closed her eyes for a moment, trying to sort them out. Suddenly she sat up straighter, and thought: My God, I agreed to marry Jack! In effect, I'm engaged to him!

This was no joke as far as he was concerned. He was very serious. He had gone on talking about getting married over dinner, constantly touching his glass of red wine to hers, and they had laughed together, flirted, been in tune on all levels.

Whilst they hadn't exactly settled on a date, she had sort of acquiesced when he had talked about a winter wedding at the end of the year. 'In New York. A proper wedding,' he had insisted. 'With your family and mine, and all the trimmings. That's what I want, Lexi.' And she had nodded in agreement.

Once dinner was over, he had helped her stack the dishwasher, and then they had gone to bed. But he had left at five, kissing her cheek and whispering that he wanted to get an early start on a large canvas for his upcoming show.

As for her, she had dreamed about another man, and in the most intimate way possible at that. *Was* there something wrong with her? This wasn't normal, was it?

Despite the camomile tea and its so-called soothing properties, she was suddenly wide awake. Glancing at the small brass carriage clock on the mantelpiece she saw that it was already ten past six in the morning.

Ten past twelve in Paris.

On an impulse, before she could change her mind and stop herself, she lifted the phone on the side table and dialled his office number, his direct line. Within a split second the number in Paris was ringing.

And then he answered. '*Allo.*'

She clutched the phone tighter. She couldn't speak. She could barely breathe. She heard an impatient sound from him, and then he spoke again.

'Tom Conners *ici.*' Then again, this time in English, he said, 'Hello? This is Tom Conners. Who is this?'

Very carefully she replaced the receiver. Her hands were damp and shaking, and her heart was thudding unreasonably in her chest. What a fool she was to do this to herself. She took several deep breaths, leaned against the cushions in the chair, staring off into space.

He was there. In his office. He was still in Paris. He was alive and well.

And if she went to Paris, to Anya Sedgwick's birthday party, she would do exactly what she had just done now. She wouldn't be able to resist. She would call him, and he would say let's have a drink, because he was like that, and she would say yes, that's great, and she would go and have a drink with him. And in consequence of that she would be genuinely lost. Floundering about once more. Yes, a lost soul.

Because to her Tom Conners was devastatingly irresistible, a man so potent, so compelling he lived with her in her thoughts, and in her heart and mind – if not all the time, for a good part of it.

Even though they had stopped seeing each other three years ago, and he had been the one to break it off, she knew that if she spoke to him he would want to see her.

But she couldn't see him. Because she was afraid of him. Afraid of what would happen to her if she fell under his mesmeric spell once again.

You're such an idiot, she chastised herself. Anger flooded her. It was an anger at herself and her lingering emotional involvement with Tom Conners. And she knew it had been foolish to make that call, even though she hadn't spoken to him. Just hearing that arresting, mellifluous voice of his had truly unnerved her.

Alexa now forced herself to focus on Jack Wilton. He loved her, wanted to make her his wife, and she had actually accepted his proposal. All that aside, he was a truly decent human being, a good man, honourable, kind, loving, and generous to a fault sometimes. His success had not spoiled him, and he was very down-to-earth in that humorous English way of his, not taking either himself or life too seriously. 'Only my work must be taken seriously,' he was forever telling her, and she understood exactly what he meant by that.

She knew he adored her, admired her talent as a designer, applauded her dedication and discipline. He encouraged her, comforted her when she needed comforting, and he was always there for her. And the truth was he had stayed in the relationship and had been exceedingly patient with her even when she had been cool towards him physically these last few months.

What's more her parents liked him. A good sign, since they'd always been very critical when it came to her boy-friends. Not picky about Tom Conners, because he'd charmed them without trying. But then again, they had never really known him, nor had they actually understood the extent of her involvement with him, because their relationship had evolved after she had left Anya's school in Paris.

Jack would make a wonderful husband, she decided. He loved her, and she loved him. In her own way.

Alexandra pushed herself up out of the chair very purpose-fully, and, turning off the lamp, she went back to bed. Jack Wilton was going to be her husband and that was that.

Sadly, she would have to forgo Anya's eighty-fifth birthday party. For her own self-protection.

CHAPTER THREE

S eated at the mahogany table in the elegant dining room of her parents' apartment on East Seventy-Ninth Street, Alexandra was savouring the tomato omelette her mother had just made, thinking how delicious it was. Hers inevitably turned into a runny mess, despite having had her mother, the best chef in the world, to teach her over the years.

'This is great, Mom,' she said after a moment, 'and thanks for making time for me today. I know you like to have your Saturdays to yourself.'

'Don't be so silly, I'm glad you're here,' Diane Gordon answered, glancing up, smiling warmly. 'I was just about to call you this morning, to see what you were doing, when the phone rang and there you were, wanting to have lunch.'

Alexa returned her mother's smile and asked, 'When's Dad getting back from the Coast?'

'Tuesday, he said. But it could be Friday. *You* know what the network is like. You grew up with networks and their schedules, lived by them when you were a child.'

'And how!' Alexa exclaimed. 'I suppose Dad's going to see Tim this weekend.'

'Yes, they're having dinner tonight. Dad's taking him to Morton's.'

'Tim'll love that, it's his favourite place in LA. I guess he's going to stay out there after all. When I spoke to him last week he sounded very high on Los Angeles, and his new job at NeverLand Productions. He told me he was born to be a movie maker.'

Diane laughed. 'Well, I suppose that's true. Remember what he was like when he was a kid, always wanting to go with your father to the television studios, to be on the set. And let's not forget that Grandfather Gordon was a very highly thought of stage director for many years. Show business is in Tim's blood, more than likely.' Diane took a sip of water, then asked her daughter, 'Do you want a glass of wine, darling?' a blonde brow lifting questioningly.

'No, thanks, Mom, not during the day. It makes me sleepy. Anyway, it's fattening . . . all that sugar. I prefer to take my calories in bread.' As she spoke she reached for a piece of the baguette, which her mother had cut up earlier and placed in a silver bread basket. She spread it generously with butter and took a bite.

'You don't have to worry about your weight, you know. You look marvellous, really well,' Diane remarked, eyeing her daughter. She couldn't help thinking how young she looked for her age. It didn't seem possible that Alexandra was *thirty*. In fact, in the summer she would be thirty-one, and it seemed like only yesterday that she was a toddler running around her feet. My God, when I was her age I had two children, Diane thought, and a husband to look after, and a growing business to run. *Thirty-one*, she mused, and in May *I'll* be *fifty-eight*. How time flies, just disappears. Where have all the years gone? David will be fifty-nine in June. What is even more incredible is our marriage. It's lasted so long, so many years, and it's still going strong. A record of sorts, isn't it?

'Mom, what *are* you pondering? You're looking very strange. Are you okay?' Alexa probed.

'I'm fine. I was just thinking about your father. And our marriage. It's amazing that we've been married for thirty-three years. And what's even more staggering is that the years seem to have passed in a flash. Just like that.' She snapped her fingers together and shook her head in sudden bemusement.

'You two have been lucky,' Alexa murmured, 'so lucky to have found each other.'

'That's absolutely true.'

'You and Dad, you're like two peas in a pod. Did you start out being so alike? Or did you *grow* to resemble each other? I've often wondered that, Mom.' Her head on one side, she gazed at her mother, thinking how beautiful she was, probably one of the most beautiful women she had ever seen, with her peaches-and-cream skin, her pale golden hair and those extraordinary liquid blue eyes.

'You're staring, Alexa. You're going to see all my wrinkles!'

'Oh Mom, you don't have one single wrinkle. I kid you not, as Dad says.'

Diane laughed, and murmured, 'As for you, my girl, you don't look a day over twenty-five. It's hard for me to believe you'll be thirty-one in August.'

'It's my new short haircut. It takes years off me.'

'I guess it does. But then short hair makes most women look younger, perkier. And it's certainly the chic cut this year.'

'You once told me short hair was the only chic style, and that no woman could be elegant with hair trailing around her shoulders. And you should know, since you're considered one of the chicest women in New York, if not *the* chicest.'

'Oh, I'm not really, but thanks for the compliment. Although I should point out that the whole world suspects you're a bit prejudiced.'

'Everyone, the press included, cites *you* as a fashion icon, a legend in your own time. And your boutiques have been number one for years now.'

'We've *all* worked hard to make them what they are, not only me, Alexa. Anyway, what about you, darling? Have you finally finished those winter sets?'

Alexa's face lit up. 'I completed the last one of the snow forest earlier this week, on Tuesday actually. Yesterday I saw blow-ups of them all at the photographic studio, and they're great, Mom, even if I do say so myself.'

'I've told you many times, don't hide your light under a bushel, darling. It doesn't do to brag, of course, but there's nothing wrong in knowing that you're good at what you do.

You're very talented, and personally I was bowled over by the panels I saw.' Diane's pale blue eyes, always so expressive, rested on her daughter thoughtfully. After a moment, she said, 'And so . . . what's next for you?'

'I have one small set to do for this play and after that my contract's fulfilled.' Alexa laughed a little hollowly, and added, 'Then I'll be out of work, I guess.'

'I doubt that,' Diane shot back, the expression on her face reflecting her pride in her only daughter. 'Not you.'

'To be honest, I'm not worried. Something'll turn up. It always does.'

Diane nodded, and then her eyes narrowed slightly. 'You said on the phone that you wanted to talk to me. What –'

'Can we do that later, over coffee?' Alexa cut in swiftly.

'Yes, of course, but is there something wrong? You sounded worried earlier.'

'Honestly, there's nothing wrong. I just need . . . a sounding board, a really good one, and you're the very best I know.'

'Is this about Jack?'

'No, and now you're sounding like all those other mothers, which most of the time you don't, thank God. And *no*, it's not about Jack.'

'Don't be so impatient with me, Alexa, and by the way, Jack Wilton is awfully nice.'

'I *know* he is, and he feels the same way about you. And Dad.'

'I'm glad to hear it. But how does he feel about *you*? That's much more important.'

'He cares.'

38

'Your father and I think he would make a good – a very nice son-in-law.'

Alexa did not respond.

Half an hour later Alexandra sat opposite her mother in the living room, watching her as she poured coffee into fine bone-china cups. She was studying Diane through objective eyes, endeavouring to see her as clearly as possible. It suddenly struck her, and most forcibly, what a unique person she was, a woman who was savvy, smart, successful, and highly intelligent as well. And she really did understand human frailties and foibles, because her perception and insight were well honed, and she was compassionate. But would she comprehend *her* dilemma, a dilemma centred on two men?

After all, there had only been one man in her mother's life, as far as she knew, and that man was her father, who Diane Carlson had met at twenty-four and married within the year; they had been utterly devoted to each other ever since. I know she'll understand, Alexandra reassured herself. She's not prudish or narrow-minded, and she never passes judgement on anybody. But how to tell her my story. Where do I begin?

It was as though Diane had read her daughter's mind, when she announced, 'I'm ready to listen, Alexa, whenever you want to start. And whatever it's about, you'll have all my attention and the best advice I can give.'

'I know that, Mom,' Alexa answered, adding, 'Thanks,' as she accepted the cup her mother was passing to her. She put it down on the low antique table between them, and settled back against the Venetian velvet cushions on the cream sofa. After a second or two, she explained, 'Late yesterday afternoon I got an invitation to go to a party in Paris. For Anya. She's going to be eighty-five.'

A huge smile spread across Diane's face, and she exclaimed, 'Good Lord, I can't believe it! She's a miracle, that woman.'

'Oh, I know she is, and aside from looking so much younger than her age, she's full of energy and vitality. Whenever I speak to her on the phone she sounds as busy as ever, running the school, entertaining and travelling. Only last month she told me she's started writing another book, one on Art Deco. She's just so amazing.'

'I'll say she is, and what a lovely trip for you. When is the party?'

'On June second, at Ledoyen. It's a supper dance, actually.'

'That'll be fun, we must find you something pretty to wear. Is it black tie?'

'Yes, it is, but look, Mom, I'm not sure that I'm going to go.'

Diane was startled, and she frowned. 'Whyever not? You're close to Anya, and you've always been a special favourite of hers. Certainly more than the others –' Diane stopped abruptly, and stared at her daughter. 'But of course! That's *it*. You don't want to go because you don't want to see the other three. I can't say I blame you, they turned out to be rather treacherous, those women.'

With a small jolt, Alexandra realized that she hadn't even thought about her former best girlfriends, who had ended up her enemies. She had been focused only on Tom Conners, and her feelings for him. But now, all of a sudden, she realized she must throw them into the equation, along with Tom. Her mother was quite right, they were indeed an excellent reason she should stay away from Paris. They were bound to be at the party . . . Anya would have invited them as well as her . . . together the four of them had been her greatest pride the year of their graduation . . . her star pupils. Of course they'd be there . . . with bells on.

'You're right, Mom, I have no desire to see them,' Alexa said. 'But they're not the reason I don't want to go to Paris. It's something else, as a matter of fact.'

'And what's that?'

'His name's Tom Conners.'

Diane was momentarily perplexed. The name rang a bell but she couldn't pinpoint the man. She leaned forward slightly, her eyes narrowing. *'Tom Conners.* Do I know him? Oh yes, now it's coming back to me. Isn't he the Frenchman you introduced to us a few years ago?'

'That's right, but Tom's *half* French, *half* American. If you remember, I did tell you about his family. His father's an American who went to live in Paris in the early fifties, married a French girl and stayed. Tom was brought up and educated there, and he's always lived in France.'

'Yes, so I recall, darling. He's a lawyer, if I remember correctly, and very good-looking. But I didn't realize there was anything serious between the two of you. I thought it was a brief encounter, a sort of fling, if you like, and that it was over quickly.'

'It lasted almost two years, actually.'

'I see.' Diane sat back, wondering how she had missed this particular relationship. On the other hand, that was the period Alexa had lived in Paris, working with Anya's two nephews in films and the theatre. However, her daughter had certainly kept awfully quiet about Tom Conners, had confided nothing. Odd, really, now that she thought about it. She said slowly, 'Somehow you're still involved with Tom Conners, I think. Is that what you're trying to say?'

'No . . . Yes . . . No . . . Look, Mom, we don't see each other any more, and I never hear from him, he's never in touch, but he's sort of there . . . inside me, in my thoughts . . .' Her voice trailed off lamely and she gave her mother a helpless look.

'Why did you break off with him, Alexa?' Diane asked curiously.

'I didn't. He did. Three years ago now.'

'But *why*?' her mother pressed.

'Because I wanted to get married, and he couldn't marry me.'

'Is he married already?'

'No. Not now, not then.'

'I'm not following this at all. It doesn't make sense to me. I just don't understand what the problem is,' Diane murmured, her bafflement only too apparent.

Alexa hesitated, wondering if she could bear to tell her mother Tom's story. It was so painful, harrowing. But when she glanced at her mother's face and saw the worry settling there, she decided she had no option. She wanted her to understand . . .

Very softly, Alexa said, 'Tom was married very young, Mother, to his childhood sweetheart, Juliette. They grew up together, and their parents were friends. They had a little girl, Marie-Laure, and seemingly, from what he told me, they were an idyllic couple . . . the poster couple, I guess. Very beautiful, very happy together. And then something bad happened . . .'

Alexa paused, drew a deep breath, and continued, 'In July of 1985 they went to Athens. On vacation. But Tom also had to see a client from Paris, who owned a summer house there. Towards the end of the vacation, Tom arranged a final meeting with his client before he took his family back to Paris. That morning he told Juliette he would meet her and Marie-Laure for lunch at their favourite café, but Tom was delayed and got there a bit late. It was chaotic when he walked into the square where the café was located. Police cars and ambulances were converging in the centre, and the human carnage was horrendous. People were dead and dying, there was blood and body parts everywhere, as if a massacre had taken place. The police told Tom that a bomb had exploded only minutes before his arrival, more than likely a terrorist's bomb that had been planted on one of those big tour buses, this particular one filled with Americans from the hotel in the square. About sixty people were on the bus, and they all died.

'As the bus was leaving the square it suddenly blew up, right in front of the café where Juliette and Marie-Laure were waiting for Tom. The impact of the blast was enormous. People sitting at the various cafés around the square were blown right out of their chairs. Many were killed or injured . . .' Alexa stopped, and it was a moment before she could continue.

After taking several deep breaths, she went on: 'Tom couldn't find Juliette and Marie-Laure, and as you can imagine he was worried and frightened, frantic as he searched for them. He did find them eventually, under the rubble in the back of the café . . . the ceiling had collapsed on them. They were both dead.' Alexandra blinked, and her voice was so low it was almost inaudible as she finished, 'Don't you see, he's never recovered from that . . . that . . . *nightmare*.'

Diane was staring at Alexandra in horror and tears had gathered in her light blue eyes. 'How horrendous, what a terrible, terrible tragedy to happen to them, to him,' she murmured, and then looking across at her daughter, she saw that Alexa's face was stark, taut, drained of all colour.

Rising, she went and sat next to her on the sofa, put her arm around her and held her close. 'Oh darling, you're still in love with him . . .'

'Am I? I'm not sure, Mother, but he does occupy a large part of me, that's true. He's there, inside, and he always will be, I think. But I'm smart enough to know I have no future with Tom. He'll never marry me, or anybody else, for that matter. Nor will he have a permanent relationship, because he can't. You see, he just can't forget *them*.'

'Or he won't let himself forget,' Diane suggested softly.

'Perhaps that's true. Perhaps he thinks that if he forgets them he'd be riddled with guilt for the rest of his life and wouldn't be able to handle it. You brought me up to be sensible, practical, and I believe I am those things. And after we broke up, I knew I had to get on with my life . . . I knew I couldn't moon around yearning for Tom. I understood there was no future in that.'

Diane nodded. 'You were right, and I think you've managed to get on with your professional life extremely well. I'm proud of you, Alexa, you didn't let your personal problems get in the way of your career. All I can say is bravo.'

'You once told me years ago that I must never negate my talent by not using it, by wasting it, and I listened to you, Mom. I also knew I had to earn a living, I wasn't going to let you and Dad support me, especially after you'd sent me to such expensive schools, Anya's in particular.'

Diane nodded. 'Just as a matter of interest, how old is he? Tom, I mean.'

'He's forty-two, Mom.'

Diane nodded, searched her daughter's face intently and wondered, 'Do you love Jack Wilton a little bit at least?'

'Yes, I do love him, in a certain way.'

'Not the way you love Tom?' Diane ventured.

'No.'

'You could make a life with Jack, though?'

Alexandra nodded. 'I think so. Jack's got a lot going for himself. He's very attractive and charming, and we get on well. We're compatible, he makes me laugh, and we understand each other, understand where we're both coming from, which is sometimes the same place. We admire each other's talents, and respect each other.' She half-smiled at her mother. 'He loves me, you know. He wants to marry me.'

'Would you marry him?' Diane asked quietly, hoping for an answer in the affirmative.

Alexa leaned against her mother, and a deep sigh escaped

her. Unexpectedly, tears spilled out of her eyes. Then she swiftly straightened, flicked the tears away with her fingertips. 'I thought I could, Mom, I really did. But now I don't know. Ever since that invitation arrived yesterday, I've been in a turmoil.'

'You won't be able to resist seeing Tom if you go to Paris, is that what you're telling me?'

'I guess I am.'

'But you're stronger than that . . . you've always been strong, even when you were a little girl.'

Alexa was silent.

After a short while, Diane said slowly, carefully, 'Here's what your loving and very devoted sounding board thinks. You have to forget Tom, as you know you should. You must put him out of your mind once and for all. He's not for you, Alexa, or anybody else, in my opinion. What happened to his wife and child was unbearable, very, very tragic, and so heart-rending. But it *was* years ago. Sixteen years ago, to be precise. And if he's not over it by now –'

'He wasn't over it three years ago, but I don't know about now –'

'– then he never will be,' Diane continued in a very firm voice. 'Your life is here in New York, not in Paris. For the most part, your work is here, and you know you can make a wonderful life with Jack. And that's what you should do . . .' Diane stopped, tightened her embrace, and said against her daughter's glossy dark hair, 'There are all kinds of love, you know. Degrees of love. And sometimes the great love of one's life is not meant to last . . . perhaps that's how it becomes the *great love* . . . by ending.' Diane sighed, but after a moment she went on, 'I know it's hard to give someone up. But, in fact, Tom Conners gave you up, Alexa. Not vice versa, so why torture yourself. My advice to you is not to go to Paris. That way you won't be tempted to see Tom, and open up all those wounds.'

'I guess you're right, Mom. You usually are. But Anya's going to be really upset if I don't go to the party.'

'I'm sure she will be.' There was a slight pause, and then Diane exclaimed, 'There *is* an alternative! You and Jack could go to Paris together. Obviously, you couldn't go looking for Tom if you were there with another man.'

Want to bet? Alexandra thought, but said, 'The invitation doesn't include a guest. Only my name is written on it. And I'm sure Anya's only invited former pupils and her family.'

'But she wouldn't refuse *you* . . . not if you said you were coming to Paris with your . . . fiancé.'

'I don't know what she'd do, actually. I have to think about that, Mom, all of what you've just said . . . and implied.'

The invitation stood propped up on the mantelpiece next to the carriage clock, and the first thing Alexandra did when she got home was to pick it up and read it again.

Down in the left-hand corner, underneath the initials rsvp was the date of the deadline to accept or decline: *April the first 2001*. And in the opposite right-hand corner it said: *Black Tie*, and underneath this: *Long Dress*. All the information she needed was right there, including what to wear; attached to the engraved invitation with a paperclip was a small rsvp card, and an envelope addressed to a Madame Suzette Laugen at 158 Boulevard St Germain, Paris.

So, she had the rest of February and most of March to make up her mind, to think about Anya's birthday and decide what to do, whether to go or not. That was a relief. But she knew she would spend the next few weeks vacillating.

Deep down she wanted to go, wanted to celebrate this special birthday with Anya, an extraordinary woman who had had such an enormous influence on her life. But there was the problem of Tom Conners, and also of her former friends . . . Jessica, Kay and Maria. Three woman once so close to her, and she to them, that they were inseparable, but they were sworn enemies now. She couldn't bear the thought of seeing any of them.

April the first, she mused. An anniversary of sorts, since she had met Tom Conners on April the first. In 1996. She had been twenty-five, he thirty-seven.

April Fool, she thought, with a wry smile. But she wasn't sure if she meant herself or him.

Placing the invitation back on the mantel, she knelt down in front of the fireplace, struck a match and brought it to the paper and small chips of wood stuffed in the grate. Within minutes she had the fire going, the logs catching alight quickly, the flames leaping up the chimney.

Pushing herself to her feet, Alexandra turned on a lamp. Along with the fire it helped to bring a warm, roseate glow to the living room, already shadowed as it was by the murky winter light of late afternoon. She felt tired. After leaving her mother, she had walked all the way down Park Avenue from Seventy-Ninth Street to Thirty-Ninth. Forty blocks of good exercise, but she had finally given in and taken a cab back to the loft.

After glancing out of the window at the lights of Manhattan slowly coming on, Alexa sat down on the sofa in front of the fire, staring into the flames flickering and dancing in the grate. Her mind was awash with so many diverse thoughts, but the most prominent were centred on Tom.

It was Nicky Sedgwick who had introduced them, when Tom had come out to the studios in Billancourt to see his client Alain Durand, who was producing the movie. It was a French-American co-production, very elaborate and costly. Nicky and his brother Larry were the Art Directors and were designing the sets, and at Anya's suggestion they had hired her as their assistant. But she had become more like an associate, because of all the work and responsibility they had heaped on her.

What a challenge the movie had been, and what a lot she had learned. It was a historical drama about Napoleon and Josephine in the early part of their relationship, and Nicky, who was in charge, was a stickler for historical accuracy and detail. Even now, when she thought of the endless hours she had spent at Malmaison she still cringed. She had taken countless notes, knew that house inside out, and had often wondered why the famous couple had ever lived there. Its parkland and closeness to Paris, she supposed. Nicky had been thrilled with her . . . with her work, her overall input, and most of all with her set designs. In general, it had been a positive experience, and she worked on most of their films and plays after that, until she left Paris.

The day Tom Conners came out to the studios shooting

was going well, and Alain Durand had been elated. He and Tom had invited the Sedgwick brothers to dinner when they wrapped for the day, and she had been included in the invitation since Anya's nephews had by then adopted her, in a sense.

She had been struck dumb by Tom's extraordinary looks, his charm and sophistication. So much so, she had felt like a little schoolgirl with him. But he had treated her as a grown-up, with gallantry and grace, and she had been smitten with him before the dinner was over. Later that night she found herself in his arms in his car after he drove her home; two nights later she was in his bed.

'Spontaneous combustion,' he had called it; not very long after this he had said it was a *coup de foudre*, clap of thunder, love at first sight. Which they both knew it was.

But that easy charm and effortless grace hid a difficult man of many moods, a man who was burdened down by the needless deaths of his wife and child, and by an acute sorrow he was so careful to hide in public.

Nicky had teased her about Tom at times, and once he had said, 'I suppose women must find his dark Byronic moods sexy, appealing,' and had thrown her an odd look. She knew what he was hinting at, but Tom was not acting. He really was in pain. But it was Larry who had been the one to warn her. 'He comes to you dragging a lot of baggage behind him, emotional baggage,' Larry had pointed out. 'So watch out, and protect your back. He's lethal, a dangerous man.'

Alexa stretched out on the sofa. Her thoughts stayed with Tom and their days together in Paris. Despite his moodiness, those awful bouts of sadness, their relationship had always been good, even ecstatic when he shed the burdens of his past. And it had only ended because she had wanted permanence with him. Marriage. Children.

She wondered about him sometimes, wondered who he was with, how his life was going, what he was doing. Still suffering occasionally, she supposed. She hadn't been able to convey to her mother the extent of that. She hadn't even tried. It was too hard to explain. You had to live through it with him to understand.

He was forty-two now, and still unmarried, she felt certain of that. What a waste, she thought, and closed her eyes, suddenly craving sleep. She wanted to forget . . . to forget Tom and her feelings for him, forget those days in Paris . . . she was never going back there. Not even for Anya Sedgwick's eighty-fifth birthday.

CHAPTER FOUR

KAY

I remember dancing with him here, right in the centre of this room, under the chandelier, she thought, and moved forward from the doorway where she had been standing.

Her arms outstretched, as if she were holding a man, Kay Lenox turned and whirled to the strains of an old-fashioned waltz which was playing only in her head. Humming to herself, she moved with rhythm and gracefulness, and the expression on her delicately moulded face was for a fleeting moment rhapsodic, lost as she was in her thoughts.

Memories flooded her.

Memories of a man who had loved and cherished her, a man who had been an adoring lover and husband, a man she was still married to but who no longer seemed quite the same. He had changed, and even though the change in him was minuscule, she had spotted it from the moment it had happened.

He denied her charge that he was different in his behaviour towards her, insisting she was imagining things. But she knew she was not. There had been a cooling off in him; it was as if he no longer loved her quite as much as before.

Always attentive and solicitous, he now appeared to be distracted, was even occasionally careless, forgetting to tell her if he planned to work late or attend a business dinner, or some other such thing. He would phone her at the very last minute, giving no thought to her or any plans she might have, leaving her high and dry for the evening. Although she seethed inside she said nothing; she was always patient, understanding and devoted.

Kay had never believed it possible that a man like Ian Andrews would marry her. But he had. Their courtship had been idyllic, and so had the first two and a half years of their marriage, which had been, for her, like a dream come true.

And these were the memories which assailed her now, held her in their thrall as she moved around the room, swaying, floating, circling, as if in another kind of dream. And as she danced with him, he so alive in her head and her heart, she recalled his boyishness, his enthusiasm for life, his gallantry and charm. He had swept her off her feet and into marriage within a month of their first meeting. Startled though she was, she had not objected; she had been as madly in love with him as he was with her. Besides, it also suited her purpose to marry him quickly. She had so much to hide.

A discreet cough intruded, brought her out of her reverie and to a standstill. She glanced at the door, feeling embarrassed to be caught dancing alone, and gave Hazel, the cook at Lochcraigie, a nervous half smile.

'Sorry to intrude, Lady Andrews, but I was wondering about dinner . . .' The cook hesitated, looking at her steadily, and then finished in a low voice, 'Will his lordship be here tonight?'

'Yes, Hazel, he will,' Kay answered, her tone firm and confident. 'Thanks, Hazel. Oh, by the way, did you see the dinner menu I left?'

'Yes, I did, Lady Andrews.' The cook inclined her head and disappeared.

But *will* he be here? Kay asked herself, walking to the window where she stood looking out across the lawns and trees towards the hills that edged along the pale blue skyline. After breakfast he had announced he was going into Edinburgh to buy a birthday gift for his sister Fiona, and it was true that it was their birthday tomorrow and they were seeing her for Sunday lunch, a birthday lunch. But she couldn't help wondering why he hadn't asked her to pick something out earlier in the week, since she went to her studio in the city three days a week. On the other hand, he and Fiona were twins and unusually close, and perhaps he felt the need to do his own selecting.

Turning away from the long expanse of window, Kay walked across the terra-cotta tiled floor, heading for the huge stone hearth. She stood with her back to the fire, thinking, as always, what a strange room this was, and yet it succeeded despite its strangeness. Or perhaps because of it.

It was a conservatory which had been added on to one end of the house, built by Ian's great-great-grandmother in Victorian times. It was airy and light because of its many windows, yet it had a cosiness due to the stone fireplace, an unusual addition in a conservatory, but necessary because of the cold Scottish weather in winter. Yet in summer it was equally pleasant to be in, with its many windows, French windows and cool stone floor. Potted plants and wicker furniture painted dark brown helped to give it the mandatory garden mood for a conservatory, yet a few choice antiques added charm and a sense of permanence. A curious but whimsical touch was the Venetian blown-glass chandelier which hung down from the beamed ceiling, and yet this, too, somehow worked in the room despite its oddness.

Kay bit her lip, thinking about Ian, worrying about their relationship, as she had for some time now. She knew why there had been this slight shift, this moving away . . . it was because she had not conceived. He was desperate for a child, longed for an heir to his lands and this house, where the Andrews family had lived for four hundred years. And so far she had not been able to give him one.

My fault, she whispered to herself, thinking of her early years in Glasgow and what had happened to her when she was a teenager. A shudder passed through her slender frame, and she turned bodily to the fire, reached out to warm her hands, shivering unexpectedly as she filled with that old familiar coldness.

Lowering herself on to the leather-topped club fender, she sat staring into the flames, her face suddenly drawn, her eyes pensive. Yet despite the sadness there was no denying her exceptional beauty: with her ivory complexion, eyes as blue as speedwells and red-gold hair that shimmered in the firelight, she was a true Celt. But at this moment Kay Lenox Andrews was not thinking about her beauty, or her immense talent, which had brought her so far in her young life, but of the ugliness and degradation of her past.

When she looked back, growing up in the Gorbals, the slums of Glasgow, had been something of an education in itself. There were times when Kay wondered if she might have been a different person if her early environment had not been quite so difficult and harsh.

She knew there were those who said environment helped to create personality and character, while others believed you were born with your character intact, that character was destiny, that it determined the roads you took, the life you ultimately led. She herself tended to accept this particular premise.

The road *she* took was the road to success. At least, that is what she repeatedly told herself when she set out to change her life. And her positive attitude, plus her determination, had helped her to accomplish wonders.

When she was a teenager, the thing that had driven her was the need to get out of the Gorbals, where she had been born. Fortunately, her mother Alice Smith felt the same way, and it was Alice who had helped her to move ahead, who had pushed her out into the bigger world. 'And a much better world than it is here, Kay,' her mother had repeatedly told her, always adding: 'And I want you to have a better life than I ever had. You've got it all. Looks, brains, and that amazing talent. There's nothing to stop you . . . but yourself. So I'm hoping to make certain you bloody well succeed, lassie, I promise you that, even if it kills me trying.'

Her mother had plotted and planned, scrimped and saved, and there had even been one moment when she had actually resorted to blackmail in order to rescue Kay and fulfil her own special plans for her daughter. Alice had enormous ambitions for Kay, ambitions some thought were ludicrous, beyond reach. But not Alice Smith. Nothing and no one was going to stop her grabbing the best for Kay; eventually, all that shoving and pushing and striving, and sacrifice had paid off. Her cherished daughter was launched with a new identity ... a young woman of background, breeding and education, who happened to be stunningly beautiful, unusually talented, and all set to become a fashion designer of taste and flair.

I wouldn't have made it to where I am today without Mam, Kay now thought, still gazing into the flames of the roaring fire, ruminating on her past life. But a moment later she was brought back into the present by the sound of loud knocking on a glass windowpane. She sat up swiftly and glanced across the room.

Kay was startled to see John Lanark, the estate manager, on the terrace, bundled up in a Barbour jacket and scarf, hovering on the other side of the French windows. Jumping off the fender, she ran to let him in, surprised he was paying a call on Saturday.

Unlocking the door, she exclaimed, 'John, come in! Come in at once. It's freezing out there.'

He flashed her a breezy smile, stepping into the conservatory quickly, pulling off his tweed cap as he did. 'Morning, Kay. I know I ought to have phoned instead of barging in, but it just so happened I was passing in the Land Rover on my way to the village, and I remembered I'd promised Ian I'd let him know about the progress on the septic tanks at the Home Farm. Would he be about?'

'No, he's not, John. He drove into Edinburgh this morning, but he'll be back this afternoon. Do you want to leave a message, a note perhaps?'

'No, no, I'll phone him later. Basically, everything's now in proper order, but I'd like to fill him in with the details.'

'I'll tell him. And how's Margo?'

'Oh she's just wonderful. Busy with the church festival for spring. It's a little way off, as you know, but she likes to get started early.'

Kay nodded, then smiled at him. She had always liked this loyal and genial man.

He said, 'Look, I'd better get off. I don't want to take up your time. And I've a lot of paperwork waiting for me.'

'That's all right, John. But like you, I have work to do and the morning seems to be escaping.'

'*Tempus fugit*,' he murmured, said goodbye and let himself out.

Kay left the conservatory and walked towards the front hall set in the centre of the house. It was a vast open space, with a high-flung cathedral ceiling and a double staircase, with carved balustrades, which ran up to the wide upper hall. The main feature of the latter was a soaring stained-glass window which bathed the front hall below in multi-coloured light, almost like a perpetual rainbow.

She took the left-hand side of the staircase, running up to

the second floor, where her design studio was located in what had once been the day nursery at Lochcraigie.

As she opened the door and went in on this bitter February morning she was glad to see that Maude, the housekeeper, already had a fire burning brightly in the grate. It was a large, high-ceilinged room with six tall windows, and it was flooded with the cool northern light she loved, and which was so perfect for her work. In this crystalline light all colours were *true*, and that made her designing so much easier.

Stepping towards the old Jacobean refectory table that served as her desk, she reached over and picked up the phone as it began to ring. 'Lochcraigie House,' she said, walking around to her high-backed chair and sitting down.

'It's me, Kay,' her assistant said.

'Hello, Sophie. Is something wrong?'

'No, nothing. Why? Oh, you mean because I'm calling on Saturday. No, all's well in the world, as far as I know. At least it is in mine, anyway.'

Kay smiled. Sophie was a darling, full of energy and life, and a joy to work with. At twenty-three she was bursting with talent, enthusiasm and ideas. 'Then you *are* the lucky one,' Kay said at last, wishing that all was well in her little world. She went on, 'I just came up to the studio, and as I'm sitting here talking to you I can see that vermilion piece which came from the mill the other day . . . I like it, Sophie, I really do. It's such a change from the colours I've been using this past year.'

'I agree. It's really vibrant, but also sort of . . . smoochy.'

'What do you mean by smoochy?'

'You know, smoochy, as in kiss-kiss-kiss.'

Kay burst out laughing.

Dropping her voice, Sophie now said confidingly, 'I called because I finally got that information for you.'

'What information?'

'About the man my sister recently heard of . . . you know we discussed it two weeks ago.'

'Oh, yes, of course. Sorry, Sophie, I guess I'm being a little bit stupid today.' She clutched the receiver more tightly, filled with sudden expectancy.

'His name is François Boujon, and he lives in France once again.'

'Where exactly?'

'Just outside Paris. A place with a peculiar name. Barbizon. My sister got me all the information. Do you want to know everything now, or shall I tell you on Monday?'

'Monday's perfectly fine, I'll be at the studio by about ten, and we can talk then. But just tell me one thing now . . . is he difficult to get an appointment with?'

'Yes, a bit, I'm afraid. But Gillian will help.'

'Can she?'

'Oh yes, very much so . . . her girlfriend Mercedes has a strong connection, which is good.'

'It certainly is, and listen, I'm very grateful, Sophie, I really am. Thanks for going to all this trouble.'

'It wasn't anything, not really. I was happy to do it, Kay. So, I'll see you Monday then.'

'That's right. Have a good weekend.'

'I will, and you do the same.'

'I'll try,' Kay answered, and after saying goodbye she returned the phone to its cradle. Resting her head against the faded red velvet covering the chair's back, she let her eyes roam around the room, her mind whirling with all manner of thoughts. Then quite suddenly she remembered the envelope which had arrived by FedEx yesterday, and she reached for the decorative wooden box on one end of the desk. Lifting the lid, she took out the envelope with its beautiful calligraphy – her name so elegantly written – opened it and slipped out the invitation.

Once again she read it carefully.

Anya's party was on the second of June, a good four months away. She wondered if she could get an appointment with François Boujon for around that time.

It would be perfect if she could, because Ian hadn't been invited, and so she could travel alone to Paris. Kill two birds with one stone, she thought, and then she sat back in the chair, frowning hard. Her vivid blue eyes clouded over, and her expression became unexpectedly grim.

They would be there and she would have to see them. No, not only see them, but socialize with them, spend time with them. Not possible. They hated her. The feeling was mutual.

Alexandra Gordon, the snob from New York. From the elite social set, Junior League, and all that ridiculous kind of thing. Always so toffee-nosed with her, stuck-up, snubbing *her*.

Jessica Pierce, Miss Southern Belle Incorporated, with her feminine sighs and languor and the dropping of lace hankies along the way. Poking fun at *her*, teasing her unmercifully, never leaving *her* alone with her taunts.

Maria Franconi, another snob, this one from Italy, with her

61

raven hair and flashing black eyes and fiery Mediterranean temperament. And all those lire from her rich, Milanese textile family, flaunting her money and her connections, treating *her* like a servant.

No, it's not possible, Kay told herself again. I cannot go to Anya's party. Because my tormentors will be there . . . how miserable they had always made her life.

She knew what she must do. She must go to Paris sooner rather than later, to meet with this man François Boujon. She hoped she would get an appointment relatively soon. She would set everything in motion on Monday, ask to see him next month. And it did not matter what it cost.

She put the invitation back in the envelope, placed this in the wooden box, dropped the lid and turned the key. Then once more she sat back in the chair, her eyes becoming soft and faraway as she thought of Ian. The man she loved. Her husband . . . who must remain her husband at all costs.

CHAPTER FIVE

Even as a child, growing up in the slums of Glasgow, Kay had always managed to escape simply by retreating into herself. When the cramped little flat where she lived with her mother and brother Sandy became overly oppressive, she would find a small corner where she could curl up, forget where she really was, and dream.

A great deal of her childhood was spent dreaming, and she found solace in her dreams. She could escape the impoverished, gloomy world she occupied and go to another place, any place she wished. It made her young life more bearable.

And she always dreamed of beauty . . . flower-filled gardens, picturesque country cottages with thatched roofs, grassy meadows awash with wildflowers, and grand open spaces with huge, canopied green trees where trilling birdsongs came alive. And sometimes her dreams were of pretty clothes, and ribbons for her hair, and sturdy black shoes, shining with boot polish, for Sandy; and a beautiful silk dress for her mother . . . a pale blue dress to match her eyes.

But as she grew older Kay's priorities changed, and she began to replace her dreams with a new-found focus and concentration, and it was these two qualities, plus her talent, which helped to make her such a great success in the world of fashion.

Now, as she sat at her desk, thoughts of Ian lingered, nagged at the back of her mind. But eventually she let go of her worries about her marriage and became totally engrossed in her work, as she usually did.

In many ways, she loved this old day nursery here at Lochcraigie more than her busy, high-tech studio in Edinburgh, not least because of its spaciousness and high ceiling, but also because of the clarity of the light which came streaming in through the six soaring windows.

After looking through a few sketches for her autumn collection, which she had just finished, she rose and went over to the swatches of fabric hanging on brass hooks attached to the opposite wall. The vermilion wool she had focused on a short while before attracted her attention again, and she unclipped it, carried it over to the window, where she scrutinized it intently.

Suddenly, a smile flickered in her eyes as she remembered Sophie's comment a short while ago. *Smoochy*, she had called the colour, as in a kiss, and Kay knew exactly what her assistant meant. It *was* a lovely lipstick shade, one which reminded her of the glamorous stars of those old movies from the fifties.

As often happened with Kay, inspiration suddenly struck out of the blue. In her mind's eye she saw a series of outfits . . . each one in a different version of vivid vermilion red. She thought of cyclamen first, then deep pink the colour of peonies, pale pinks borrowed from a bunch of sweet peas, bright red lifted from a pot of geraniums, and all of those other reds sharpened by a hint of blue. And mixed in with them she could see a selection of blues . . . cerulean, delphinium and aquamarine, as well as deep violet and pansy hues, a softer lilac and the lavender shade of hydrangeas.

That's it, she thought, instantly filling with excitement. A winter collection of clothes based on those two colours – red and blue – interspersed with other tones from these spectrums. What a change from the beiges, browns, greens, taupes and terra-cottas of her spring season.

Turning away from the window where she still stood, Kay went over to the other fabric samples and searched through them quickly, looking for the colours she now wanted to use. She found a few of them and carried them back to her desk, where she spread them out. Then she began to match the samples to the sketches she had already done for her winter line, envisioning a coat, a suit or a dress in one of the reds, purples or blues.

Very soon she was lost in her work, completely oblivious to everything, bubbling inside with enthusiasm, her creative juices flowing as she began to design, loving every moment of it.

At twenty-nine Kay Lenox was one of the best-known young fashion designers on both sides of the Atlantic. In London her clothes sold at her boutique on Bond Street, and in New York at Bergdorf Goodman. She had a boutique in Chicago and one in Dallas, and another on Rodeo in Beverly Hills.

Her name was synonymous with quality, stylishness and wearability. The clothes she designed were elegant, but in a relaxed and casual manner, and they were extremely well cut and beautifully made.

The fabrics Kay favoured gave her clothes a great sense of luxury . . . the finest light wools, cashmeres, wool crepes, soft Scottish tweeds, suede, leather, crushed velvet and a heavy silk which she bought in France. Her flair and imagination were visible in the way she mixed these fabrics with each other in one garment – the result a look entirely unique to her.

Kay worked on steadily through the morning, and so concentrated was she that she almost jumped out of her skin when the phone next to her elbow rang.

Picking it up, she said, 'Lochcraigie,' in a somewhat sharpish tone.

'Hello, darling,' her husband answered. '*You* sound a bit snotty this morning.'

'Ian!' she exclaimed, her face lighting up. 'Sorry. I was lost in a dress, figuratively speaking.'

He chuckled. 'Is your designing going well then?'

'I'll say, and I had a brainstorm earlier. I'm doing the entire winter collection in shades of red running through to palest pink, and blue going to lilac to violet and deep purple.'

'Sounds good to me. Did John phone by any chance?'

'He stopped by, actually. He wanted you to know that the septic tanks at the Home Farm are under control.'

'That's a relief.'

'Did you find a gift for Fiona?'

There was a moment's hesitation before he said, sounding vague, 'Oh, yes, I did.'

'So you're on your way home now?'

'Not exactly,' he replied, clearing his throat. 'Er, er, I'm a bit peckish, so I'm going to have a spot of lunch. I should be back about fourish.'

The brightness in her vivid blue eyes dimmed slightly, but she said, 'All right then, I'll be here waiting for you.'

'We'll have tea together,' he murmured. 'Bye, darling.'

He hung up before she could say another word, and she stood there puzzled, staring at the receiver in her hand, and then she went back to work.

Later that afternoon, when she had eaten a smoked salmon sandwich and drunk a mug of lemon tea, Kay put on a cream fisherman's-knit sweater from the Orkneys, thick woollen socks and green Wellington boots. In the coat room near the back door she took down her dark green coat of quilted silk, pushed her red-gold hair under a red knitted cap, added a matching scarf and gloves, and went outside.

She was hit with a blast of freezing air, and it took her breath away, but her clothes were warm, the coat in particular, and she set out towards the loch, in need of fresh air and exercise.

This was one of her favourite walks on the estate, which in its entirety covered over three thousand acres. A wide path led down from the cutting garden just beyond the back door, past broad lawns, and thick woods bordering one side of the lawns. In the distance was the narrow body of glassy water that was Loch Craigie.

At one moment Kay stopped and stood staring across at the distant hills, partially obscured this afternoon by a hazy mist on their peaks and lightly covered in snow. Then her eyes settled on the great stone house where she lived, built in 1559 by William Andrews, the new laird of Lochcraigie. From that time onwards, the eldest son had inherited everything through the law of primogeniture, and fortuitously there had always been a male heir to carry on the Andrews name. An unbroken line for centuries.

Ian was the laird now, although no one ever used that old Scots name any more, except for a few oldtimers from his grandfather's day who still lived in the village.

Apart from these vast lands, the Andrews family had many other interests, primarily in business, including manufacturing, publishing and textiles. Everything belonged to Ian, but he was a low-profile millionaire content to lead the quiet country life.

Kay began to walk again, striding out at a steady pace, her eyes thoughtful as she contemplated her own past. She couldn't help wondering what Ian would say if he knew of her mean and poverty-stricken beginnings. He would be horrified, shocked, perhaps even disbelieving . . .

She let these thoughts float away, up into the air, and took several deep breaths . . . her troubles began when she was a teenager, but she had always known they would end, that she would have a different life when she was older.

And now she did. She had everything she had ever wanted,

had ever dreamed about . . . a husband who was not only young and handsome but an aristocrat, an ancient historic house she called home, a big career as a fashion designer, fame, success . . .

But no child.

No heir for Ian.

No boy to be the laird of these vast estates and holdings, one day in the far distant future, when Ian was dead and they proclaimed a new Master of Lochcraigie.

She sighed under her breath. It was an old story. After a moment she increased her pace, almost running down to the loch. The body of water was flat and grey, leaden under the wintry sky, and she did not plan to linger long. The air had grown much colder and there was a hint of snow on the wind. But she walked along the edge of the water for fifteen minutes, always enjoying the tranquil view, the sense of peace that was all-pervasive here.

On her way back, she took the paved path which led her past the Dower House where Ian's mother lived. For a moment she thought of dropping in to see her mother-in-law, but changed her mind. It would soon be four o'clock and Ian would be home; she longed to see him, to assuage her anxiety about him. She had plans for tonight, big plans, and she wanted him to be in the right frame of mind. If she were absent when he arrived, he could be put out.

And so she passed the Dower House and climbed the narrow steps, thinking of Ian's mother. She was a lovely woman, with impeccable manners, manners bred in the bone, and a kind and loving heart. She had always been *her* champion, and for that Kay was grateful.

Margaret Andrews had been born a Hepburn, and her family was somehow distantly related to the ill-fated James Hepburn, Earl of Bothwell, third husband of Mary Queen of Scots, who had died a terrible death in Denmark, imprisoned in the dungeons of a remote castle. Kay hated the story of Bothwell's death. It always upset her; she couldn't bear to think of that virile, vigorous and handsome man dying in such a ghastly way. And yet the story haunted her . . . She chastised herself now for her morbid thoughts of Bothwell, and ran across the lawn to the terrace in front of the conservatory. A second later she let herself into the house.

Kay knew at once that Ian was in a good mood as he walked into the conservatory just after four. He was smiling, and when she went to greet him he hugged her close and kissed her cheek. 'You look bonny,' he said to her as he moved away, went and stood with his back to the fire.

She smiled back at him. 'Thank you. Hazel just brought the tea in, Ian. Shall I pour you a cup?'

He nodded. 'It was a long drive back, and I thought I was going to hit snow, but so far it's held off.'

'Not quite,' Kay said, and pointedly looked towards the window. 'It's just started.'

He followed her gaze, saw the snowflakes coming down heavily. But he laughed and said, 'It looks as if we might get snowed in, Kay.'

'I don't care! Do you?'

'No. Well, let's have tea then.'

They sat down on the wicker furniture grouped in front

of the fire, and Kay poured for them both, looking across at him surreptitiously as she did.

Ian appeared to be happier this afternoon than he had in a while, more lighthearted and carefree than was usual. He also looked younger, unusually boyish today, but perhaps that was because his fair hair was tousled from the wind and he wore an open-neck shirt under a pale blue sweater with a vee neckline. Very collegiate, and vulnerable, she thought, and smiled, thinking of her plans.

Ian said, 'Actually, I hope the snow doesn't stick. It really would be quite awful if we had to cancel tomorrow's birthday lunch.'

Kay nodded in agreement. 'Let's not worry about the lunch now. I heard a weather report earlier on the radio, and it's supposed to be sunny tomorrow, and also much warmer.'

Ian smiled at her, and surveyed the tray of sandwiches and fancy cakes. 'My goodness, Hazel's done us proud this afternoon,' he murmured and reached for a sandwich, bit into it. 'Mmmmm . . . this is delicious. I see she's put out most of my favourite things.'

'By the way, Ian, what did you end up getting Fiona?'

'What do you mean?'

Kay gave him a baffled look, and exclaimed, 'The gift, for her birthday. What is it?'

'Oh yes . . . a pair of earrings. Rather nice, I'll show them to you later.'

They fell into a companionable silence, sipping their tea and eating the little sandwiches and cream cakes in front of the blazing fire. Outside the windows it was snowing heavily now, and settling on the ground, but neither of

71

them noticed, preoccupied as they were with their own thoughts.

Kay couldn't help feeling taut inside, even though Ian appeared to be so relaxed and at ease with himself and with her.

He was more like his old self, and this was a good omen. She planned to seduce him later, planned a night of lovemaking, and it was important that he was in the right mood. She believed he was . . . at least at the moment. She prayed it would last. And with a little luck she would get pregnant. She must. So much depended on it.

For his part, Ian was thinking about his trip to Edinburgh. It had been interesting, to say the least, and he was glad he had made the effort to go. And he was happy with the purchases. He hoped Fiona would like his gift, certainly it had been carefully chosen. He looked at his wife, and couldn't help thinking how beautiful she looked today, and desirable . . . he let *that* thought slide away . . .

Kay broke the silence when she confided, 'The FedEx envelope I received yesterday was an invitation . . . an invitation to go to Anya Sedgwick's eighty-fifth birthday party in Paris.'

'I don't have to go too, do I?' Ian asked, frowning, looking worried. 'You know how I hate travelling.'

'No, of course not,' she answered quickly. She didn't even bother to tell him that only her name was on the invitation. But she did think to add, 'I'm not going to go either.'

Ian stared at her, apparently puzzled and surprised. 'Whyever not?'

'I don't really want to see people I haven't seen in seven years . . . I lost touch with my friends when I graduated.'

'But you've always admired Anya.'

'That's true, she's the most fascinating woman I've ever met, a genius, too.'

'Well, then?' He raised a sandy brow.

'I don't know . . .'

'I think you should go to her party, Kay, just out of respect.'

'Perhaps you're right. I'll think about it.'

CHAPTER SIX

B y the time they had finished their tea the snow had settled on the ground, and it was continuing to fall steadily. Outside, it was growing darker and darker; the dusky twilight of late afternoon had long since been obliterated, and already a few sparse early stars sprinkled the sky.

But in the snug conservatory all was warmth and cosiness. The fire roared in the great stone hearth, constantly replenished with logs and peat by Ian; the table lamps cast a lovely lambent glow throughout, and in the background music played softly.

Ian had turned on the radio earlier, to listen to the weather report, and after hearing that heavy snow was expected, he had tuned in to a station playing popular music. Now the strains of *Lady in Red*, sung by Chris De Burgh, echoed softly around the conservatory.

The two of them had been silent for a while, when at one moment Ian looked across at Kay intently, his eyes narrowing. 'You're very quiet this afternoon, and you look awfully pensive. Sad, even. Is something the matter, darling? What are you brooding about?'

Kay roused herself from her thoughts, and shook her head. 'Not brooding, Ian. Just thinking . . . people *do* suffer for love, don't they?'

His brows drew together in a small frown, but his expression was hard to read. After a split second he answered her. 'I suppose some do . . .' He paused and shrugged offhandedly. 'But what are you getting at *exactly*?'

'I was thinking of Bothwell earlier, and the way he loved Mary. How he died because of her . . . well, in a sense, he did. And that awful death . . . chained like a poor dog to a pole for years . . .' Her voice trailed off and she let out a long sigh. '*He* suffered for love. It's so heartbreaking, that story, when you think about it.'

'But it happened hundreds of years ago. I do believe my mother's been filling your head with stories again –'

'Yes, but they're all part of Scottish history,' she interrupted peremptorily. 'I can never get enough of it. I guess I didn't pay enough attention at school . . . but your mother's rectified all that. She's been a wonderful teacher.'

His searching hazel eyes rested on her, and then he half smiled. 'My mother's the best teacher I know. A genius at it, especially when it comes to history, and the history of the clans. She held me enthralled when I was a child.'

'She's told me a lot about the noble families, but so much

more as well. I've learned a great deal about the Stuarts. How extraordinary they were, so bold and courageous, so very beautiful to look at.'

'And very ill-fated,' he shot back pointedly. 'At least some of them were. Foolish Mary, led by her heart and not her head. She was no match for crafty Elizabeth Tudor, I'm afraid. Not in the long run. Her cousin was so much cleverer.'

'The problem with Mary and Bothwell is that they were so entangled in the politics of the times. It doomed them.'

'*That's* an old familiar story, isn't it?' Ian shook his head, laughed a bit cynically. 'She was trying to keep a throne and protect her heir, and he wanted to sit next to her on his own throne, and the lords were in rebellion. God knows, it was a dangerous and hellish time to live.'

'Your mother explained everything. She's such an expert on Scottish history . . .' Kay paused, added: 'And a bit of a nationalist.'

He laughed. 'So are you!'

'Something must've rubbed off.'

He smiled at her indulgently.

There was a small silence.

Eventually Kay murmured, 'Your mother once told me that suffering for love is a noble thing. Do you agree with her?'

Ian burst out laughing. 'I'm not so sure I do! And let's not forget that my mother is something of a romantic, always has been, always will be, just like you are. But come to think of it, no, I don't want to *suffer* for love. No, not at all. I want to relish it, enjoy it, wallow in it.'

'With me?'

'Is that an invitation?' he asked, eyeing her keenly.

She simply smiled, beguilingly.

Ian rose and crossed the room, took hold of her hands and brought her to her feet. And then he led her over to the fireplace, pulled her down on to the rug with him.

He smoothed his hand over her red-gold hair, shimmering in the fire's glow, and held strands of it between his fingers. 'Look at this . . . Celtic gold . . . it's beautiful, Kay.' She was silent. Her eyes never left his face. He began to unbutton her white silk blouse, leaned forward, kissed her cheek, her neck, and her mouth, then moved her down. He kissed her with mounting passion.

But after only a moment, Kay pushed him away. 'Ian, stop! We can't. Not *here*! Someone might come in.'

'No, they won't.'

'Maude might, or Malcolm. To clear away the tea things.'

He laughed dismissively. But, nevertheless, he got up and walked over to the door set in the wall, to the right of the fireplace. This led to the main house.

Risk, Kay thought. He loves taking risks, taking chances. It excites him. And I mustn't fight him now. He wants to make love . . . I must seize this moment.

She heard him locking the door, and his footsteps echoing on the terra-cotta tiles as he came back to her.

Ian knelt on the floor next to Kay. He took her face in both of his hands, brought his lips to hers gently, gave her a light kiss.

'What about the French windows?' she asked, pulling away, glancing worriedly towards the terrace.

'Nobody's going to be out in this weather, for God's sake! There's a snowstorm brewing!'

He doesn't care, she thought. He doesn't care if someone sees us through the windows. Or walks in. But she knew this wouldn't happen. He was right. Everyone was snowbound tonight, safe in their homes. His mother down the hill in the Dower House; his sister Fiona ensconced in her cottage by the loch; John Lanark and his family secure in the estate manager's house close by the Home Farm. No one would venture out unless there was an emergency.

Ian had taken off her cardigan and white silk blouse, and was fumbling with the hooks on her bra. She helped him to unfasten it, then reached out for him, pulled him into her arms. They fell back on the rug together, and she kissed him hard, deeply. He responded with ardour, and then almost immediately sat up, pulled off his sweater, struggled out of his shirt, threw them to one side.

Kay followed suit, and within a few seconds they were both completely undressed, naked on the rug in front of the fire. Ian sat back on his haunches looking down at her. She never failed to stir his blood. She was such a beautiful woman, tall, slender, long-limbed; and her skin was pale as ivory. But now, in the firelight, it had taken on a golden glow and her red hair was like a burnished halo around her narrow face. How very blue her eyes were.

Staring back at him, Kay saw the intensity in his luminous hazel eyes, twin reflections of her own filled with mounting desire. She lifted her arms up to him.

In answer, he stretched himself on top of her. How perfectly we fit together, he thought.

'I want you,' she whispered against his neck, and her long, tapering fingers went up into his hair.

He wanted her as much as she wanted him, but he also wanted to prolong their lovemaking. Sometimes it was too quick. He was too quick. Tonight he had the great need to savour her, to pleasure her, before he took his own pleasure with her.

And so he kissed her very slowly, languorously.

As he began to caress her breasts, her hands moved down over his broad back, settled on his buttocks. Smoothing his hand up along her leg, he slipped it between her thighs; her soft sighs increased as he finally touched that damp, warm, welcoming place. She arched her body, then fell back, moaning.

Now he could hardly contain himself and he parted her legs and entered her swiftly, no longer able to resist her.

Kay began to move frantically against him, her hands tightly gripping his shoulders, her whole body radiating heat and a desire for him he had not seen in her before. Excited beyond endurance, he felt every fibre of his being exploding as he tumbled into her warmth, and she welcomed him ecstatically.

William Andrews, who inherited Lochcraigie on the death of his bachelor uncle, had had a growing family, and so it was necessary to provide a larger dwelling to accommodate them all. To this end, he built a new house which was finished in the late summer of 1559, and for the past four hundred and forty-two years it had stood unflinching on the small hillock above the loch.

Across all these decades the large bedroom, which over-looked the long body of water and the rolling hills beyond, had been called the Laird's Room. From William's day on it had always been the private enclave of the head of the family, from the moment he inherited the title and property until he died.

Like the rest of the rooms in this great stone manse, the bedroom had a grandeur and dignity about it. Of spacious proportions, it had eight windows, one placed on each side of the central fireplace, and three set in each end wall. The fireplace itself was grand and soaring, with an oversized iron grate to hold big logs and slabs of peat, the kind of massive fires necessary in the dead of the Scottish winter. Its mahogany mantel matched the dark beams which floated across the ceiling and the highly polished, pegged-wood floor.

The elegance of the room was not only to be found in its beautiful proportions, but in its furnishings as well. Set against the main wall, and facing the fireplace, stood the mahogany four-poster bed, with its carved posts, rose silk hangings and coverlet.

The same rose brocade, with a self-pattern of thistles, covered the walls and hung as curtains at the many windows. It was faded now, having been chosen by Ian's great-great-grandmother, the famous Adelaide, renowned in the family for her installation of the Victorian conservatory.

Although she had taste and a great eye for decorating as well as for fashion, Kay had not tampered with anything in the master bedroom. For one thing, Ian loved the room just the way it was, and so did she. So there was no good reason to upset him by making changes to a setting already quite beautiful, and one loaded with tradition and family history.

In particular, she admired the handsome antique chests, dressing table and other smaller pieces from the Jacobean period, and the Persian rug in the centre of the room. This was very old, its rose and blue tones faded, but it looked perfect against the dark pegged wood; it was priceless, she knew that. A beautiful gilded mirror over one of the chests, antique porcelain lamps and vases, and a charming old grandfather clock standing in one corner were items in the bedroom which Kay cherished as much as Ian did.

Several comfortable chairs were arranged near the fireplace, and Kay curled up in one of them now.

It was late, well past midnight.

Ian was already fast asleep. She could hear the faint rise and fall of his deep breathing; the only other sounds in the room were the crackle of the logs in the grate and the ticking of the clock in the corner.

Kay was thinking of Ian. She had been overwhelmed by his passion tonight, not only in the conservatory after tea, when he had taken her by surprise and made amazing love to her on the floor, but then later in their bed, when desire had overtaken him yet again. He had been unable to get enough of her, or so it seemed.

She had found herself responding in kind, meeting his passionate sexual needs, as wild and demanding as he was.

Hope rose in her that she had conceived.

Kay wanted a child as much as her husband did. Not that Ian ever made reference to his longing for a son. But she knew, deep within herself, how much he yearned for an heir, a boy to follow in his footsteps as the Laird of Lochcraigie.

What would happen if she didn't conceive? Not ever? Would he divorce her and find another woman to bear him a son? Or would he shrug and hope that his sister Fiona would marry, and provide a male child to inherit the title and vast family holdings? The awful thing was, she had no idea what Ian would do.

Rising, Kay walked over to the window and looked out. It was still snowing; there was a high wind that sent the crystalline flakes whirling about, and on the ground they were still settling. There was a blanket of white below, and under the pale moon this pristine coverlet seemed woven with silver threads. The wind rattled the windows, but the house stood firm and solid as it always had. William Andrews of Lochcraigie had built a manse that had defied time and the harsh Scottish winters.

If only she had someone to talk to, Kay thought, pressing her face against the cold windowpane. She had never discussed their childlessness with Ian, for fear of opening Pandora's box; or with her mother-in-law for the same reason. If only Mam were still alive, she thought, and unexpectedly a surge of emotion choked her. Her mother had made her what she was, and put her where she was, in a sense, but her mam was no longer around to reap the benefits or share the joy. Her brother Sandy was long gone, having emigrated to Australia eight years ago, and she never heard from him any more. Sadly.

I have no friends, at least not close friends, she realized, and thought instantly of Alex Gordon. They had been so very close once, until their terrible quarrel. Sometimes, when she wasn't closing her mind to those wonderful days at Anya's school, memories of Alex enveloped her, and she found herself missing the American girl. Not the Italian though; Maria had been a pain in the neck. And Jessica, too, had been difficult. Jessica had been mean to her, teasing her and putting her down. Miss Jessica Pierce was cruel and vindictive.

A long, rippling sigh escaped from her throat, and she felt a sadness settle over her. But there *was* Anya Sedgwick. She had always been good to her, not only as a teacher and mentor, but as a true friend, almost like a loving mother. Perhaps she should go to Anya's party after all. If she went a few days before the party she could meet with Anya privately, unburden herself perhaps. But why wait until June? she now wondered. And thought instantly of François Boujon. Once she had an appointment with him she could make a date for lunch or tea or dinner with Anya, who would be thrilled to see her, she had no doubts about that.

Suddenly, boldly, Kay made a decision. She would go to the party anyway. Out of respect for Anya, as Ian had suggested earlier.

She couldn't help wondering how her three former friends would behave towards her. She had become a fashion designer of some renown, after all. And although she seldom used her title away from Scotland, she was, nevertheless, the Lady Andrews of Lochcraigie now.

CHAPTER SEVEN

JESSICA

Jessica Pierce was in a fury.

She stood in the elegant den of her Bel-Air house, looking down at her boyfriend Gary Stennis. He was almost falling off the cream velvet sofa, sprawled out across the cushions, dead drunk.

Her cool grey eyes swept around the room.

Everything looked neat, undisturbed in the superbly decorated room. Except for the messy jumble of things he had managed to accumulate on the low, antique Chinese coffee table in front of the fireplace. A piece that had cost her the earth.

The unusual ebony table, beautifully inlaid with mother-of-pearl orange blossom trees, was littered with a number of highball glasses, one of her best Baccarat crystal goblets, a bottle of Stolichnaya Cristall, half full, and an empty bottle of her Château Simard Saint-Emilion 1988. One of my better red wines, she thought, as her eyes settled on an antique crystal dish. With a flash of irritation she saw that this valuable signed piece of Lalique, a gift from a client, had been carelessly used as an ashtray. It was full of cigarette butts. And God knows what else.

Sighing under her breath, Jessica picked it up and sniffed. The unmistakable aroma of cannabis was missing. For once he had not been smoking pot with his friends and colleagues. She put it down, relieved.

A frown furrowed her brow, and she leaned closer to the coffee table, staring at the crystal goblet. It bore traces of lipstick on the rim. But it had been a business meeting, of that she felt sure.

Pages of his new script were scattered on the floor, along with a yellow legal pad on which innumerable notes had been scrawled. In his handwriting.

Straightening, now focusing all of her attention on Gary, she studied him at length, through dispassionate eyes. His salt-and-pepper hair was mussed, his face was gaunt and pale, with dark smudges under his eyes. In sleep, his mouth had gone slack, was partially open, and with his furrowed neck it made him look curiously old, worn out.

Washed up, she thought, and felt a tinge of sadness.

But no, he wasn't that. At least, not yet.

Gary was still a brilliant screenwriter, one of the best, if not *the* best, in the business, and his past was filled with tunes of glory. And Oscars.

He had written many of the greatest screenplays ever put on celluloid and for some of the most talented stars, male stars especially. During his most-celebrated career he had made, lost and made several fortunes, married two famous movie stars, divorced them, and fathered a daughter with one who no longer spoke to him.

And now, at the age of fifty-one he was courting her and entreating her to marry him.

When he was sober.

Quite frequently these days he was drunk. And because of this addiction, which he refused to admit was an illness, she knew deep down she would never marry him. In her innermost soul she knew she would never be able to cope with an alcoholic on a long-term basis, and that was what he was on his way to becoming, if he wasn't already there.

Constantly Jessica begged him to go to AA, but he merely laughed at her, and somehow managed to charm her into believing he didn't need Alcoholics Anonymous. In her quiet moments, when she was alone, she knew with absolute sureness that he did. Just as she knew she should break up with him.

On two occasions Jessica had thrown him out; he had managed to charm his way back into her life. Well, he was a charmer personified, everyone knew that, and *the* master when it came to words. He had earned millions and millions from his words, hadn't he?

'Don't forget, he's a writer, he knows exactly what to say to press *your* buttons,' her friend Merle was always saying. Her retort to Merle never varied. 'And don't *you* forget that Jeremy's an actor. He knows which role to play to punch *yours*. Once an actor always an actor, Merle.'

Merle usually laughed, and so did she. They knew their men, that was a certainty. And they're both wrong for us,

Jessica thought; she turned swiftly on her high heels, went out of the den and closed the door quietly behind her.

She was still furious with Gary for being in this inebriated state when she got home, and the best thing was to let him sleep it off.

Jessica had been in Santa Barbara for five days, supervising an installation at a client's new house, and Gary had promised her dinner tête-à-tête at home tonight . . . no matter what time she arrived. A dinner he would cook. He was a great chef when he wanted to be, and a great lover when he was stone-cold sober.

Yes, she loved him, with certain qualifications. Nevertheless, he made her madder than a wet hen at times. Like right now.

When she reached the circular front hall, with its glassy black granite floor and elegant, curving staircase, Jessica picked up her hanging clothes bag and overnight holdall and headed upstairs to her dressing room next door to the bedroom.

As she went into the octagonal-shaped room she caught sight of herself in one of the four mirrors, and after hanging up the clothes bag and putting the other one in a corner, she turned and stared at herself in the nearest glass.

Stepping closer, she moved her long blonde hair back over her shoulders, then straightened her jacket. What she saw was a tall young woman of thirty-one, not bad-looking, quite elegant in a white gabardine trouser suit and high-heeled mules, with a string of pearls around her neck and pearl studs on her ears. But it's a slightly tired woman tonight, she muttered, then went back downstairs.

Jessica's brown leather handbag was on a Louis XIV bench in the front hall. Picking it up as she walked past the bench, she hurried down the carpeted corridor to her office. Pushing open the door, she turned on the light switch and moved forward to her eighteenth-century French *bureau plat* in front of the window.

The first thing she saw, propped up against the Chinese yellow porcelain lamp, was a FedEx envelope.

Jessica sat staring at the invitation for a long time, lost in her thoughts as she found herself carried back into the past.

A decade fell away.

She was young, just twenty-one, and starting out at the Anya Sedgwick School of Decorative Arts, Design and Couture, on the rue de l'Université in Paris, where she had gone to study interior design.

In her mind's eye she could see herself as she was then . . . tall, very thin, with straight blonde hair falling to her shoulder blades and a skin without a blemish. A small-town Texas girl on her first visit to Europe. An innocent abroad.

She had been captivated by Paris, the school, Anya, of course, and the little family *pension* on the Left Bank where she lived. It had all been new, different, and stimulating. So very exciting, and far removed from San Antonio and her parents. She missed them a lot, whilst managing to enjoy every new experience at the school and in her daily life.

And it was in Paris that she met Lucien Girard and fell in love for the first time. It was at the end of her first year that she and Lucien were introduced by Larry Sedgwick, Anya's nephew. She was just twenty-two; he was four years older, an actor by profession. She smiled now, thinking of the way she teased Merle unmercifully about living with an actor.

Lucien and she had been the perfect match, completely compatible. They liked the same movies, books, music and art, and got on so well it was almost uncanny. They shared the same philosophy of life, wanted similar things and were ambitious for themselves.

Jessica had believed she knew Paris well – until she met Lucien; he had quickly shown her she knew it hardly at all. He took her to wonderful out-of-the-way places – charming bistros, unique little boutiques, art galleries and shops, and obscure pretty corners filled with peacefulness. He showed her interesting churches, little-known museums, and he had taken her on trips to Brittany, Provence and the Côte d'Azur.

Their days together had been golden, filled with blue skies and sunshine, tranquil days and passion-filled nights.

He had taught her so much, about so many different things . . . sex and love . . . the best wines and food, and how to savour them . . . with him she had eaten mussels in a delicious tangy broth, omelettes so light and fluffy they were like air, soft aromatic cheeses from the countryside, and tiny *fraises des bois*, minuscule wood strawberries fragrant with an indefinable perfume, sumptuous to eat with thick clotted cream.

With him, everything was bliss.

He had called her his long-stemmed American beauty, had utterly loved and adored her, as she had him, and their days together had been sublime, so in tune were they, and happy. They made so many plans . . .

But one day he was gone.

Lucien disappeared.

Distraught, she tried to find him, teaming up with his best friend Alain Bonnal. His apartment was undisturbed, nothing had been removed. His agent had no idea where he was and was as baffled and worried as they were. He was an orphan; they knew of no family member to go to, no one to appeal to for information. She and Alain checked hospitals, the morgue, listed him as a missing person. To no avail. He was never found, either living or dead.

That spring of 1994 Lucien Girard had disappeared off the face of the earth. He might never have existed. But she knew very well that he had . . .

Suddenly jumping up, Jessica hurried across the office to the large French *armoire* where she kept fabric samples, opened the drawer at the bottom and pulled out a red leather photograph album. Carrying it back to the desk, she sat down, opened the album and began turning the pages . . . it was a full and complete record of her three years in Paris studying interior design. Almost everyone she had met and cared about was in here.

There we are, Lucien and me, she said under her breath, staring down at the photograph of them on the banks of the Seine, just near the Pont des Arts, the only metal bridge in Paris. She peered at the picture, instantly struck by their likeness to each other; Lucien had been tall and slender also, with fair colouring and bluish-grey eyes. The love of my life, she thought, and swiftly turned the page.

Here were she and Alexa, Kay, Maria and Anya, in the garden of Anya's house. And here was a fun picture of Nicky and Larry clowning it up with Alexa, and Maria Franconi looking mournful at the back.

Jessica experienced an unexpected feeling of great sadness . . . Lucien had disappeared and everything had gone wrong after that. '*Les girls*', as Nicky Sedgwick called their quartet, had quarrelled and disbanded. And it had all been so . . . so . . . silly and juvenile.

Jessica closed the album. If she went to Anya's birthday party she would undoubtedly run into her former friends. She shrugged . . . not knowing how she really felt about them. Seven years. It had all happened seven years ago . . . a long time, a lot of water under the bridge.

And could she actually face being in Paris? She didn't know. Paris was Lucien.

Lucien no longer existed.

That had to be true, because he had never surfaced, never reappeared. She still heard from Alain Bonnal occasionally, and he was as baffled as she continued to be; they had come up with every scenario they could think of, and were never satisfied with any of them, never sure what could have happened.

Accept the invitation. Go to Paris, just for the hell of it, she told herself. Then changed her mind instantly. *No, decline. You're only going to open up old wounds*.

Jessica closed her eyes, leaning back in the chair . . . Her memories of Paris and Lucien were golden . . . filled with happiness and a joy she had not experienced since her days with him.

Better to keep the memories intact.

She would send her regrets.

* * *

Gary said from the doorway of her office, 'So you finally decided to come home.'

Startled, Jessica swung around in the chair and stared at him. He was leaning against the door jamb wearing crumpled clothes and a belligerent expression.

He's an angry drunk, she thought, but said, 'You look as if you've been ridden hard and put away wet.'

He frowned, never having liked her southern Texan humour. 'Why did you get back so late?' he demanded.

'What difference does it make? You had passed out dead drunk on my sofa.'

He let out a long sigh and slid into the room, came to stand by her chair, suddenly smiling down at her. 'I guess we got to celebrating. Harry and Phil were crazy about the first draft of the script, and after making our notes, a few changes, we were pretty sure it was almost good enough to be a shooting script. So . . . we decided to celebrate –'

'I guess it just got out of hand.'

'No. You just got back very late.'

'Nine o'clock isn't all that late.'

'Why *were* you late? Did Mark Sylvester detain you . . . in some way?' He glared.

'Don't be so ridiculous! And I don't like the innuendo. He wasn't even there. And I was late because there was a lot of traffic on the Santa Barbara freeway. And how was Gina?'

'Gina?' Gary frowned, then sat down on the sofa.

'Don't tell me Gina wasn't here tonight, because I smelled her perfume in the den. And she's always at your script meetings, drinks my best red wine and leaves her lipstick on the wine glass. Harry hasn't taken to wearing lipstick has he?'

'Your sarcasm is wasted on me, Jessica. And I fail to understand why you're always so hard on her. Gina's been my assistant for years.'

And partner in bed when you see fit, she thought, then said, 'This ain't my first rodeo . . . I know what's what.'

Gary leapt to his feet, colour flooding his face. He looked apoplectic as he said, 'I can see the frame of mind you're in, and I'm not staying around to get in the way of your whip, Missy. I'm going to my place. I'll get my stuff tomorrow. See you around, kid.'

Jessica did not respond. She merely stared at him coldly, understanding, suddenly, how truly tired she was of having him use her. And misuse her house.

He strode out and slammed the office door behind him. A moment later she heard the front door bang and the screech of wheels as he drove out of her front yard at breakneck speed.

And at this precise moment, Jessica Pierce realized that she actually didn't care that he had left in a temper . . . or that she had pushed him at a bad moment, and he had almost snapped.

She opened the red leather album again and turned the pages, staring at the photographs of her three years in Paris, and with a flash of unexpected insight she recognized how little Gary Stennis meant in her life. Yes, she had feelings for him, and in the early stages of their relationship she had truly believed they had a chance of making it together on a long-term basis. But now the odds of it working were remote.

If she were honest with herself, she knew she shouldn't string him along any more. It wasn't fair to him; or to herself, for that matter. She ought to end the affair.

Well, maybe she just had. He had left in a huff and might never come back.

She thought again of Lucien, gazing at a photograph of him standing between her and Alexa outside Anya's school on the rue de l'Université. How young we all look in the picture, she thought. Young, innocent, with life ahead of us . . . how unconcerned we were about the future . . . about our lives. We thought we were invulnerable, immortal.

'Lucien,' she murmured out loud, tracing a finger over his face. 'What really happened to you?'

She had no answer for herself, just as she never had. His disappearance was a mystery. It was one that would never be solved.

94

CHAPTER EIGHT

To Jessica the Pacific had never looked more beautiful. The deepest of blues, glittering brilliantly in the afternoon sunlight, it was dazzling to the eye as it stretched into infinity.

Her gaze remained on the ocean as she fell down into her thoughts, asking herself what her life was all about, where she was heading and where she would end up.

In the last twenty-four hours she had felt extremely depressed about her relationship with Gary, which she now believed was doomed to failure. The end was coming, of that she was sure; she could only hope it would not be too messy.

It was Monday afternoon, and Jessica was sitting in the small, antique gazebo which she had shipped from a stately home in England. It now stood at the tip of Mark Sylvester's property in Santa Monica.

On a bluff facing the sea, the gazebo was a peaceful spot, a place for reflection and tranquillity, as she had known it would be. Mark loved it, just as he loved the new house. She had been quite certain he would approve, but it was a relief, nonetheless, to know he was actually thrilled with it. He was moving in next weekend, and today she had walked him through for the first time since the furnishings had been installed.

Everything's gone right with the house; everything's gone wrong in my personal life, she thought, her mind settling on Gary. She had called him yesterday, wanting to be conciliatory, to make amends, but he had not picked up. Nor had he returned his messages. At least, not hers.

So be it, she suddenly thought. I must get on with my life; move on. I have to, in order to save myself. Instinctively, Jessica felt that Gary Stennis would only drag her down with him. She paused in her thoughts, frowning to herself. There it was again, the frightening idea that Gary was on a downward spiral.

Slowly, she walked up towards the house, through the beautiful gardens which had been planned and executed by one of the world's great landscape designers from England. They were in perfect harmony with the new house, built where the old one, a Spanish hacienda, had once stood.

In its place, shimmering in the sunlight, was a Palladian villa of incomparable symmetry and style. Built of white stone, it had the classic temple façade of arches and columns made famous by Andrea Palladio, the Renaissance architect.

Jessica paused for a moment, stood gazing at the new villa, and realized once again how much it reminded her of one of the great houses on southern plantations. But, as she well knew, these, too, had been Palladio adaptations, as were so many of those lovely Georgian mansions in Ireland.

Jessica had hired an architect renowned for his expertise in Palladian architecture to design the villa, and she had worked very closely with him to achieve what she knew Mark liked and wanted. Inside, the central hall was the pivotal point, with all of the rooms grouped around it for total symmetry, following Palladio's basic rule.

Once the house was completed, Jessica had decorated the interiors in her distinctive style, using lots of pastel colours and cream and white, for the most part. Her well-known signature was a room based on a monochromatic colour scheme, the finest antique furniture and art money could buy, combined with luxurious fabrics, carpets, and stylish objects of art. Since Mark had given her carte blanche and an unlimited budget, she had been able to create a house of extraordinary beauty and style, and one totally lacking in pretension or overstatement.

Walking along the terrace, Jessica opened the French doors leading into the library, and found herself coming face to face with Mark.

'Where did you disappear to?' he asked, looking at her curiously.

'You became so involved with your business call, I thought I'd better leave you in peace. I went for a walk.'

'I didn't need privacy, you could have stayed,' he replied, and sat down on the sofa.

She took a seat on the opposite sofa, and said, 'I'm glad I put the gazebo down there on the bluff . . . I enjoyed a few minutes of perfect quiet, just whiling away the time, watching the ocean.'

'It's a great spot . . .' His voice trailed off, and he eyed her for a moment, before saying, 'You've looked awfully troubled all morning, Jessica. Want to talk about it?'

'Not sure,' she murmured.

'He's been around the block too many times for you, and he's –' Mark cut himself off, stared at her, suddenly looking chagrined.

She stared back at him, her eyes wide with surprise.

'I'm sorry, Jessica, I shouldn't have said that. It's none of my business. I overstepped the boundaries there.'

'No, no, it's okay,' she said swiftly, offering him a small smile. 'I was staring at you only because I'd thought the same thing myself yesterday. I'm afraid Gary and I are at odds at the moment, and I'm not sure the situation will change.'

'Leopards and their spots, and all that,' Mark volunteered, and shook his head. 'I guess he's drinking again.'

'No, no, not at all, it's not that,' Jessica was quick to say. 'We're at odds because of other things. To tell you the truth, it's partially my fault. I've been so involved with my work in the last six months, I'm afraid he's come in for a bit of neglect. And also, I think we've just grown apart.'

'That can happen when there are two careers going strong. Separations, preoccupations.' He rose and walked over to the built-in bar at one end of the library. 'Would you like something to drink? A coke? Water?'

'I'll have a cranberry juice please, Mark.' She laughed. 'I know there's a bottle there, I put it in the refrigerator on Saturday morning.'

He nodded, stood for a moment pouring their soft drinks, wondering why Jessica had ever become involved with Gary Stennis in the first place. She deserved so much better. He was a nice guy, and still good-looking in a washed-out, faded sort of way. That was partially due to the booze and hard living over the years. In one sense, Gary was bordering on the edge now; almost, but not quite, a has-been in the business.

It's one helluva cruel town we live in, he thought, pouring cranberry juice into a tall highball glass. He knew full well what the industry thought of Stennis; that he had only a couple of scripts left in him, and that was about it. Once he had been the greatest, in Mark's opinion. But the booze and the women had taken their toll, got to him, laid him out flat at times. Life could be pretty tough on the fast-track of Hollywood fame and fortune, accolades and alcohol.

He smiled to himself. You had to have the strength, will-power and ruthlessness of a Ghengis Khan to survive here.

As he walked across the room he couldn't help thinking what a good-looking woman Jessica was. Her appearance was wonderful today. She wore a pale lavender-coloured suit with a shortish skirt and very high-heeled shoes; he had always admired her long silky legs. She was a bit too thin for his taste, but striking, nevertheless, and her colouring was superb.

'Thanks, Mark,' she said as he put the drink in front of her on the glass-topped coffee table.

His thoughts stayed with her as he went back to the bar to get his ginger ale. Jessica Pierce was one of the nicest people he knew. There was a sweetness and kindness in her nature that was most commendable, and which he admired.

He *knew* that she *knew* that Gary was drinking heavily, and that she had avoided agreeing with him, admitting this, in order to protect Gary in his eyes. Honourable, loyal girl. Too nice for Stennis, as it happened.

When he returned and sat down opposite her, Mark raised his glass. 'Cheers, Jessica. And thank you for making this place so beautiful. You're just . . . miraculous.'

She smiled at him, her eyes suddenly sparkling with pleasure. 'Thanks, Mark, I'm glad you love your new home. Cheers.' There was a moment's pause. 'And thanks for trusting me, giving me carte blanche to do what I wanted.'

'I'm a bit in awe of you, you know. In awe of your knowledge, your taste, your restraint, your flair, your style. You're just the . . . the . . . whole enchilada, Jess.'

She laughed at his turn of phrase, took a sip of her drink and studied him for a moment. She found herself wondering for the umpteenth time why Kelly O'Keefe had left him, had sued for divorce last year. He was such a nice man, at least he was with her; fair, reasonable and a pleasure to work with, plus he had a good reputation in Hollywood. But she was aware he was a tough businessman, which is why he was a successful producer. Wimps didn't make it in the movie business. At least not to the big time.

Jessica knew Mark Sylvester was forty-five, but he didn't look it. In fact, he seemed much younger, like a man in his mid-thirties; he was lean, tanned, somewhat athletic in appearance, with a pleasant if angular face, and very knowing, alert brown eyes. Kind eyes that could turn as hard as black pebbles if he was displeased. She'd seen that look directed at one of his associates a couple of times, and she was glad it was not her who was on the receiving end.

'You're staring at me, Jessica.'

Laughing self-consciously, she admitted, 'To be honest, Mark, I was thinking about you and Kelly, and your divorce, wondering why on earth she would leave you.'

He gave her a quick, speculative look and replied, 'I let that idea penetrate the town. But in actuality, Jessica, I was the one who asked for the divorce.'

'Oh, I didn't know.'

'Nobody did. Nobody does. They think she wanted it.'

'I see.'

Mark sat back on the sofa, and looked off into the distance for a split second, a reflective expression entering his dark eyes. As if coming to a sudden decision, he sat up straighter, and said, 'I've never really explained about the divorce. Not to anyone, Jessica. However, I trust you in a way I can't quite explain. So, here goes. I had a problem with Kelly. She drank a lot and that was hard for me to take. In fact, she was well on the way to becoming an alcoholic.'

Jessica was so startled to hear this that she exclaimed, 'But I would never have guessed! She was always so . . . *proper*.'

'Leave it to an actress. She was pretty good at hiding it.'

'But you were . . . the *perfect* couple.'

'Wanna bet?' he asked, shaking his head. 'Anyway, I let her down as lightly as possible. It was all relatively amicable. She got a nice chunk of dough from me, and off she went to New York. I think she's managed to get herself back on track there, and in a sense she's a little more anonymous, although not much.'

'Is she still drinking?'

'She's eased off a bit. I think the break-up of our marriage and the divorce really . . . sobered her up. If you'll forgive the pun.' He grinned wryly. 'She seems to be making a big effort and I just hope she continues to do so.' He leaned back in his seat, crossed his long legs. 'In the meantime, I've got to get on with my own life . . . And what are you going to do, Jessica?'

'I've got a couple of houses to remodel in Beverly Hills, and –'

'I meant what are you going to do with your life . . . *and* Gary Stennis?'

Letting out a long sigh, she slumped down on the sofa. 'I don't know. Well, that's not true, I know what I *should* do, and that's end the relationship. It's over really, Mark, it's just a case of easing out of it.'

'I've known Gary for years, he's written several movies for me in the past. He's a great guy, don't misunderstand me, but he's always been a tad self-destructive.'

'Do you really believe that?' She gave him a hard stare.

'I do. And he is. Listen to me, there's no way you can ease out of this situation. You've got to bail out. Just go. Take a deep breath and jump.'

'I guess you're right about that. Pussyfooting around doesn't solve a thing, and it can be more painful in the long run.'

'You'd better believe it, Jess.'

She nodded, and then changing the subject, she asked, 'And what're you going to do now you've got the new movie in the can?'

'There's a play I want to buy. It's in rehearsal, about to go on in New York. I think it'll be a big hit on Broadway. It's dramatic, and it would make a good movie, my kind of movie. Unfortunately, the playwright won't let his agent deal with me. He wants to do that himself. So I'll be going to see him in about two weeks. Then I'm going to Paris on movie business. I might be shooting there later this year.'

'I just received an invitation to go to a party in Paris.'

His eyes lit up, and he exclaimed, 'Will we be there at the same time?'

'I don't know. I don't think so. My party is on the second of June. It's for my former teacher, who's going to be eighty-five.'

'Sounds great, but what a pity, I'll probably have left by then. I would have taken you out one night. We could've painted the town pink, if not bright red.'

She half smiled, then turned her head, looked across at a painting.

Observing her intently, he said, 'You've got that sad look on your face again.'

'Receiving the invitation sent me spinning backwards in time . . . seven years back, actually. And it opened up a lot of old . . . *wounds* I guess you could call them. I haven't been quite the same since.'

'Brought back memories, did it?'

'Yes.' Unexpectedly, tears filled her eyes.

Mark leaned forward. 'Hey, honey, what's all this? Tears? It has to be a man.' A dark brow lifted questioningly.

Jessica could only nod.

'An old love . . . a broken romance . . . yearning for him?

Do you want to talk about it? I have a good strong ear for listening.'

Sighing, she said slowly, 'Yes, an old love, a wonderful love. We made so many plans. Actually, we planned a future together, and then it ended.'

'From the sound of your voice, he broke up with you.'

'No, he didn't. He disappeared.'

'What do you mean?'

'One day he disappeared. It was just as if he'd dropped off the edge of the world without a trace. I never saw him again.'

'Tell me the story, Jessica.'

And so she did. Speaking slowly and carefully, she told Mark everything there was to tell about Lucien Girard – their first meeting, their relationship, and how she and Alain Bonnal had tried so hard to find him after his disappearance.

When she had finished, Mark said in a thoughtful tone, 'We have three choices here. Either he was killed and his body disposed of remarkably well, or he's alive and walking around with amnesia. Or he chose to disappear on purpose.'

'But why would he do that?' she exclaimed, her voice rising. She sounded aghast.

'Anyone who disappears has their own reasons for doing so. And usually it's hard to find them, because they've thought everything out very carefully. They're only ever found when they want to be.'

'Someone who disappears obviously does so because they want to start a new life,' she began and stopped. Leaning back against the antique Aubusson cushions on the blue linen sofa, she sat thinking for a few seconds. Then looking across at Mark, she volunteered, 'Alain and I wondered if he'd been mugged, or killed, and his body taken out to sea. We both accepted at the time that it would be relatively easy to dispose of a body. Like you, we'd even thought of memory loss.'

'People have been known to recover their memories.' He rubbed his chin with his hand, went on, '*Random Harvest*. Memory loss always evokes that movie in my head. Greer Garson, Ronald Colman. A good movie, a classic now, and one of my favourites, as far as old movies go. *Very* sentimental, though.'

'I never saw it.'

'You're too young.'

'No, I'm not. You're not much older than me, Mark.'

He grinned. 'Fourteen years. Anyway, if ever you see it advertised on late-night television, tune in.'

'I will.'

He continued, 'Anyway, I always think in terms of movies, you know. It's just a peculiar little quirk I have. But getting back to your friend Lucien . . . please take me through it again, Jess. I mean the part about him saying he had to go away for a few days.'

'We were having dinner, it was the last time I saw him, actually. Over dinner he said he'd be out of town for a few days, that he was going to Monte Carlo to shoot a commercial. I thought that was great and told him so. We made plans for the following week. Oh, and he told me he was leaving for Monte Carlo the next day.'

'Did he call you from there?'

Jessica shook her head. 'No. I didn't really expect him to, since I knew he'd be extremely busy. But after a week's silence I grew anxious. I phoned his apartment, there was no answer. Then I spoke to his friend Alain Bonnal, who was also perturbed because Lucien hadn't shown up for a lunch date they'd made. We went over to Lucien's apartment building, and spoke to the concierge. She told us he was still away. And she mentioned that she had seen him leave, that she spoke to him as he went out with his suitcase.'

'And no one else had heard from him?' Mark asked quietly.

'No. As a matter of fact, Alain and I went to see his agent and he was as baffled as we were.'

'It's all very odd. And the police never came up with anything? Never had any information for you?'

'No, they didn't. And neither did the hospitals or the morgue. Alain continued to check with them for a long time, even after I left Paris and came home to America. But there was never anything.'

'How upsetting it must've been for you, no wonder you were so distraught.' He shook his head, looking perplexed. 'I hate that kind of situation, one that doesn't have a satisfactory explanation.'

Jessica said nothing, but the look she gave him was full of gratitude.

Mark leaned back against the cushions, and after a split second he asked her in a somewhat cautious tone, 'Is there any reason you can think of, *any* reason, why Lucien might want to engineer his own disappearance?'

'None at all, Mark. I've racked my brains about what happened to him for years now, but the thought that he had done a disappearing act never crossed my mind. He wasn't that sort of man, he had a true sense of honour. Lucien had more integrity than anyone I knew. Or know.'

'I certainly trust your judgement. Obviously you knew him well enough to know what he was capable of doing or not doing.' There was a brief pause, before he asked her, 'Have you ever been back to Paris since then?'

Jessica shook her head. 'And I'm not even sure that I'll be going to the party.'

'Oh but you must!' he exclaimed. 'To toast your former teacher, wish her well ... becoming eighty-five is quite a milestone in somebody's life.'

'I know it is, but Paris does not hold happy memories for me, Mark, as you can imagine. To me, Paris is Lucien ... I don't think I could bear to feel the pain of losing him, experience the hurt all over again. I'm sure I wouldn't enjoy the trip at all.'

'I understand what you're saying, but we've all got to live with pain of some kind or other. Life is hard, Jess, and it's always been hard. Nobody ever said this world was an easy place to live in, it's hazardous and full of dangers. People suffer such terrible things. Actually, you'd be surprised what a person can live through. Human beings are tremendously resilient, you know. The secret is to be strong, to keep on fighting.'

'I just don't know. About going, I mean.'

He said, 'I've got an idea. Would you like me to come with you in June? Hold your hand?'

So startled was she by this offer, she gaped at him speech-lessly. Finally, she answered, 'You'd come to give me courage?'

'If you want to put it that way.'

Jessica was truly touched by such generosity of spirit on Mark's part and she fell silent. They were genuinely good friends; she had designed several of his homes and his offices, and they had become close buddies. That he would want to help make her visit to Paris easier, if she did go, was something that took her breath way. 'Thank you for making such a lovely and generous gesture . . . I'm grateful, Mark, really I am.' A sigh trickled out of her. 'I do love Anya Sedgwick, and she was an extraordinary influence on my life . . . but . . . Oh, I don't know . . .' She shook her head several times and gave him a helpless look.

'Sometimes having another person with you makes a tough trip much easier. And, in fact, I might well be in Paris then anyway, since I'm hoping to shoot part of my next movie there.'

'So you just said,' she answered. 'But I haven't made a final decision about attending Anya's party. I only found the invitation waiting for me, when I got home on Saturday evening. But whatever I decide, you'll be the first to know.'

Mark gave her a warm smile; he was filled with affection for her. But he did ask himself why he had suddenly insinu-ated himself into her life. He had startled himself as well as her, and he was puzzled by his actions.

As for Jessica, she was wondering the same thing. And asking herself whether or not she had the guts to go to Paris to confront the past. She simply didn't know.

CHAPTER NINE

MARIA

Her life had changed. Miraculously. Overnight. She could hardly believe it had happened.

For the last few days she felt as though she were walking on air. Her demeanour was more positive than it had been for a long time; she was excited and filled with anticipation, in a way she had not been for years. In a certain sense, it was as if she had suddenly been reborn.

The change in her had started last Friday, when she had returned to her office after lunch. On her desk was a FedEx envelope from Paris. Momentarily baffled, unable to read the sender's name and address properly, she had pulled the little tag on the back and taken out the white envelope inside.

The way her name was written in beautiful calligraphy told her at once that this was an invitation. She could not imagine what event it could be for, and when she had removed the card from the white envelope she had been thrilled as she quickly scanned it, reading every word.

Her heart had tightened and she had felt a rush of genuine happiness running through her . . . how wonderful to be invited to this very special occasion for Anya; what an honour to be a guest at the festivities for her.

Anya Sedgwick was a unique person in Maria's life, and also a favourite teacher; she had done more for her than anyone else. Except for Fabrizio. And Ricardo, of course.

It was Anya who had taken her under her wing when she had started at the school, who had encouraged her creativity, led her into new areas of design, and opened up the worlds of art, music, and culture in general. She had been like a mother to her at times, as well as her champion, and a truly good friend.

When she had first begun to attend the Anya Sedgwick School of Decorative Arts, Design and Couture, Maria had made a lot of other friends – besides the three who had eventually become her closest friends, until the quarrel.

In her opinion, it had been about nothing of any great consequence. The parting of the ways should have never happened . . . they had been at loggerheads with one another at one moment in time, and there appeared to be no other alternative but to go their separate ways. She had been upset after this break in the friendships, and at a loss, floundering a little without the other girls in her life.

Surely they would attend Anya's eighty-fifth birthday party? How could they bear to miss it?

She hoped they would be there; she couldn't wait to see them again, whether they wanted to see her or not. She was exceedingly curious about them and their lives. Having not heard from any of them for the last seven years, she couldn't help wondering if they were married, divorced, had children or not. And she was equally interested to know if they had pursued the careers they had chosen, if they had been successful.

Seven years later there could be no animosity left, could there? *Perhaps*. Maria shrugged. One never knew about people; they could be very strange, as she knew only too well, and to her bitter disappointment.

Maria Pia Francesca Theresa Franconi, called simply Maria by her family and friends, fully intended to go to Paris to celebrate with Anya. In fact, she had not had to think about it twice.

Her reaction to the invitation had been positive, and she had already mailed the reply card, saying she would attend.

The invitation to the party, and the prospect of the trip, were the reasons her depression had fled; she was so buoyed up and excited she could hardly contain herself. To her, the invitation was somehow like the spending money she had received every week when she was a child. Her Grandmother Franconi gave it to her each Thursday, but she wasn't able to spend it until the weekend, when her mother took her into Milan. And so the money had burned a hole in her pocket.

She had looked at her lire as a child, counted the money over and over again, then put her little purse in a very safe place. She had hardly been able to wait until Saturday and her trip to the shops.

Quite apart from wanting to attend Anya's party, Paris was Maria's favourite place. And also, the idea of escape appealed to her enormously . . . escape from her domineering family, a job which bored her, a family business she had not the slightest interest in, and a personal life that was dull and uneventful.

She *was* going to go to Paris, and she fully intended to have a good time when she got there.

It would not be merely a weekend visit, just to attend the celebration. She planned to take her holiday in June, and she would stay in Paris for a week. Perhaps even two. Maybe even three.

Three weeks in Paris. The mere thought of it took her breath away. What a wonderful idea.

Now on this Thursday evening, almost a week since she had received the FedEx envelope, Maria was still soaring as if she had inhaled some kind of high-octane gas. She couldn't wait to tell Fabrizio about the party, and the trip she was planning. Her brother was coming to dinner; he usually did on Thursdays if he was in Milan.

As it was, Fabrizio had been away for the past two weeks, visiting some of their clients in Vienna, Munich and London. He was the head of sales in their company, Franconi and Sons, manufacturers of textiles par excellence since 1870.

With lightness and speed, Maria moved around the high-tech, stainless-steel-and-glass kitchen in her modern apartment, checking the pasta she had just freshly made from her own dough, stirring the Bolognese meat sauce she had put in a glass bowl a few minutes before. Moving to the refrigerator, she took out the mozzarella cheese and tomatoes, began to slice them. Once she had done so, she arranged them on two plates, and added basil leaves. Later she would drizzle oil on top.

As she worked, Maria glanced out of the window, thinking what a pretty sky it was. Ink-black, filled with crystal stars and a perfect orb of a moon, it was without cloud tonight.

She could see from the delicate, lacy pattern of the frost on the windowpane that it had turned icy outside. But then it usually was cold in Milan in February.

Maria was glad Fabrizio was coming to dinner. She had missed him whilst he had been away. He was not only her favourite in the family, but her ally in the business. Not that she really needed one these days, since she was now twenty-nine and able to stand up for herself. However, he took her side whenever she had a strong opinion, and agreed with most of the major points she made at meetings. Her grandfather usually did not.

Frequently her father supported her, since he, too, saw the necessity for a number of their lines to be updated. This was something Maria continually fought for, but she was not always successful, much to her irritation.

In the years since she had graduated from Anya's school in Paris, she had become one of the top designers at Franconi, and Fabrizio, in particular, was forever acclaiming her talent, giving her accolades for her textiles.

Deep down, she didn't really enjoy her work any more, feeling at times that she was in a rut. And her frustration forever got the better of her.

Thinking suddenly of this, she sighed, then immediately clamped down on these negative feelings, focusing instead on her brother. His arrival was imminent. This instantly cheered her up. Fabrizio enjoyed her cooking, and they usually had a good time together, no matter what they did.

Like her, Fabrizio, who was thirty-one, was single; like her, he was also forever being nagged at by their mother . . . marriage being the reason for the incessant nagging. Their mother and their Grandmothers Franconi and Rudolfo couldn't wait to bounce *bambini* on their laps, and were therefore vociferous about this. In fact, none of the older females in the family let the two of them forget that they were in dereliction of their duty.

Their elder brother, Sergio, who was thirty-four next week, had been married and divorced and was childless. Obviously he was beyond the pale, as far as the grandmothers were concerned; mostly this was because of his marital history, his taste for the fast-track and flashy women.

Sergio was the heir apparent. But Maria knew that Fabrizio was the true favourite in the family. And she fully understood why. He was the best-looking. Tall, blue-eyed and blond, he was a true Franconi in appearance, while she and Sergio were dark and took after the Rudolfos. Furthermore, Fabrizio was the smartest, the brightest, and he worked the hardest. Without even trying, he endeared himself to everyone. Even strangers quickly fell under his spell.

No blots on his page, she thought, smiling. Fabrizio was the star, and she did not resent this one bit. She loved and admired her brother more than anyone in the world. And she trusted him implicitly. He had two characteristics she put great store in: honour and integrity.

*   *   *

Ten minutes later, Fabrizio stood leaning against the door jamb of her kitchen, watching her as she finished cooking, sipping a glass of dry white wine, looking nonchalant.

He was filling her in about his trip, and she turned and smiled at him, glowing inside, when he told her that it was her revamping and updating of their famous Renaissance collection which was making such a difference to the company.

'The reorders are tremendous, Maria,' he explained. 'And so I toast you, little one, for designing a line that has been such an extraordinary success.' He raised his glass.

Picking up her own goblet of white wine, she touched it to his. 'Thank you, Fab. And won't Grandfather be surprised? He was so against my ideas.' She laughed delightedly. 'I can't wait to see his face when you tell him.'

'Neither can I. Not only that, the customers were really singing your praises. They like what you have done with some of the other older styles as well. I told them I would be showing them a whole new line next season. A line not based on any of the company's standards.'

'You did!' She stared at him, her dark eyes holding his.

'Yes. And so I am looking to you, Maria, to produce a collection that bears *only* your signature.'

'That's quite a challenge! I'll try.' She paused for a moment. 'Fabrizio . . . ?'

'Yes?' He stared at her alertly, detecting a new note in her voice. 'You sound excited.'

'I am. I got an invitation last week to go to Anya's eighty-fifth birthday party in Paris.'

Fabrizio stiffened slightly, although he tried to disguise

this, and his face did not change when he asked, as casually as possible, 'And when is this party?'

'Early June.'

'I see . . .' He let his voice trail off noncommittally, wanting to hear what else she had to say.

'I'm going, of course. I wouldn't miss it for the world. I've already sent in the reply card, accepting, and I plan to stay for two or three weeks.'

Her brother frowned. 'Two or three weeks!' he exclaimed and looked at her askance. 'Whatever for?' This announcement *had* surprised him.

'Because I love Paris, and I want to have my summer holiday there.'

'But we always go to the house in Capri in the summer.'

'Not this year . . . at least I won't be going.'

'*They* won't like it.'

'I don't care. I'm twenty-nine, almost thirty years old, and I think I can spend a holiday alone for a change. Don't you?'

'But yes, of course, you're an adult.' He smiled at her gently, decided to say no more, and swallowed the rest of his wine without further comment.

Later, after dinner, he would have to tell her she could not go to Paris. He dreaded the thought.

CHAPTER TEN

Maria watched her brother surreptitiously, pleased that he was savouring his food, obviously enjoying the dinner she had so painstakingly prepared for him.

After eating a little of the spaghetti Bolognese, which was one of her specialities, she then put her fork down and reached for her glass of red wine.

'I am feeling so much better, Fabrizio, much less depressed. I know it is receiving the invitation to go to the party that has cheered me up.'

Lifting his head, he looked at her intently, swallowing his dismay. 'I'm glad you're feeling better. But perhaps this change is really due to the way Father has been backing you and your ideas lately.'

'It's nothing to do with work. Nothing at all!'

'All right, all right, you don't have to get excited.'

'I'm not excited. I'm simply telling you the way it is. And I do know what makes me happy. The thought of going to Paris has been . . . very liberating these last few days.'

This was the last thing Fabrizio Franconi wished to hear, and he took a few more forkfuls of the pasta before pushing the plate away. 'That was delicious, Maria, and thank you, you're the best cook I know.'

'You'd better not let either of our grandmothers hear you say that,' she shot back, smiling at him. Then rising, she took their plates out to the kitchen.

'Can I help you?' her brother called after her.

'No, no, everything is under control.' Maria returned a few seconds later, carrying a plate of warm cookies. 'I didn't make dessert, because you never eat them. But I did make coffee. Would you like a cup?'

He shook his head. 'No thanks. I'll savour my wine.'

'How was London?' she asked, sitting down opposite him.

'Cold and wet. But it was good to be back even for a few days. You know, I do have genuinely happy memories about my days at school there. I enjoyed that period of my life, my days at Harrow. Didn't you enjoy your schooldays in England?'

'Yes, I suppose so. But to be honest, I loved the time I spent at Anya's school so much more.' Her face changed, became animated as she added, 'By the way, her birthday party is black tie. I'll have to get a new evening dress. I can't wait to go shopping for something special.'

For a second her brother was silent, wondering how to begin. After a few moments of reflection, he said in a soft voice, 'I wish you hadn't already accepted that invitation, Maria. I think it was a little premature on your part.'

'What do you mean?' she asked, her voice rising slightly. She had detected something odd in his voice, detected trouble brewing. 'Oh my God! You think our mother will interfere, that she'll try to stop me going!'

'You know very well she won't do that. You're twenty-nine, as you just pointed out to me.'

'Then why do you say I was premature?'

He was silent, staring into his glass of red wine. When he looked up his expression was unreadable. Very carefully, he began, 'You know you can't go to Paris because –' And then his voice faltered.

She stared at him.

He stared back at her.

The face he looked into was one of the most beautiful faces he had ever seen. The face of a Madonna, worthy of being painted by a great artist. She had huge, soulful eyes as black as obsidian, clouds of thick glossy black hair falling to her shoulders, a perfect oval of a face with dimples in her cheeks when she smiled. And each feature was delicately and clearly defined as if carved from ivory by a master sculptor.

Maria's eyes impaled Fabrizio's as she murmured shakily, '*You* don't want me to go because I'm so . . . heavy. That's what you mean, isn't it?'

'I can't stop you going, if you want to go so badly. After all, to quote your friend Jessica, whom *you* are always quoting, you're free, white and twenty-one. But that is just my reason, Maria. *Jessica*. And also Alexandra and Kay. Three very good reasons why you ought not to go to

Paris. You are not merely heavy, you are *fat*, and I know you will feel awkward and *humiliated* when you see your friends. Because they are bound to be as svelte and good-looking as they always were.'

'You don't know that!' she cried, and then closed her eyes convulsively. *Of course he was right.* They would look gorgeous, she had no doubts about that. And she would feel like a beached whale, a big ball of blubber. Yet she wanted to go to Paris so much, she couldn't bear the idea of declining the invitation, and so she said, somewhat defiantly, 'I can still go. I don't care what they think.'

Fabrizio got up, walked over to the sofa, and said, 'Come and sit here with me, let's talk this out, little one.' He gave her an encouraging smile, and she smiled back, although the smile instantly wavered as she rose.

Once she had joined him on the sofa, he took her hand in his, and looked into her eyes lovingly. 'Since you do want to go so badly, there is a way. However, it is going to be tough.'

'What do you mean?'

'First of all, let's talk about your love of cooking. It is an enjoyable hobby, I know, but you do it because you are frustrated about many things.'

'But I cook for you,' she protested.

'That is true, but you also cook for yourself. You comfort yourself with food, Maria.'

She did not say a word.

Fabrizio continued: 'If you're going to go to Paris then I suggest you lose some weight. You have a good three months to do that. You will look so much better, and you will feel better.'

'Diets don't really work for me,' she mumbled.

'They would if you really stuck to them,' he shot back swiftly. 'You have to stop all of this cooking. *Immediately*. Cooking for me, for your friends and most importantly, you've got to stop cooking for yourself.'

'Do you think I could stick with a diet, Fab?' she asked, sounding suddenly hopeful.

'I certainly do. I will take you to a diet doctor tomorrow, and she will put you on a regime that is suitable for you. Then you can enrol at my gym, and start working out every day. Quite apart from your trip to Paris, and getting in shape to meet old friends, your health will benefit.'

She almost visibly shrank back against the sofa, and gaped at him, her eyes wide, her expression fearful. 'I don't think I could cope with everything all at once, Fabrizio . . .'

He shook his head impatiently. 'Oh Maria, you *can*. I know you can.'

Tears gathered in her eyes and she began to weep. 'It's too hard for me to diet and work out. And diet and work out. It's so monotonous, and I'm always hungry.'

'Then I suggest you cancel your trip to Paris, because you won't enjoy the trip looking the way you do.'

Later, after Fabrizio had left, Maria stood in front of the full-length mirror, staring at herself through self-appraising eyes.

For the first time in several years she saw herself as she truly was. The blinkers were off, and she faced reality. And finally she admitted that her brother was right. She had put on a lot of weight in the last few years.

Yes, I'm fat, she said to herself. No, not just fat. Very fat.

Staring at her body totally naked, she saw that she was huge, her arms thick from the shoulders down, her thighs wide, like the great hams hanging in her grandmother's winter larder.

She blinked several times as tears welled, and turned away from the mirror, filled with self-loathing. Reaching for her silk robe, she drew it on quickly and went and lay on her bed, pushing her face into the pillow.

She let the tears flow, sobbing as though her heart would break, until finally there were no tears left in her. Exhausted, she lay there on the damp pillow, consumed by her longing to go to Anya's party, her weight problem, and her current plight. What to do? What to do? she asked herself repeatedly.

Fabrizio was correct. The ideal thing would be to use the next few months to get the weight off, but she was so afraid of failure and of the hardship of exercise and dieting, she was ultimately paralysed. And she was aware that she would feel exactly the same tomorrow. She always gave up before she even started.

Ricardo, she suddenly thought. It all began when they pushed Ricardo Martinelli out of my life. Closing her eyes, Maria looked back into the past, as if down a long, dark tunnel, seeing him standing at the end of it. How she had loved him, and he her, but her parents had considered him to be unsuitable, and they had broken up the love affair. He had gone away and she had never seen him again. Four years ago it had happened.

That was when she had started to put on weight, after Ricardo had exited her life. One thing was true, she *did* eat for comfort and consolation. She pampered herself with food because she had lost him, because her parents and grandparents were domineering, always trying to control her, and also because she was desperately lonely. She hated her job, was sick and tired of designing textiles, found the whole experience constraining.

Escape.

That was what she really wanted.

Permanent escape from Milan. From her family. From her job.

But you can't escape from yourself, Maria, she reminded herself, sitting up, pushing her hair away from her face. You have a big, terribly fat body that is ugly and ungainly, and no man is going to love you with your elephantine shape. You can't blame the family for your eating, at least only indirectly. You and only you are responsible for what you put into your mouth.

She thought of this over and over again as she sat propped up against the pillows, and then after a while she left her bed and went to sit at her Venetian mirrored dressing table, staring intently in the looking glass.

She saw herself as she really was; it was a beautiful face staring back at her. If only she did not have this awful body . . . all hideous rolls of fat. Everywhere.

You *can* do it, she insisted in her head. You *can* lose weight. You have great motivation now. Going to Paris . . . to see Anya . . . to make friends again with Jessica, Alexandra and Kay. And maybe if you get thin enough you can go and see

Ricardo. She knew where he was, what he was doing; she knew he was not married.

Perhaps her lover still yearned for her, as she yearned for him. She wondered about this for a few minutes, then she got up, threw off her robe and went again to stare at herself in the full-length mirror. She was gross. What man would want you with a body like this? she asked herself.

Turning away in disgust, she wrapped herself in the robe and went through into the kitchen. Snapping on the light, she opened the refrigerator door; her hand reached in for the large slab of cheese. Instantly, she withdrew her hand, closed the door, turned away empty-handed.

Slowly she walked back to her bedroom, vowing to herself that she would *try* to lose weight.

She wanted to go to Paris so much . . .

'I'm going to go!' she exclaimed out loud to the empty room. But she was fully aware that she would only make the trip if she shed some weight . . . how could she let her glamorous former friends see her looking like this? Or Anya? Or Ricardo?

Motivation, she whispered to herself later, as she began to fall asleep. Motivation . . .

PART TWO

Doyenne

CHAPTER ELEVEN

Anya Sedgwick was so startled that she sat back on the sofa and stared at her visitor seated opposite. There was a questioning look in her eyes and her surprise was evident.

After adjusting her back against the antique needlepoint pillows, she frowned slightly and asked, 'But whatever made you do it so . . . so . . . *impetuously*?' She shook her head: 'It's not like you . . .' Her voice trailed off; her eyes remained fixed on his handsome face.

Nicholas Sedgwick cleared his throat several times. 'Please don't be angry with me, Anya.'

'Good heavens, Nicky, I'm not angry.' She gave him the benefit of a warm smile, wanting to reassure him, to know that he was still in her good graces. He was her favourite in the family, and although he was not her child, not even of her blood, she thought of him as a son. He was very special to her.

'All right,' she continued. 'You're giving me a birthday party, and you've already sent out lots of invitations, which perhaps precludes cancelling it. So you'd better tell me about it. Come along, I'm all ears.'

'I wanted to do something really special for your birthday, Anya,' he replied, leaning forward with an eagerness that brought a boyish look to his face. 'I know how much you enjoy Ledoyen, so that was my restaurant of choice. I went to see them and I've booked the entire restaurant for the evening. There's going to be a cocktail period, then supper and dancing afterwards. And a few surprises as well, along the way.'

'I'm sure there are lots of surprises in the works, knowing you,' she laughed.

'So far I've invited seventy-five people, but we can have a lot more, double that amount, if you wish.'

'Seventy-five already sounds a few too many!' she exclaimed, but immediately smiled at him when she saw his crestfallen expression. 'I'm only teasing, Nicky. Continue, darling.'

'After I visited the restaurant, did a tour of it, I was filled with all kinds of ideas for the party, and I suppose I got overly enthusiastic. I went ahead and created an invitation, which I had printed, and I had the calligrapher address the envelopes. Once they were ready I posted them. But I panicked the day I put them in the mail. It struck me that I had pre-empted the rest of the family, that I took control, so to speak.'

'As you usually do,' she asserted in a mild tone.

He nodded; he was relieved she sounded so benign. She was

obviously surprised by his actions but definitely not annoyed with him.

'Anyway, Anya, I was going to phone you in Provence that day, but I decided against it. Sometimes speaking on the phone is very unsatisfactory.' Nicky lifted his hands in a helpless gesture, and finished: 'So, here I am telling you now, and hoping you won't want me to cancel it.'

'I don't know.' She gazed across at him, shaking her head. 'I really don't know, Nicky.'

'You *must* have a celebration for your eighty-fifth birthday. It's such a milestone . . . and you should be surrounded by everyone you care about.'

'Do I care about so many . . . *seventy-five* people?' She frowned, screwed up her mouth, looking reflective.

'Let me rephrase that, Anya. I've tried to include those who love you, and the people who have been special in your life, in one way or another.'

'Well, there are quite a few of those still alive,' she conceded, her reflective expression intensifying. 'Did you bring the invitation list?'

'Yes, I did.' He smiled wryly as he added, 'I'm afraid I was sneaky. I had Laure take most of the addresses from your files.' Not waiting for a comment from her, he rushed on, 'Here's the list.' Pulling it out of his jacket pocket, he rose and went to join her on the sofa.

After lunch, when Nicky had finally left, Anya went back to her upstairs sitting room. It was a room she had continually gravitated to ever since she had come to live here over half a century ago now, a place to entertain family and friends, relax and read when she was alone, or listen to the music she loved so much.

And, just as importantly, it was her preferred place to work, surrounded by comfort, her beloved photographs, books and possessions gathered over a lifetime and so meaningful to her. The large antique desk piled with papers, which stood in one corner, was testimony to her lifetime ethic of disciplined hard work.

Walking briskly across the floor, Anya paused briefly at the window, staring down into the yard below, thinking how bleak her garden looked on this cold February afternoon.

A painting in grisaille, she murmured under her breath, as usual thinking in terms of art. *All those greys and silvers mingling . . .*

The trees were skeletal, bereft of leaves, were dark etchings against the pale grey but luminous Paris sky. And the wet cobblestones in the yard gleamed with a silvery sheen after the recent downpour.

Mature sycamores and lime trees encircled the house, and there was a lovely old cherry tree in the middle of the courtyard. Now its spreading bare branches cast an intricate pattern of shadows across the yard. But in spring it bloomed softly pink, its branches heavy with cascades of luscious blossoms; in the heat of summer its cool, leafy canopy offered welcome shade.

As bleak as the garden was today, Anya was well aware that in a month or two it would be glowing green with verdant grass and banks of ferns, dotted with the variated pinks of the cherry blossoms and the little impatiens set in borders around the lawn.

By then, the picket fence enclosing the lawn and garden at one end of the courtyard would be gleaming with fresh white paint, as would the many planters and the ancient wrought-iron garden furniture. A sudden transformation took place every spring, just as it had for as long as she could recall. She had been here in the summer of 1936, when she was twenty years old, witnessing it for the first time.

Now Anya's glance took in the tall, ivy-covered wall which, along with the many trees, made the garden and house so secluded and private, shielded as it was from its neighbours. She had always been enchanted by the garden, the quaint courtyard and the picturesque house with its black-and-white half-timbered façade. It was a house that looked as if it had been picked up lock, stock and barrel in Normandy and deposited right here in the middle of Paris.

It stood just a stone's throw away from the busy Boulevard des Invalides, and around the corner was the rue de l'Université where her now-famous school was located.

Anya smiled, thinking of the surprise most people had when they came in from the street through the great wooden doors, and confronted the courtyard. The ancient house, which had stood here for over a hundred years, and the bucolic setting so reminiscent of Calvados country, usually took everyone's breath away.

As it had hers, when she had first visited this house, the day she was celebrating her twentieth birthday . . . so many years ago now . . . sixty-five years, to be exact.

She had come here with Michel Lacoste. To meet his mother. He had been the great love of her youth, her first husband, the father of her two children, Dimitri and Olga.

This house had belonged to his mother, Catherine Lacoste, and to Michel after his mother died. Michel and she had begun to raise a family here . . . and then the house had become hers when Michel died.

Too young to die, she muttered under her breath as she turned away from the window.

Of late, so many memories and recollections of the past were constantly assailing her. It was as if her whole life were being played out for her on a reel of film, one which passed before her eyes too frequently. Perhaps that was part of growing old, remembering so many things that had happened long ago. And not remembering the events of yesterday.

However, she could not dwell on the past at this moment. Nicholas Sedgwick, her great-nephew through her second husband Hugo Sedgwick, had forced her to look to the future. To June the second, to be precise, and the fancy party he had planned for her.

In fact, her birthday was actually on June the third, and she had reminded him of that over lunch. Naturally Nicky had known. He should never be underestimated. But, as he had carefully explained to her, he was not able to book the restaurant for the actual night of her birthday, June the third being a Sunday.

Seating herself at the desk near the fireplace, glad to have the warmth of the blazing logs nearby, Anya looked again at the invitation, thinking that it was tastefully done. But then Nicholas was known for his great taste. She turned her attention to the guest list which he had prepared, focusing on the names.

His choices had been correct, and in some instances rather

clever, since he had thought of certain old friends she rarely saw these days. But would like to see again, she decided suddenly.

There were about ninety people on his original list, although Nicky had posted only seventy-five invitations so far.

He played it safe, she thought shrewdly, and studied the names once more. She approved of the family and friends he had already invited, along with some of her former pupils from different years. Always the best and the brightest.

In particular, she was pleased to see he had included four brilliant girls from the class of 1994: Jessica Pierce, Kay Lenox, Maria Franconi, and Alexandra Gordon. Most especially Alexandra. Her favourite pupil during the 1990s, perhaps even her most favourite pupil of them all over the many long years she had owned the school. My special girl, she thought.

Anya sat back in the chair, thinking of Alexandra with love and affection, and of her involvement with that poor, bedevilled Tom Conners. All Nicky's fault, since he had introduced them. Well, if she were honest, that wasn't exactly the way it was. Tom had come to the studio to see a client, if she remembered things correctly. So she could not blame the meddling hands of her nephew. Not this time.

And was it ever anybody's fault when lives went awry?

Surely it was fate, destiny stepping in . . . She considered her own life and the role fate had played in it. She was absolutely certain it was her destiny to end up where she was today, having lived the life she had lived. She did not worry about what might have been. She never had.

CHAPTER TWELVE

Although she enjoyed the milder climate of Provence in the winter months, and frequently went there, Anya was, nevertheless, glad to be back in Paris. And back in her house which meant so much to her, filled as it was with her life's history.

This room in particular told the whole story. Encapsulated within its walls were mementoes gathered over the years. Some she had bought, others were gifts, yet more were inherited; certain things she had even created herself.

The decoration of her sitting room depicted a woman of discernment, taste and talent, a woman with an exotic background who had ventured forth courageously when young.

She had followed her heart and her dreams, given free rein to her creativity, believing in her destiny as a woman and an artist. She had lived her life to the fullest, had never regretted anything she had done, only the things she had not found time to do or to accomplish.

After studying the guest list for her birthday party, and making notes, adding a few names, she had put it to one side. But she had continued to work at her desk, going over papers which had accumulated during the couple of weeks she had been in Provence. Finally growing a little weary, she put down her pen, sat up straighter in the chair, and glanced around.

Anya smiled, thinking that at this moment the room had a lovely golden haze to it, even though it was grey outside and dusk was rapidly approaching. But then it had a sunny feeling at all times, as she had fully intended.

Although she had started her professional life as an artist, Anya was talented in many areas, and she had a great flair for interior design. Years ago, wanting to introduce a mood of summer sunshine into this large, high-ceilinged sitting room, she had covered the walls with a yellow-on-yellow striped fabric. This had long since faded from a sharp daffodil to a very pale primrose, but it was nonetheless mellow and warm.

In vivid contrast to these now muted yellow walls were great swathes of scarlet taffeta, which Anya had selected for the full-length draperies at the two windows. They hung on rings from wooden poles, falling straight, but then halfway down they softly billowed out like the skirts of ball gowns.

Anya loved these curtains, the stunning effect they created, and when the bright colour faded she simply replaced them with new ones made of identical fabric. She was forever fussing with them, puffing them up with her hands, and sometimes even stuffing tissue paper behind them for the desired bell shape.

These draperies were her pride, gave her immense pleasure. Even though Nicky tended to tease her about them, he secretly admired her nerve, knowing that only Anya Sedgwick would have dared to use them, secure in the knowledge that they were a knock-out. She had wanted to surprise, and she had succeeded admirably.

Naturally, Anya paid no attention to his teasing, confident in her own taste and choice of colours. In fact, this whole room was a play on scarlet and yellow, with white accents showing up in the paintwork. Also cooling the strong colours was a pale apple-green silk used on several French *bergères*, these elegant chairs scattered around the room. Anya believed that these muted tones balanced a room essentially commanding because of its vibrant colours.

In front of the fireplace there was a large, overstuffed Chesterfield sofa covered in scarlet velvet; the same fabric was used for two huge chunky armchairs, typical Anya Sedgwick touches. She always opted for comfort as well as style. Even the rectangular coffee table was of her own invention. It had originally been an old wrought-iron garden gate, which she had found at a local flea market. She had hired a metal worker to weld on short iron legs, and then she had topped it with a thick slab of glass. She was very proud of her unique coffee table, and glanced at it now, nodding her head in approval.

The fire blazing in the hearth added to the sense of warmth and intimacy on this wintry afternoon, and Anya considered herself blessed to have such a wonderful haven for herself; she had only been back from Provence for two days, and she had felt the cold immediately she had arrived. She still felt cold at times, even though the house was warm.

Old bones, she mumbled as she pushed herself to her feet. Old bones . . . getting *older*. She moved around the desk, and went towards the fireplace, but then paused for a second to admire some of her things.

It was as if she had momentarily forgotten how beautiful her possessions were, during her absence in the south, and she wanted to reacquaint herself with them, touch them, remember who had given them to her, remember what they meant to her.

That's not in the right spot, she thought, as her sharp eyes settled on a silver samovar. This had been put on a circular table, skirted in a red-and-yellow *toile de Jouy*, standing between the two windows.

Leaning forwards, she pushed the samovar into the centre of the table, where it was meant to be, then stood back, gazing at it lovingly; it was very special to her.

This samovar had been resolutely carried out of Russia when they had left for good, by her mother, a woman who had been determined that certain precious family objects would not be left behind.

Anya had no recollection of this event, but her mother had recounted it countless times to her, and to her siblings, and so it had become part of her family history.

As she walked past a console table she stopped to admire her mother's collection of icons, some of them ancient, and all of them very valuable. These had also been in their luggage when they had fled the Bolsheviks, deemed so bloodthirsty by her father.

At the other end of the console, family photographs from Russia were displayed. These were in gold Fabergé frames encrusted with green malachite and blue lapis stones, and had been deeply treasured by her parents. How they had missed their families, whom they had left behind in Russia; they had missed Mother Russia, too, despite the country's ills, the turmoil and bloodshed of the revolution.

And these photographs of handsome men, finely dressed, and beautiful women in fashionable gowns and splendid jewels were poignant reminders of the murdered Romanov monarchy, a lost aristocracy, a vanished world of money, power and privilege, a decimated society which had once been theirs.

Anya turned away from those evocative family photographs, which had been her parents' legacy to her, along with so many other things they had brought out of Russia.

Briefly, her eyes scanned the bookshelves along a wall at the far end of the room. All were filled with a diverse and eclectic mix of books, some of which she had written, while others had been penned by her friends. Soon, she hoped, another of her works would be on a shelf over there, her book on the Art Deco period, which she was finishing at this moment. It would go to the publisher in a month.

It was an automatic reaction, the way her eyes then swung to a striking painting, one which exuded dominant force, and hung on the wall adjoining the bookshelves. It was a landscape, all sharp angles and planes, a modern painting awash with deep greens, rich yellows and dark reds, these colours balanced by earthy browns and coppery, autumnal hues. It was a most powerful painting, by her father Valentin Kossikovsky, the great Russian artist. It held her eyes, as it always had and always would. She was full of admiration for the extraordinary talent that had been his.

Finally she looked away, moved on.

There were a couple of her own paintings hanging here. One in particular stood out. She had painted it over sixty years ago, and it was the full-length, life-sized portrait of a young woman.

Hanging above the fireplace, it was the focus of interest at this end of the room; everyone was drawn towards it, instantly captivated when they caught sight of it.

Anya now approached the fireplace, stood staring up at the canvas, and as usual her eyes were critical. Yet she could never fault this painting, even though it was one of her own works, which she generally had a tendency to overly criticize.

The painting was of her sister Ekaterina, Katti for short, painted when she was just twenty years old. What a beauty she had been.

And there was her own name, Anya Kossikovskaya, and the date, 1941, in the left-hand corner, at the bottom of the painting.

She herself had been twenty-five when she had asked Katti to sit for the portrait, and reluctantly her sister had agreed. For a great beauty she was singularly without vanity, and modest in her opinion of herself.

When the painting was finally finished her father had been amazed, and momentarily rendered speechless. When he had found his voice at last, he had marvelled at Anya's work, and he had called the painting a treasure. Immediately, he had asked the renowned London art gallery which represented him and handled his own work to show it, and they had obliged him. They had even gone as far as to give her an exhibition of her other paintings; this had immediately sold out, much to her surprise and delight.

Many people had tried to buy the painting of her sister. But she had wanted to keep it for herself. For a short while, at least.

In the end, even after the show was over, she had still not been able to let it go. The painting was special to her, meaningful and extremely personal. It was important in a way she found hard to explain, except to say that it had become part of her.

And over the long years many other people had tried to buy it, but her answer was always the same: *Not for sale*.

Anya focused appraising eyes on the painting, studying it, endeavouring to be objective, wanting to analyse its extraordinary appeal to so many different people.

Here was her darling Katti, blonde, beautiful, with high, slanting cheekbones, a broad forehead, wide-set eyes and an impossibly slender, aristocratic nose. Her sister appeared literally to shimmer in the clear light that she had somehow managed to capture on canvas. The painting virtually glowed with incandescent light, a hallmark of her work.

Katti's eyes were a lovely blue, like bits of sky, and they reflected the colour of the blue taffeta gown she was wearing.

Even now Anya felt, as she had always felt, that if she

reached out to the painting her fingers would touch silk not canvas, so real did the fabric appear to be with its folds and shadows and silvery sheen. She could almost hear it rustle.

Once more, it struck her how English her sister's appearance was; actually, the entire painting had a sense of Englishness to it.

And why would it not? she asked herself. She had painted the portrait on a sunny afternoon at the height of summer in the garden of a manor house in Kent. The background had a hint of Gainsborough about it, even though she did say so herself. Not that she was comparing herself with the master, that great eighteenth-century portraitist, but rather with the way he had painted English landscapes of the time. Somehow he had been able to marry the landscape to the human subjects in his portraits, which was rare. It was this technique she had attempted to emulate, and nothing else. No one had ever been able to compete with that extraordinary artist Thomas Gainsborough, except perhaps for Sir Joshua Reynolds, another great master of portraiture in eighteenth-century England.

Were people drawn to this painting because of the girl portrayed in it? she wondered. Or was it for its Englishness? Or perhaps the shimmering pastoral landscape depicted behind the girl? Or the mood of a bygone age which it seemed to capture? She had no idea; she had never known what it signified to other people, what powerful emotional response it evoked in them. But it did, that was certain.

Her thoughts stayed with her sister. Katti had been born in England, but deep down, Anya believed, she had a truly Russian soul. She was so like their mother Natasha had been, almost a carbon copy. Their brother Vladimir, also born in London, was wholly English and did not appear to have a hint of his Russian heritage in him. He was three years younger than Katti, eight years younger than she.

Both her siblings were alive, and for this she was inordinately grateful. She knew they would be thrilled to come to her birthday party; the three of them had remained close and loving over the years, had been there for each other when they were needed. They did not live far away, just across the English Channel, in the beloved country of their birth.

Obviously Nicky had placed them at the top of the guest list, along with the rest of her extended family. Anya laughed out loud when she thought how large it was, and its eclectic mix. She considered it something of a genuine gypsy stew.

Her sister Katti and her husband Sacha Lebedev, another Russian born in England of émigré parents from Moscow via Paris, and their sons Charles and Anthony, and their daughter Serena. And Serena's husband, and the wives of the Lebedev boys. Her brother Vladimir, his wife Lili, and their three sons Michael, Paul and Peter, and their wives.

And then came her closest, her children by her first husband, Michel Lacoste. Her daughter Olga and Anya's son Dimitri; there would be Olga's children, her granddaughters Anna and Natalie, by Olga's former husband Adam Mattison, with whom she was still friendly. Anya had seen his name on the list, and she was glad of that. She had always liked Adam. Dimitri would bring his wife Celestine, and their daughter Solange and son-in-law Jean-Claude.

Oh, and then there was the Sedgwick tribe, whom she had inherited from Hugo, her second husband, and whom she loved as much as her own. Larry, his wife Stephanie; Nicky, her special favourite, and his wife Constance. But no, perhaps Constance would not come, since she and Nicky were apparently at loggerheads, estranged at the moment. She had not noticed Connie's name on the guest list. And of course there was their sister Rosamund, who had never married, although she had often been engaged. She was expected, along with her current partner Henry Lester.

It was indeed a complex mixture, but they were all members of her family, and she cared for each and every one of them. The party's going to be fun, she thought, sitting down on the scarlet velvet sofa. She leaned back against the soft cushions, enjoying the warmth of the fire, the floral smell of the scented candles, the comfort of the surroundings in general, the tranquil atmosphere which prevailed here.

The painting of her sister Katti had triggered innumerable memories . . . memories of the past, of people she had loved who were gone for ever . . . others whom she loved and who, fortunately, were still alive . . .

Eighty-five, she thought, I can't believe I'm going to be eighty-five in just three months. I feel so much younger inside.

Anya smiled to herself, and looked up at the painting of Katti. She felt as young as that girl there, who gazed back at her with such innocent eyes . . .

She had been born in St Petersburg in 1916, virtually on the eve of the Russian Revolution, although she had no recollections of that city as it was then. Nor did she know of the tumultuous events of 1917 and 1918, which had led her parents to flee their country.

But her father, Prince Valentin Kossikovsky, had recounted everything to her when she was old enough to understand. The politics of these chaotic times was his favourite subject, and besides this he was a mesmerizing raconteur, one who held her fascinated with his tales and reminiscences.

Her parents were from Russia's most elite and privileged society; her father was a man of ancient lineage, great wealth derived from vast family-owned lands in the Crimea, a variety of industrial holdings in Moscow, and financial interests abroad. Her mother Nathalie, always called Natasha, was the daughter of Count Ilya Devenarskoe, also a landowner and man of wealth.

At the time of her birth Anya's father was acquiring a name for himself as an artist of formidable talent. His mother and siblings regarded his painting as more of a hobby than anything else; in fact, his mother, Princess Irina, thought it was an avocation rather than a vocation.

But, as it eventually turned out, she was totally wrong. Valentin Kossikovsky *had* found his true *vocation* when he had begun to paint seriously, and in time he would astound art lovers around the world with his work; he was to become as famous as his contemporary, Marc Chagall.

Within fifteen years of his departure from Russia, Valentin would be acclaimed as one of the great Russian painters of the twentieth century.

But in 1917 Valentin was not thinking of fame but of escape. Anya was now a year old, and he was worried about the safety of his child and young wife Natasha. To a certain extent, he was involved in politics, as were other Russians of his ilk, and he was well aware of trouble brewing. Smart, intuitive and well informed, he was certain that Russia was about to plunge into disaster and turmoil from which it would never recover. He had long anticipated the revolution, had seen it coming, and accordingly he had made certain financial plans.

At this time, as Anya learned in later years, her father believed that they had been brought to the brink of ruin by the German wife of the Tsar, who was born Princess Alix of Hesse. Until the day he died, Valentin Kossikovsky tended to blame Tsarina Alexandra for the revolution, as did so many of his contemporaries and some members of the imperial Romanov family. Within the circle of his small family, he quietly castigated her, characterizing her as deluded, manipulative, controlling and interfering. As for Tsar Nicholas II, Valentin thought he was weak, vacillating, and under the thumb of his wife.

And yet Prince Valentin Kossikovsky also knew, as most educated Russians knew, that basically Nicholas was a good man and not the tyrant he was purported to be by the Bolsheviks. History would prove Valentin to be correct on this score; in time Tsar Nicholas II was deemed a martyr.

As matters drew to a head within the Duma, the national government, at the beginning of 1917, Valentin held his breath, worrying, waiting, weighing the odds, wondering what moves to make.

Then unexpectedly, in March of that year, Tsar Nicholas II

abdicated on behalf of himself and the Tsarevitch, in favour of his brother, Grand Duke Michael Aleksandrovich.

For a short time, Valentin thought that disaster had been averted, that Michael would become a constitutional monarch, like his first cousin, King George V of England. This is what the government said they wanted.

Valentin, like most of the aristocracy, admired Grand Duke Michael, who was a celebrated war hero, a forthright man of honour, honesty, and great ability, who favoured constitutional monarchy, had advocated it in the past to his brother.

Valentin often told Anya when she was growing up that he had met Grand Duke Michael with her Uncle Sergei, who was in the army and stationed at Gatchina, where Michael was stationed. 'We frequently ran into each other at the riding school of the Blue Cuirassiers. He would have made a good emperor.'

Although she knew the story by heart, Anya always pleaded to hear it again. 'What happened to Michael, Papa? Tell me the story, please, please.'

And her father would explain: 'Michael was Tsar for only a day. He abdicated immediately, because that was what the Bolsheviks wanted him to do. Since *he* wanted to prevent bloodshed he signed the papers of abdication. But he didn't prevent the killing or the terrible bloodbath, Anya. Michael was the last Emperor and Autocrat of All the Russias, and the first of the Romanovs to be murdered, just a few weeks before his brother Nicholas and his family were killed in cold blood, in that cellar in Ekaterinburg.'

Grand Duke Michael was murdered at two a.m. on June

13, 1918. The ghastly murder of Michael and his secretary Nicholas Johnson took place in the woods outside Perm, the town where they had been under house arrest in the local hotel. But the murders were not known about then; news of Michael's death did not come out for a long time. At first it was assumed he had managed to escape with Johnson, and that they had fled Russia.

Valentin and Natasha had not believed this story. They were convinced there had been foul play on the part of the Bolsheviks. Five weeks later, when the Tsar and his family were so brutally murdered, the news leaked out almost immediately. Valentin made his moves with great speed. He went to see his Uncle Sandro, his father's first cousin, who was a very close friend of Admiral Kolchak, at that time the Supreme Commander of the White Army.

A lot of strings were pulled by a lot of people, and Valentin, Natasha and their daughter Anya were finally able to leave Russia six months later, in January of 1919, getting out via Finland. From Helsinki they went to Sweden, and from Stockholm they travelled to Oslo. After spending several weeks in Norway, they were finally able to board a British merchant ship and set sale for Scotland.

Waiting for them there was Valentin's older sister Olga, who in 1910 had married a wealthy English banker, Adrian Hamilton, and moved to London.

Anya's first conscious memories from her childhood were of England, and, in particular, her aunt's beautiful manor house in Kent, where years later she would paint the portrait of Katti on the terrace.

It was in this house, Haverlea Chase, that the Kossikovskys

lived until they found a place of their own. Valentin and Natasha spoke several languages, including English, and so they adapted quickly to life in the bucolic English countryside. And for the first time in years they felt safe from harm at last.

After six months of living in Kent, Valentin knew he must move on. He and Natasha quickly found a small but attractive house in Chelsea; what made it so attractive to them was the conservatory in the garden. Built almost entirely of glass, this was ideal as a studio in which Valentin could paint.

Fortunately, Valentin Kossikovsky had wisely moved money out of Russia in 1912. It ended up in England, where it was well invested by his banker brother-in-law. And so, unlike many other White Russian émigrés who had fled to London and Paris, they were not destitute.

It was in this lovely old house in Chelsea that Anya grew up, surrounded by the possessions her mother had managed to bring out of Russia . . . the silver samovar in which she made tea every day . . . the icons arranged on a table in the sitting room, alongside the family photographs in their Fabergé frames.

Anya ate Russian food, learned Russian history from her father, and the language from her parents who spoke only Russian when they were alone.

In essence, she was raised as a Russian aristocrat would have been brought up in St Petersburg. And yet she was also an English girl who grew up in the ways of her adopted country. She went to a private kindergarten as a young child, and then to one of the best boarding schools; later she became a student at the Royal College of Art.

'I'm a funny mixture,' she said to Michel Lacoste, when she first met him in Paris. 'But deep down I know that my soul is Russian.' And she continued to believe this for the rest of her life, just as her father, the prince, had intended.

CHAPTER THIRTEEN

The rain did nothing to dampen Nicholas Sedgwick's good mood. As he walked across the Boulevard des Invalides, heading towards the rue de l'Université, he dismissed the sudden downpour as merely an April shower that would stop at any moment. And it did, almost before he had completed this thought.

Closing his umbrella, he hooked it over his arm, and marched on at a brisk pace, humming under his breath. He had just finished the sketches of sets for a new movie to be shot at the studios in Billancourt and in the Loire Valley, and he was thrilled that the producer and director had liked his designs; actually, they had both been bowled over by them.

Nothing like a little success to put a man in a happy frame of mind, he thought, as he crossed the boulevard, making for Anya's school.

And then his expression changed and a shadow crossed

his handsome face, settled in his bluish-green eyes, clouding them over. Professionally, he was at a high point; but in his personal life happiness had eluded him for a long time, and this troubled him greatly.

As far as he was concerned, his marriage to Constance Aykroyd, the English stage actress, was over. He had tried to make it work, but he simply became more and more estranged from her as the months went by, and all he wanted now was to end it. And as peacefully as possible.

But Connie did not want a divorce; she clung to him and to the marriage. He took the line of least resistance, did nothing legally, because he had no real reason to push for the divorce at the moment. There was no other woman in his life; he was so busy with his work he didn't have much time to start seeing lawyers, setting the legal wheels in motion. Although deep within himself he knew that this was an inevitability, if he was going to get his freedom. Certainly Connie was not about to set him free of her own accord, even though he had moved out many months ago.

Nicky sighed, thinking how difficult and temperamental Connie had become. And anorexic. He was really so upset by her these days. She was so painfully thin that she appeared to be starving herself to death, looked like one of those tragic Holocaust victims released from Belsen at the end of the war. He shuddered involuntarily; just *thinking* about her ghastly appearance appalled him. She was a walking skeleton.

Nicky was thankful there were no children involved in this disastrous marriage. It would be a clean break, when it finally happened, and with no additional casualties of the divorce, thank God.

And he was only thirty-eight.

He could start again. He hoped. Hope springs eternal . . . that was the favourite line of Hugh Sedgwick, his uncle. Hugo, as he was commonly called, was Anya's second husband; he had been a rather special man, a business genius and the linchpin of the family, the man around whom everyone and everything revolved. Charismatic, reliable and strong, he had been steady as a rock, and the most enduring influence in Nicky's life.

At least my work is going well, Nicky thought, as he turned the corner. He and his brother Larry were busier than they had ever been, and their design company, with offices in Paris and London, was thriving.

Not only that, he was particularly enjoying teaching this season. He gave two classes a week, on set designing and decorating, at Anya's school, and this year he had discovered that he had several brilliant students in his class. Consistently, they took his breath away with their work.

Larry, who stood in for him when he was away on a film, agreed with him about their unique talents, was also full of praise.

Nicky had always found it rewarding to encourage and nurture students who showed promise, and he took pleasure in showing them how to develop their work and achieve their goals.

Halfway down the rue de l'Université he finally came to the huge, wooden double doors that led into the courtyard of the school. He went in through the small side door designed for pedestrians; as he closed it behind him he hoped Anya would be happy with the designs he had created for her birthday party. He was going to show them to her later today.

Nicky went up in the old-fashioned lift to his office on the fourth floor. This was in the building where the original school had first started, and had been housed from the twenties to the forties, which was when adjoining buildings were acquired.

As he stepped out of the lift and walked along the corridor, he couldn't help thinking about the history of this place. The school would be seventy-five years old later this year and what a success story it was.

If only walls could talk, he thought, going into his office. He put his umbrella in the cupboard, sat down at his large desk and began to look at the sketches he had made for Anya's party. But his mind drifted off after a while, his thoughts on the school, and what it had become, all because of Anya Sedgwick.

Originally it had been a modest little school of art run by Catherine Lacoste, Anya's mother-in-law.

The young widow of the renowned French sculptor, Laurent Lacoste, who had started the school in 1926, she had struggled to keep it going after Laurent's death in the early thirties.

Despite being small, it had a good reputation because of the gifted teachers it employed, mostly artists themselves who needed to earn a steady income to support their art. Even in those days it had a certain prestige because of Laurent Lacoste's name.

Incredibly, and to her credit, Catherine had even managed to keep the school open during the war years and the German Occupation of Paris. Somehow it had been able to survive in the terrible and troubled times of the Nazis' domination of Paris, the many deprivations and hardships.

After the end of the Second World War, the school had begun to blossom more fully once again. But in 1948 Catherine realized she could not run it by herself for much longer. She was growing increasingly debilitated by arthritis, and less mobile than ever. Eventually she had asked her young daughter-in-law to take over the school and run it for her. Anya had agreed, knowing she would have the advice and guidance of her mother-in-law at all times.

Anya and Catherine had always been unusually close. They had initially bonded in 1936, when Michel had taken Anya to meet his mother for the first time. It had been her twentieth birthday, and Anya had once told Nicky that they had sat in the garden drinking champagne and giggling like schoolgirls as they got to know one another. Apparently they had hit it off in no uncertain terms; Catherine had even predicted, that very afternoon, that Anya and her son would marry one day.

During the war, Michel Lacoste, a journalist by profession, was based in London, where he was a member of the staff of General Charles de Gaulle, leader of the Free French forces, who was headquartered in London.

Anya and Michel, who had fallen in love in Paris before the war, continued to see each other in war-torn England. They were married in 1941 during the Blitz. The wedding took place at the Kossikovsky house in Chelsea, in an austere and badly bombed-out London. Anya was twenty-five, Michel thirty-one.

In 1946, some months after the war was over, Michel had taken Anya and their two young children, Olga, aged three, and Dimitri, aged two, back to Paris.

Life in France in 1946 was full of post-war problems and shortages, just as the rest of Europe was. Because of the shortage of available housing, and their shaky financial situation, Michel and Anya had moved in with his mother. Catherine had been thrilled; she welcomed them warmly, excited and delighted to have her son's young family with her at long last. The war years had been hard and lonely; she welcomed their company, cherished her beautiful grandchildren.

They had all lived compatibly in the lovely old black-and-white half-timbered house where Anya still lived. The house was big enough for them all, and the garden a boon, a place for the children to play and run free, especially in the warm weather.

At Catherine's request, Anya had gone to teach part-time at the school; much to her amazement, she had discovered she had a gift for teaching. And then two years later, when Catherine had asked her to take over, she had agreed to do so, confident in her abilities.

Anya was an astute young woman, and soon, under her guidance, the school began to prosper. Anya had a talent for organization, management and promotion, plus a keen nose for sniffing out exceptional teachers. Like Catherine before her, she always sought out artists who needed to support themselves in a compatible environment, whilst continuing their own creative careers. It was a policy that had always paid off.

But, perhaps most importantly, Anya had a vision. In her mind's eye she could see so many marvellous possibilities, exciting ways to expand the little art school by developing its curriculum, adding new courses which taught some of the other important decorative arts.

However, out of respect for Catherine, Anya did not make any really serious changes until after Catherine's death in 1951.

It was at this time that she slowly and cautiously began to upgrade the school, adding the new courses which taught fashion and textile design, as well as costume and theatrical design.

The classes in art and sculpture were still the mainstay of the school, and as always the most important to Anya. But students began to enrol for the other courses, and she and Michel were thrilled.

Her innovations, long in the planning stages, were working, and both of them were surprised how popular the new courses were becoming. So much so, they acquired the adjoining building when it became vacant, and another a year later.

And then in 1955 tragedy struck.

Michel suddenly and unexpectedly died of a massive heart attack; he was forty-five years old. He and Anya had been married for fourteen happy years, and she staggered with the terrible shock and devastating loss.

Stunned and grief-stricken as she was by Michel's untimely

death, Anya continued to run the school. In a way, it held her together, helped to get her through those heartbreaking months. When Nicky once asked her how she had managed to do it, she had replied: 'I just kept plodding on. Even though my heart was breaking, I knew I couldn't give in, or collapse. I had so many responsibilities at the school, and many people depended on me for a livelihood, especially the staff, and the teachers. There were my two young children also . . . to raise and educate, and I had a living to earn. I had to keep going, you know. But it was the plodding that did it . . . that was the secret. Anyway, I felt I owed it to Catherine's memory to keep the school open.'

Two years after Michel's death, in 1957, Anya met Hugh Sedgwick, an English businessman living and working in Paris. A widower and childless, he had been introduced to Anya by mutual friends, who thought these two single people were a good match. Hugo came from a theatrical family; his brother Martin and his sister Clarice were both actors, and Hugo himself was a bit of an amateur artist, painting in his spare time. They seemed to have a lot in common.

Hugo and Anya had dined together several times when she let the friendship drift away. She was far too involved with her children and the school to be bothered with developing a relationship, and, as she later said, the time was not right for her.

A year later, they ran into each other by accident at an art exposition, discovered how much they enjoyed each other that evening, and soon began to see each other once more. Very quickly, they became involved, and in 1960 they were married in Paris.

Hugo was an enterprising businessman of unusual acumen and foresight. When Anya asked him to help her with the financial management of the school, a year after they were married, Hugo agreed. He happily took over these duties from Anya, who was overburdened. Within a year the school turned yet another corner; it became highly profitable for the first time in its history.

Not only that, its reputation began to grow in the ensuing years. More than ever before, students were flocking to the school, many of them from abroad. It had acquired a certain cachet, not least because many of its graduates had become famous in their given fields. And Anya's own fame as a teacher and nurturer of young talent had begun to spread. A place at her school had become expensive, and much sought after.

By the mid-sixties it was called the Anya Sedgwick School of Decorative Arts. A few years later the name was changed again, this time to the Anya Sedgwick School of Decorative Arts, Design and Couture. And it went on growing, turning out truly exceptional graduates, and Anya's fame was magnified. She had become a legend in her own time.

The shrilling telephone startled Nicky to such an extent he almost jumped out of his skin. He had been so lost in thought it took him a moment to recover and reach for the receiver.

'Nicholas Sedgwick.'

'It's Anya, Nicky.'

'*Hello!* I was just thinking about you, or rather, the history of the school.'

'And what *exactly* were you thinking?'

'To tell you the truth, I was wondering if you were planning on giving some sort of reception later in the year? After all, the school is celebrating its seventy-fifth anniversary in November.'

She began to laugh. 'Don't you think my birthday party is enough celebrating?'

Laughing with her, he answered, 'One thing has nothing to do with the other. Just a *small* reception, Anya.'

'I don't know, Nicky. Let me think about it.'

'Yes, do that. And we can talk later. Now, what time shall I come to your office, to show you the sketches for the theme of your party?'

'I don't want to see them, Nicky, that's why I'm phoning you. Frankly, I would much prefer the party to be a *total* surprise . . . every aspect of it. I'll leave it all to you to make the choices and the decisions.'

'But Anya –'

'No, no,' she cut in. 'I trust you implicitly, darling boy. You have the best taste of anybody I know.'

'That's very flattering, I must say, but I do think I'd feel better if you saw them,' he protested.

'I want to be surprised. Nothing much does surprise me these days, I must admit, so indulge me. I know I'm going to love everything.'

'I sincerely hope so,' he muttered, then added, 'But to be honest, I really was looking forward to seeing you.'

'Then you can take me out to tea. That would be *nice*, Nicky, and we can have a little chat. We haven't done that lately.'

'What a good idea, and it'll be my pleasure. What time shall I stop by your office to pick you up?'

'I'm not at the school. I'm . . . out. So why don't we meet at the Hotel Meurice, it's very beautiful after its redecoration. Have you seen it lately?'

'No, I haven't.'

'Then we'll meet there. At four o'clock, oh, and Nicky, the main entrance is now on the rue de Rivoli.'

'I'll be there. Four sharp.'

CHAPTER FOURTEEN

They sat together in the *Jardin d'Hiver* – the winter garden – just beyond the lobby of the newly refurbished Hotel Meurice on the rue de Rivoli opposite the Tuileries.

Palm trees in tubs and many other exotic plants helped to create the garden feeling so prevalent in this charming and comfortable spot where lunch and tea were served. Floating above, set in the centre of the large curved ceiling, was a glass roof in the shape of a dome, interlaced with metal work. The milky opaqueness of the glass filtered the natural daylight and gave this garden-inspired room a softness which was unique.

'They discovered that glass roof when they started to tear the hotel apart,' Anya suddenly announced, looking up at the ceiling and then glancing across at Nicky. 'It had been covered up, plastered over and painted for many years. No one had any idea that the central dome was actually made of glass, until the restoration and refurbishment began several years ago.'

'How amazing! And what's even more amazing is the condition of the glass,' Nicky exclaimed, following her gaze. 'It *can't* be the original, can it?'

'No, actually it is not. It's new glass, and, of course, a totally new dome, Nicky, made in the Art Nouveau style, as you can see,' Anya informed him. 'The architects and designers had the original copied. You see, when they found the glass roof up there it was cracked and broken, ruined. It had been damaged by the plaster and paint which had been slathered on for God knows how many years. But it's beautiful now, isn't it? I've always been a trifle partial to Art Nouveau, haven't you?'

Nicky nodded, and gave her a curious look. 'How do you know all this, about the roof I mean?'

Anya smiled a little bit smugly. 'One of the directors is a friend of mine, and he told me about that glass roof when he showed me around the hotel recently, then took me to dinner here.'

Laughing, Nicky shook his head. 'Why do I ever ask you a single question when it comes to such things? I might have known you got your information from the horse's mouth.'

She made no comment, merely gave a slight nod, and then sat back in the chair, glancing around her. 'Catherine Lacoste always loved this hotel,' she confided after a moment. 'She used to bring me here for tea. Or champagne. It became a favourite of mine, too. Of course, when the war came she never set foot inside the place. How could she? During the Occupation, the hotel was the headquarters of the German High Command, you see. How Catherine hated *les boches*.'

'As did the rest of France.'

'Well, thank God for one thing . . . the Nazis didn't destroy Paris, although they could have.'

'I shudder at the mere *thought* of that. It would have been ghastly, a true desecration.'

'Hitler ordered historic buildings destroyed in 1944, when Allied troops were approaching. But General Dietrich von Choltitz, the occupying governor, was not able to perpetrate such sacrilege. He surrendered the city intact to General Leclerc, liberator of Paris,' she explained.

'Hugo once told me something about that,' Nicholas said and picked up his cup, took a sip of tea, eyed Anya over the rim, thinking how well she looked this afternoon. She was wearing a crisply tailored, pale blue wool suit, and her much-loved string of large, South Sea pearls and matching earrings, which were a must with her, and had become her trademark, in a sense.

Her softly waved, short dark-blonde hair was as elegantly coiffed as it usually was, and she looked positively radiant, just wonderful to Nicky. She forever sang the praises of her sister Katti, considered her to be the more beautiful, but in his opinion this was not the case. They were very similar in appearance, the two Kossikovskaya sisters, but Anya's looks were decidedly the more striking, Nicky believed. Her eyes were larger, and a lovely blue, her nose better shaped, and her high cheekbones, even at her age, were quite sensational. She looked twenty years younger than she really was. One thing on her side was her marvellous health, which she attributed to her Russian genes.

Breaking into his thoughts, Anya asked, 'Have you had many acceptances for my party so far, Nicky?'

'A lot, yes indeed, and I'm expecting more this week. The first of April was the deadline I gave, but some people will be late, that's normal.'

'Have you heard from Alexa? Has she accepted?'

'No, she hasn't, not yet. But I'm sure I'll be hearing from her any day now.'

'She might not come. She's not been back to Paris since she broke up with Tom Conners, and if you remember, that was three years ago, just about the time she stopped working with you and Larry. I saw her in New York when I was there last year to receive that award . . .' She paused, gave him a very pointed look, and finished, 'I rather got the impression Alexa was avoiding France . . . Paris in particular. Because of him.'

'You're implying she's carrying a torch.'

'I believe she is.'

Nicky sighed. 'I always warned her about him, and so did Larry. Repeatedly. Tom's hauling far too much emotional baggage. No woman needs that, Anya.'

'Perhaps he's discarded some of it? By now?'

'You'd think so, wouldn't you . . . but I just don't know . . .' His voice trailed off lamely, and then he threw her a helpless look. 'Tom was always an odd chap.'

'In what way?'

'A loner. Kept his thoughts to himself. Standoffish. Yes, I suppose that's what I mean. He was very independent and self-contained. Not at all confiding.'

'Don't you ever see him these days?' Anya leaned forward, her blue eyes on him. 'I was under the impression he represented quite a few people in show business.'

'That's absolutely true, he did. Probably still does. But I haven't run into him for the longest time, for at least a year. Maybe longer even.' His eyes narrowed slightly. 'Why? What are you getting at?'

'I do so want Alexa to be at the party. I was just wondering if there was any way we could make it easier for her.'

'By inviting him too?'

'No, no, don't be so silly, Nicholas! That wouldn't make her feel more comfortable, quite the contrary. What I meant was that perhaps he's left Paris.'

'I doubt it.' Nicky sat up, an alert expression setting on his face.

'But if he no longer lives here, we could tell her that, don't you see?' Anya pressed.

'Yes, I do. But I'm pretty sure he's still a resident of this fair city. He was born here, it's where he belongs.'

'Some people retire, move location, go south to Provence, somewhere like that.'

'Not Tom, take my word for it. Incidentally, I did hear from that nice Italian girl, the one who was in Alexa's class. Maria Franconi. She was practically the first to accept.'

A wide smile spread itself across Anya's face. 'I'm so glad she's coming! She's such a lovely person. And she has such enormous talent, wasted probably these days.'

'What do you mean?' Nicky asked, frowning.

'She could be doing a lot more than designing textiles for that antiquated family business she's stuck in, I can tell you that, darling boy. The girl's an extraordinary artist.' Not giving him a chance to make any kind of comment, she continued, 'Kay Lenox will come, that I am certain of, but not Jessica. I don't think she'll be able to face Paris, in view of what happened to her.'

'You mean Lucien's disappearance?'

'I do. That was a mystery, one that's never been solved, and I don't suppose it ever will be. *C'est dommage.*'

'I agree with you. And so you think Jessica will forgo your party because Paris holds bad memories, too much pain for her?'

Anya nodded and sat back in the chair. 'I really do, Nicky, I've never seen anyone so distraught. I remember it so very clearly, it might have happened only yesterday. One minute she was full of life, happy, madly in love, looking to a future with him, and the next she was plunged into the most horrendous anguish and despair.' She shook her head. 'I honestly thought she would never recover. It's different when the person you love dies. There's an awful finality to death. But it is final. The end. And there's the funeral, family gatherings, grieving, all of those necessary rituals, and they help, believe me they do. Somehow you go on living, by rote perhaps, and for a long time it's by rote. Eventually, though, you begin to feel a little bit better. Life *is* for the living, you know. I've come to be a firm believer in that cliché. But when the object of your love just . . . *disappears*, as if into thin air, then everything becomes impossible, and in a peculiar way there's actually no way to deal with the grief and the pain.'

'Because there's no closure,' Nicky suggested.

'Correct. No body. No burial. No grieving as such. There-fore no closure. No end to the pain, because you don't know what happened to him. It's as simple as that. For Jessica it was a nightmare. I was really concerned for her, worried to death. To be very frank, I thought she was in danger of becoming . . . well, mentally ill. For a while, she *was* demented, couldn't come to grips with the loss, and since Lucien Girard had no family there really was no one for her to grieve with, or be consoled by in the way she needed. Alain Bonnal was wonderful, but like her he was nonplussed, confused, and, not unnaturally, very baffled. Still, they were supportive of each other, helped each other for a while.'

'And nothing has ever turned up? No body has been washed ashore? Or found anywhere else? No information was ever forthcoming from the police?'

'None. I would have told you. Look, Nicky, it was as if Lucien never existed.'

For a moment Nicky did not respond. He had known Lucien, and Larry had introduced the young actor to Jessica. What a strange story it was. Finally, he said, 'I remember her parents came to Paris to be with her, and then they took her back to Texas. But what actually happened to Jessica, Anya? Did she ever marry? Do you hear from her?'

'Oh yes, I do, I get notes and cards from her from time to time, or a clipping from *Architectural Digest*, when one of the homes she has designed appears in it. She's enormously talented, one of the great interior designers of today, and that's partly because of her classical background. And no, she hasn't married. She lives in Bel-Air, does a lot of designing for the rich and famous. But she never misses sending me a

Christmas card with a lovely message. In fact, I get Christmas cards from Kay and Maria as well.'

'And Alex?'

'Oh, she's constantly in touch. I get letters, cards, photographs, and phone calls. Alexa has always been very devoted to me, warm, loving.'

'You saw her in New York last year. How was she? How's her personal life shaped up?'

'Very well, but you know that, Nicky. You know what a success she's had in theatrical design. I thought she'd been in touch with you.'

'That's true, she has. But she never discussed her personal life. Never.'

'And you never mentioned Tom Conners?'

'Sure I did. Once. She bit my head off, was really rather snotty. Therefore, I learned my lesson. Hell hath no fury like a woman in love with a man she can't have because he's a jerk.'

'Is that what you really think about Tom?' She gave him a hard stare, her brows puckering.

'Yep.' Then he shook his head, looking slightly chagrined. 'No, no, not really. In many ways he's a good man. But Tom had a great tragedy in his life and he's let it ruin his life, ruin any chance of happiness with a woman. And that's certainly being a jerk, isn't it?'

'Yes, I tend to agree. And what's more, I can't imagine any man letting a gorgeous young woman slip through his fingers the way he did Alexa.' Anya lifted her cup, sipped her tea, then continued, 'It's funny isn't it, how one girl in particular becomes very important in one's life. I've had some truly wonderful students, male and female, over many years of teaching, but there's never been anyone quite like her. At least, not for me. She was . . . the *perfect girl*. No, not perfect, I don't really mean that exactly, because she was flawed then, as she is now, I've no doubt. But she was the embodiment of everything I thought a young woman should be. Do you understand what I mean, Nick?'

'Yes, I do, only too well. I think I was always a bit in love with Alexa when she worked with Larry and me.' He smiled ruefully, took hold of her hand. 'Maybe I still am. Do you know the reason why?'

'No, I don't.'

'It's because Alexandra Gordon is so like you, Anya. That's why you love her yourself, you know. She might have been cast from the same mould as you, and she's a lot more like you than Olga is, and I mean that in the nicest way; I'm not being critical of your daughter. What I'm trying to say is that Alexa is a reflection of you, quite by accident. Or maybe she modelled herself on you. In any event, she has a lot of your special talents.'

'She does, yes, I think you're right.'

He laughed. 'I'm positive. She's creative but also very competent, that was most obvious when she worked for us. You know, she can do so many other things as well as design sets. You could give her this school to run, and she'd do it very well. She could design costumes, or fashionable clothes, even decorate a house. She's that kind of person, and her work will always be excellent. Yes, she's like you in that sense.'

'I think you might be a bit biased, Nicky,' she answered with a small smile. 'And listen to me, on reflection I don't think we should meddle in her life. I shouldn't have suggested it.' She patted his hand still holding hers, and gave him a stern look. 'Meddling can be dangerous. We mustn't play God, Nicky.'

'Like I sometimes do?'

'Exactly. Hugo used to say to me, what will be, will be. And he was right. You know, life does have a way of taking care of itself. So let us leave everything to life, let things take their course. If we don't hear from Alexa in a week or so, I'll phone her, ask her to come to the birthday party. For me.' Her eyes were warm and loving as she went on, 'I'm glad we're doing this, Nicky, I've been worried about you, worried about the way you've looked, so strained lately. I know there are problems with Constance. Can you not work them out?'

'I doubt it. The marriage is over, only she won't accept that. But she'll have to eventually. I moved out a long time ago. Now I've got to move on, get on with my life.'

'Is there anyone else?' Anya asked softly. He was very handsome, dark, striking, as Hugo had been, and she knew most women found Nicky irresistible.

'No, there's no one. I'd tell you if there was.' He let out a long sigh. 'Look, she and I have grown apart, and quite apart from anything else, I've really been put off by her dieting. Actually, it's gone beyond that. She's anorexic. Connie looks really ill, like a skeleton, as if she's stepped out of one of those wartime concentration camps.'

'Let's give those horrendous places their correct name, Nick. *They were death camps.*'

'I know.'

'It's an illness, anorexia. You know that, just as bulimia is, too. She needs help. Can't you get Connie to see a doctor, one who treats eating disorders?'

'I've tried, so has her sister. She's very resistant to the idea, it's like she has blinkers on.'

'That's part of the illness, I'm told.' Anya leaned back against the chair. 'If there's anything I can do, you only have to ask.'

'Thanks, Anya.'

A companionable silence fell between them. But eventually, Anya murmured in a reflective voice, 'Life is strange, unpredictable, so is this world we live in. Here we are, Nicky, sitting in the Meurice so relaxed, having afternoon tea. But just think, sixty years ago the Nazis were installed in this very hotel, running the German Occupation of France. Why, they had the very destiny of France in their hands. How they were feared and hated. And then, suddenly, they are finished. The conquerors are defeated. French resistance forces march into Paris and liberate the city. And everything changes yet again.'

'Uncle Hugo used to say that the only thing that's permanent *is* change.'

PART THREE

Quest

CHAPTER FIFTEEN

Anya had convinced her to change her mind.

And so, here she was, in Paris in the spring. In May, to be exact. Three weeks before the birthday party on June the second. Far too early. On the other hand, Alexandra Gordon knew she had plenty to occupy herself with during this period.

She planned to spend some special time with Anya; she was going to do quite a lot of serious shopping, wanting to treat herself to new clothes, which she needed, and felt she deserved after the many long months of hard work on the Broadway play. Also, since she had just agreed to work with Nicky on a new movie, which would start shooting in October, it was imperative that she have a number of meetings with him immediately.

And then there was her hidden agenda.

Tom Conners.

She fully intended to seek him out. She needed to understand where he was at this stage in his life. And where she
stood with him. And there was something else . . . she had to
know how she actually felt about him. After all, she had not
seen him for three years; perhaps when they did finally come
face to face her feelings would be quite different now.

In her own mind – most of the time – it was over.

He *had* ended it, telling her there was no future for her with
him, that he could not marry her, would not. Nor anyone
else. Seemingly, his past had claimed his future.

And yet in a certain way it *wasn't* over for her. Part of her
still secretly yearned for him. He occupied a large part of her,
continually crept into her thoughts when she least expected.
But lately she had come to recognize that none of this was
very healthy, and that she could not live with the situation
any longer.

Alexa accepted that she had to be emotionally free, in order
to move forward, that she could not marry Jack Wilton until
she had confronted the demons that haunted her. It wouldn't
be fair to Jack, who was such a decent human being, or to
herself, for that matter.

If she was going to marry Jack, it must be with a free heart,
with love in her heart only for him. Anything else would be
shoddy.

And so she had come to slay the dragon in his lair.

After that, perhaps she could turn the page, and get on
with her life. After all, she was almost thirty, and it seemed
to her that time sped by faster than ever these days.

Alexa had admitted to herself that she had felt much more
relaxed, once she had made the decision to see Tom. Not

only comfortable about coming to Paris for Anya's landmark celebration, but more at ease within herself. It was as if just making the decision about Tom had lifted a burden from her.

She had arrived in Paris on Thursday morning, having taken a night flight from New York, and after unpacking and resting for most of yesterday she was now ready for action.

It was eleven o'clock on Friday morning, May the eleventh, and the temptation to call Tom Conners was strong. But Alexa resisted picking up the receiver. She was not quite ready to start dealing with him just yet.

And so she glanced around the bedroom, making a last-minute check, and picked up her handbag. On the desk, where she had put them yesterday, were her dark glasses, her address book, a notepad, and her cellphone, plus the door key.

Scooping everything up, dropping them into her bag, she left the room and headed for the lift.

A few seconds later she was walking across the elegant, marble-floored lobby of the Hotel Meurice, which Anya had recommended several weeks ago. She was glad she had taken Anya's advice; her room was comfortable and pleasant, and the hotel's location was ideal for her.

Alexa went through the revolving door and down the steps, stood outside the hotel for a moment, undecided what to do. She was invited to Anya's house for lunch at one o'clock, so she had two hours to fill. And lots of options.

She was in her most favourite city in the world, and she

knew it well; and since she had not been here for three years she was filled with excitement, enormous nostalgia.

If she turned left, she could walk down to the Louvre where one of her favourite paintings hung, and it would certainly give her a great deal of pleasure to see it again.

Or she could turn right, walk along the rue de Rivoli, looking in shop windows until she came to the Place de la Concorde, the Champs Elysées beyond, with the Arc de Triomphe at the top. Always a heart-stopping sight to her.

Then again, the Place Vendôme was just behind the hotel, as was the rue du Faubourg St Honoré, where some of her favourite boutiques were. But she was not really in the mood for shopping, trying on clothes. She would do that another day. All day. Making a snap decision, she set off walking towards the Louvre.

What a glorious day it was.

Paris shimmered under a shimmering sky. It was brilliant, awash with sunlight, and there was not a cloud visible. The sky appeared to be high flung, a great arc that looked like an upturned bowl with its inside glazed a soft powder blue. There was no breeze; it was not sultry either. It was, very simply, the most perfect weather.

How magnificent Paris looks today, she thought, as she glanced around her, walking along the rue de Rivoli at a steady pace. Then she made a mental note to visit Le Louvre des Antiquaires in the Place du Palais Royal nearby. She hoped that in this unique gallery of antique shops she would find something really special and original for Anya's birthday. There might be something Russian or English, some small memento which would evoke all the right kinds of memories in Anya.

A flood of her own memories engulfed Alexa; they made her heart clench with their bittersweetness. Memories of Tom and the two years they spent together . . . their sensual lovemaking, their joy in each other. Memories of working on different movies with Nicky and Larry. Such exciting days with them, from whom she had learned so much . . . such exciting nights with Tom, from whom she had also learned so much . . . including heartbreak, heartache . . .

She was assaulted all of a sudden by the fragrant, mouthwatering smell of fresh coffee. Tantalizingly, it hung on the air, floated to her. Abruptly she came to a stop outside a pavement café; immediately she sat down at one of the tables, unable to resist.

'*Café au lait, s'il vous plaît*,' she said to the smiling waiter, who instantly appeared in front of her.

'*Mais oui*,' he said, hurrying off.

Alexa sat back in the metal chair, thinking how wonderful it was to be here; how foolish she had been to stay away for so long.

A few seconds elapsed, and then the waiter was back, placing a pot of coffee and a jug of steaming hot milk in front of her. '*Voilà, madame!*' he exclaimed with a nod.

'*Merci*,' she said, smiling back at him as he put down a basket of bread, and then she picked up the pot, poured coffee into the large cup, added the frothy milk.

The first sip was delicious; then she eyed the basket of different breads. She could smell the fresh croissants, which had also miraculously appeared on the table, along with small slabs of creamy-looking butter on a plate, plus a dish of dark, raspberry jam.

Oh what the hell, why not? she thought, and took a croissant, broke a piece off, added a touch of butter and a generous blob of the jam. It seemed to melt in her mouth, and she thought of all those breakfasts she had had, just like this one, when she had been a student here.

Nine years ago. She had been just twenty-one when she had started at Anya's school. And from the first day to the last she had enjoyed every moment, never once been disappointed.

There was an extraordinary atmosphere in the school. The series of adjoining buildings along the rue de l'Université were filled with a special kind of . . . *happiness*. That was the only word she could think of to describe the mood in the many different classrooms and art studios. This feeling of genuine euphoria and excitement enveloped everyone who came there. Of course it emanated from Anya, who else? And yet the other teachers were just as inspired, and as inspiring, as she was.

They all inculcated a love of learning in her and the other pupils. They were the best, always the greatest experts in their given fields, and specially chosen by Anya Sedgwick for a variety of qualities as well as their talents.

How wonderful those years were, she thought now, leaning back in the chair, reminiscing, letting her mind fill with memories of those days. They had been filled with wonder, anticipation, expectation, and a sense of adventure. Everything was ahead of her, her whole life, and the future glowed before her eyes. It held so much promise, glittering prizes.

Yes, all of her dreams, hopes and ambitions had been

encouraged here, by Anya and her other teachers. And what dreams of glory she'd had.

Thanks to Anya, so many of them had come true . . . at least as far as her work was concerned. But so much else had gone wrong . . . in her personal life. But that wasn't Anya's fault. And now she aimed to put it right. She had come to deal with unfinished business.

CHAPTER SIXTEEN

The woman was so striking and dramatic that heads turned as she passed.

She was tall, about five feet ten inches in height, well built but not overly heavy, and there was a certain regality to her posture, fluidity in the way she moved with a measured grace.

But it was her face which made people look at her again. The woman was startlingly beautiful, with a thick mane of jet-black hair falling halfway down her back, perfectly curved black eyebrows above dark eyes that were huge, set wide apart, and a most voluptuous mouth.

Her clothes were simple yet elegant in their cut. She wore a black, light-gabardine trouser suit, a tailored shirt of white silk, and high-heeled black sandals. A black leather bag was slung over her shoulder and she carried a pair of dark glasses in one hand.

This simple elegance was carried through to her jewellery. There was nothing ostentatious about the watch she wore on her left wrist, the gold bracelet on the other, or the small diamond studs in her ears.

This morning she moved at a slow, leisurely pace through the quiet halls of the Louvre, stopping now and then to gaze at a painting that caught her eye, in no great hurry to get to the picture she had actually come to see. She had plenty of time before she had to leave, to keep her luncheon date at the Ritz Hotel in the Place Vendôme.

The woman became aware of the stir she caused as she meandered along, self-contained and slightly aloof. She marvelled to herself about this. Three months ago she would not have believed it possible that she, of all people, could create such an astonishing reaction in others.

But Maria Franconi had undergone an enormous transformation – one so extraordinary, so radical, that her brother Fabrizio could only describe it as unbelievable and miraculous. And indeed it was both. The miracle was not accidental. It had occurred because of tremendous hard work, rigid discipline, many deprivations, and total dedication to a cause: *Immense weight loss in the shortest possible time*.

It had taken Maria not quite three months to lose forty-eight pounds, two pounds short of her goal. She had accomplished this with the help of a doctor, a nutritionist, a personal trainer and her brother – and a focus so intense it took over her life.

During this time she had thrown herself wholeheartedly into a brutal regimen comprised of punishing workouts, a diet totally free of fat, sugar and carbohydrates; wine and alcohol of any kind were forbidden, as were chocolates, sweets and most desserts.

If she was hungry more often than not, the very visible results of the dieting were worth it and kept her going, were actually inspiring to her. Through most of February, March and April she thought of nothing else but going to Paris to Anya's party, and it was this incentive and her extraordinary willpower that enabled her to continue. She even surprised herself at times.

One day, halfway through her programme, there was a sudden and remarkable change in her face. She had always been good-looking, she was well aware of that, but now her face had become dramatically beautiful. There was not an ounce of excess fat on it, and the high cheekbones were more apparent than ever. Her neck was thinner, and therefore looked longer and more elegant, added to the shapeliness of her head.

It soon became apparent to Maria that she was mostly losing weight in her upper torso first. Her shoulders, arms and back were growing more slender by the day, and her breasts were not so large any more. What disappointed her was the slowness of the weight loss on her hips. But her trainer had assured her that the weight would eventually drop off, most probably when she least expected it. All she had to do was keep strictly to her regime. And this she did. Vanity was the goad, and it kept her going.

Very simply, Maria Franconi was beginning to like herself, and she could hardly believe the incredible transformation in herself. She also discovered that being beautiful was really quite addictive.

Through her nutritionist, Maria learned all about behaviour modification, as well as gaining an understanding of the right foods to eat, ones which would keep her healthy. And thin.

And so there was no more cooking for her brother, no more dinner parties for her friends. She virtually locked the doors of her fancy, modern kitchen, took her friends to lunch or dinner in restaurants, where she herself ate frugally and stayed away from wine.

Several weeks before she left Milan for Paris, Maria visited a well-known dressmaker recommended by her brother, Sergio, who had innumerable women friends who went there. The dressmaker instantly understood the problems and created several well-tailored trouser suits, skirt suits, and a few elegant, simply-cut dresses, all in beautiful fabrics.

The clothes were specifically designed to play up her good points, and also conceal certain parts of her body. The secrets were the longer jackets, which stopped just below the thigh, cut edge-to-edge without buttons; the narrower trouser legs, and the pencil-thin, narrow skirts on the dresses and suits.

These styles helped to slim her lower body; by illusion, gave her a leaner and more elongated look. The dark colours she chose, mostly black and various tones of grey, played into this camouflage, and also suited her dark colouring, and olive-tinted complexion. In a very short time she had acquired a certain kind of chic, and this, along with her glowing health and lovely looks, made heads turn. She felt gratified. All of her hard work and focus had paid off admirably.

* * *

Even though she was now in Paris, Maria did not let up on her regime. She knew she would have to follow it for the rest of her life if she was to remain slim. At the moment it was less arduous, but nevertheless she was very disciplined and dedicated. She visited the spa in the hotel every day, swam, did exercises, and worked on the treadmill. All this gave her extra strength and muscle tone, which pleased her.

She also remained on her strict diet, despite the tempting French food she had always enjoyed, ever since her days here as a student.

Although Fabrizio had been supportive, and had helped her to achieve her goal, he had been against her spending the better part of June in Paris, which she had originally planned to do.

The entire Franconi family went to their spectacular villa in Capri at the beginning of June, where they spent most of the summer. Fabrizio was insistent that she accompany the family, and after a great deal of discussion, sometimes heated, she had finally agreed.

But she was determined to spend three weeks in Paris, which she had promised herself, having that much-needed vacation on her own, doing exactly as she pleased.

And so she had arrived on the third of May, and she planned to stay until the fifth of June, when she would join the family in Capri, travelling via Milan.

Maria had been busy since she had arrived. She had been to visit her beloved Anya several times, had lunched at the house with her and taken her out to dinner at Chez Benoît. She had gone shopping, spent time in art galleries, and been to Versailles, a favourite place of hers.

She had enjoyed every minute of her freedom, far away from her job and her domineering family.

I escaped, she thought now, as she slowly began to approach the painting she had come to see. If only I didn't have to go back . . . if only I could stay in Paris. *Always*. She instantly pushed these longings to one side, not wishing to fall down into unhappy thoughts today.

The painting was sublime. Incomparable.

Maria stood in front of it for a very long time, gazing at it as if in a trance. It usually had this effect on her . . . held her spellbound.

The Mona Lisa.

Painted hundreds of years ago by Leonardo da Vinci, the greatest artist there had ever been on this planet, with the exception of Michelangelo, in her opinion anyway.

To be able to paint like that was the greatest gift in the world, she marvelled, mesmerized by the woman's face captured so beautifully on canvas . . . how eloquently it spoke to her.

How truly gifted da Vinci had been, one of the world's greatest geniuses. She had known a lot about him before she had attended Anya's school. Coming as she did from Milan, she was familiar with the Church of Santa Maria delle Grazie where in its refectory Leonardo had painted the *Last Supper*. It was more than likely the most famous *Last Supper* in the world.

It was Anya Sedgwick who had taught Maria much, much more about da Vinci in her classical art classes – her Master

Class. And Maria had never ceased to marvel at his extraordinary achievements in so many other fields. He had been an architect as well as a painter and sculptor, an expert in the art of weaponry, hydraulics, optics, anatomy and mechanics.

What an amazing man he was, Maria thought. A man of the Renaissance, who was perhaps *the* Renaissance man of all time.

To be able to paint like that, she thought, a small sigh escaping her. It was a sigh of absolute yearning. She stepped closer in order to look more intently at the Mona Lisa.

As she did so, out of the corner of her eye she caught a glimpse of a woman heading her way. Her heart dropped. But she swung her head to make sure she was not mistaken, then swiftly turned back to face the painting.

After one last look at the da Vinci Maria hurried off in the opposite direction.

His table in L'Espadon faced the door, and he saw her the minute she arrived. He pushed back his chair and rose long before she reached the table, a broad smile of welcome on his face.

When she came to a standstill he took hold of her arm, almost possessively, kissed her cheek and then stared at her intently for a moment.

Maria smiled at him, and said, as she slid into the chair, 'I'm sorry I'm late.'

He sat down opposite her, and shook his head. 'But you're not late, and even if you were, you're certainly worth waiting for. You look very beautiful, Maria.'

'Thank you,' she murmured, dipping her head slightly.

'I ordered grapefruit juice for you,' he went on, 'I hope that's all right.'

'It's perfect, thanks.'

Lifting his wine glass, he said, '*Santé*.'

'*Santé*,' she responded, lifting her glass, touching it to his.

'So what did you do this morning?'

'I went to the Louvre. To see the Mona Lisa, in particular. I'm always mesmerized by that painting.'

As I am mesmerized by you, he thought, but said, 'What a genius Leonardo was. He was lucky enough to be born with a brain fully equipped to explore and comprehend all human knowledge.'

The maître d' arrived with the luncheon menus, and they studied them for a few moments. He knew what he was going to order; he assumed Maria did also. Since he was usually on a strict diet, as she was, they seemed to choose the same dishes. The other evening she had told him all about her strenuous dieting, and her exercise programme, had confided a great deal about herself over their second dinner. He had listened attentively, been impressed with her honesty, been sympathetic.

He had seen quite a lot of her since her arrival in Paris, and he wanted to continue seeing her. He was smitten with her, in a way he had not been taken with a woman for years. But he was aware that at this moment in time caution was in order.

'You are staring at me.'

'I'm sorry,' he apologized. 'I just can't help it. Your face is quite . . . *sublime*. That's the only word to describe it.'

Maria laughed lightly, and shook her head. 'I don't know about that . . . I only use that word when I think of the Mona Lisa . . . now that truly *is* a beautiful face.'

'Yes, it is, and actually *you* should be painted by a great artist, a modern-day da Vinci.'

The waiter arrived at the table before she could respond. She ordered oysters on the half shell and steamed turbot, as did he. That they had decided on the same food amused him.

When they were alone, Maria volunteered, 'I saw Alexandra Gordon at the Louvre this morning.'

His eyes narrowed; he glanced at her alertly. 'How was she? She must have been pleased to see you.'

Maria sighed. 'I didn't speak to her. I suddenly felt shy, a little nervous, and I slipped away before she spotted me. At least, I don't think she did.' Maria shook her head, added, 'It was foolish perhaps. After seven years, I would like to spend time with her and the others.'

'Was it such a bad rift between the four of you?' he asked, riddled with curiosity.

'It seemed like it then. But now it all seems somewhat childish, even silly . . .' Her voice trailed off lamely.

Understanding that she did not wish to pursue the subject, he moved on. 'You're enjoying Paris enormously, aren't you, Maria?'

'Yes, I am. Thanks to you. You've been so wonderful to me. I was so thrilled to come to Paris, to be on my own, away from the family. But, you know, I do think I might have been lonely if you hadn't been around and taken pity on me.'

'Anya would have taken you under her wing.'

'I like being under your wing, you –' She stopped abruptly, cut her sentence off, looked abashed.

He saw the faint pink blush rising on her neck to flood her face, and he exclaimed quietly, 'Don't be embarrassed.' Reaching out, he took hold of her hand on the table, squeezed it. After clearing his throat several times, he said in a low voice, 'I'm very smitten with you, Maria. And I was hoping you felt the same way.'

After a moment's silence, she said, 'I do. Oh, Nicky, I *do*.'

He tightened his fingers on hers. 'I'm so very glad this is not a one-way street.'

She merely laughed and looked at him, her dark eyes holding his.

They sat holding hands across the table, staring at each other in silence with great intensity until the oysters were served.

Finally releasing her hand, he picked up his oyster fork, and wondered to himself what was happening to him. Here he was, thirty-eight years old, an experienced man of the world, and feeling like a schoolboy. Daft, he thought, I'm daft. But he knew exactly what was happening to him, and he discovered he was glad.

After eating several oysters, Maria put her fork down, and leaned across the table, levelling her gaze at him again. 'When I came to Paris over a week ago, I thought I'd take the train to London for a day. To see Ricardo. As I told you, he's working there. But I don't want to do that, not now, Nicky.'

'Because of me?' he ventured carefully.

'Yes.' She lifted her eyes to his, stared back at him.

Nicky saw desire reflected there, a yearning for him, and his chest tightened. Slowly, he warned himself. Take this very, very slowly. Don't frighten her off. He wanted to possess her; he could not wait to take her to bed; but he knew he must pick the right time.

CHAPTER SEVENTEEN

Coming back to Paris *has* been a mistake, Jessica thought, as she walked up the narrow street which ran alongside the Plaza Athénée Hotel where she was staying. Just as she had always known, there *were* too many memories here, and obviously most of them were associated with Lucien Girard.

They evoked in her an immense sadness for what might have been . . . a marriage that had never happened, children that were never born, a life not lived with the man she had truly loved.

Now she wished she had not phoned Alain Bonnal from Los Angeles last week, to make this date for lunch today. She had done so because she had become nervous about being in Paris alone, after an absence of seven years. Afraid of memories, she supposed, and recurring sorrow, and the pain of old wounds opening up.

Alain Bonnal and she were friends because of Lucien, but he was not someone she was close to any more. She had seen him only twice in the last few years, when he had been in California on business. On the other hand, in the past he had been kind, considerate and helpful, and she had never forgotten his compassion for her when she was full of sorrow.

He was a connection to the past, a past she had not been able to let go of apparently, if she were honest with herself. Lucien, and their intense love affair, had haunted her ever since he had disappeared. And haunted any other relationship she had attempted to have. She truly understood that now. Gary Stennis had been a casualty of her past, in certain ways, even though his behaviour had been deplorable. Ultimately. He had given her plenty of reasons to end it. Not one regret, she thought, I don't have one regret about saying goodbye to Gary.

Of all the men she had known, Lucien had had the most impact on her. It's not a question of unrequited love, she said to herself as she hurried on, but of an unrequited life. Lucien and I made so many plans, sketched out a future for ourselves together. We even chose names for the children we planned to have. All of those nights we dreamed our dreams and built our future . . .

But it wasn't meant to happen, she thought, heading in the direction of Chez André, where she was meeting Alain. Even his choice of restaurant was a nod to nostalgia, to their shared past with Lucien, since the three of them had frequently gone there together, when she was a student at Anya's school.

She had not had a chance to visit Anya yet, but they had spoken on the phone several times. Perhaps tomorrow she would be able to run over to the house, to have tea or drinks, as Anya had suggested. Jessica realized how much she wanted to see her old teacher and mentor; despite her misgivings about making the trip, she *had* come to Paris after all, in order to honour Anya.

Jessica had arrived in Paris three days earlier, but her work had taken up all of her time. She had accepted an assignment some weeks earlier, a redecorating job for a valued client, who wanted her Bel-Air house to be redone. Jessica had suggested a theme built around French Provincial antiques and fabrics, and the client had agreed.

For the last couple of days she had been seeing the best of the antique dealers; seeking out fabrics in keeping with French country style; scouring the leading rug dealers for Aubusson and Savonnerie carpets. That very morning she had accidentally fallen on a collection of antique *toile de Jouy* fabrics, and had purchased them immediately, along with an extraordinary tapestry she knew would make an elegant wall hanging in the entrance foyer of the house.

Well pleased with her success, she had returned to the hotel to drop off her briefcase, retouch her make-up, and brush her hair. After changing into a lighter-weight navy-blue gabardine suit, she had raced out, realizing she was running late.

But within a few minutes she was pushing open the door of Chez André, and hurrying into the noisy, bustling bistro, which had a typical old-fashioned Parisian charm with its marble-topped bar, polished brass and air of bygone days. It was full of customers at this hour, but as she glanced around she spotted Alain at once.

He waved when he saw her, and came around the table to greet her. He made a big fuss of her, and after they had embraced and kissed affectionately they sat down together on the banquette.

Alain exclaimed, 'You are more beautiful than ever, Jessica!' He shook his head wonderingly. 'You *never* age. Unlike me.'

'Thank you, Alain, for those kind words, but you've always been prejudiced. Anyway, you look pretty good to me.'

'A few grey hairs these days, *chérie.*'

'But a young face, nevertheless,' she shot back, smiling at him, thinking he was just as attractive as ever.

'An aperitif, perhaps?'

'Thanks, that would be nice. I'll have the same as you,' she answered, eyeing his *kir royale*.

After he had beckoned the waiter and ordered her drink, Alain turned to face her and went on, 'I know you've come to celebrate your former teacher's birthday, but you said something about buying antiques, carpets and art for a client's house. How can I be of help?' Alain Bonnal had always admired Jessica; he was genuinely interested in her life. He had also shared her great sense of loss after Lucien Girard had disappeared, and had been as baffled as she by that strange and mysterious tragedy.

'It's a house in Bel-Air, actually,' Jessica replied. 'A beautiful house, Alain, and one I believe should have been decorated with French country antiques originally. Now the owner has finally decided to go that route.' She laughed lightly. 'Sometimes when clients ask me to redecorate, they want exactly the same thing they've been living with for years, except *newer*.'

'I know what you mean. People do seem to hate change.'

Jessica lifted her glass, which had materialized in front of her while they had been talking. 'Cheers, Alain, it's nice to see you after all this time.'

'Two years. And *à votre santé*, Jessica. Welcome to Paris.'

'So you're still not married,' she remarked, after taking a sip of champagne mixed with *cassis*.

He chuckled. 'I'm afraid I'm a confirmed bachelor. Never found the right woman, I suppose.'

She smiled at him, shook her head. 'I know a lot of beautiful women I could introduce you to, when you come to Los Angeles again,' she teased.

He smiled, sipped his drink. After a moment, he continued, 'You asked me if I had any really interesting paintings, and as it happens we just received a collection from an estate which is being sold, because of the death of the owner. His son wants to sell some of the truly good art, and I think you ought to see the collection. It is most unusual, and I believe you would make some good purchases.'

'I'd love to do that . . . to come to see them.'

'Would you like to visit the gallery after lunch today?'

Jessica thought for a moment. 'No, I don't think so, Alain, but only because I'm running out of steam. Jet lag, I guess.'

'Then I must feed you immediately.' He motioned to the waiter hovering nearby, who brought them the menus, recited the day's specials, then left them in peace to make their choices.

'Oh my goodness, my favourite!' Jessica exclaimed, as she stared at the menu. '*Cervelle au beurre*. That's what I'm going to have.'

'I recall how you and Lucien used to love brains. But not for me, I shall have a steak. And what would you like to start with? I see they already have white asparagus.'

'That's for me, Alain. Thank you.'

Once the food had been ordered, Alain asked for two more *kir royales*, and the wine list.

'Oh no wine for me, thanks. I'm afraid I can't drink too much during the day,' Jessica explained.

'I will order a dry white wine, a Pouilly Fumé, and if you wish you can have a glass later.'

'I'll see how I feel. Are you available tomorrow, Alain? Or perhaps the gallery is closed on Saturday?'

'No, we are open. I will be happy to see you then, and I do think you will be impressed by some of the paintings.'

As they sipped their aperitifs, waiting for the first course, Jessica talked to Alain about art and her own preferences, which he enjoyed, since she was knowledgeable. Madame Sedgwick's art classes had been worthwhile, he decided, as he listened to her hold forth with confidence.

Alain Bonnal worked with his father and brother in their family-owned gallery, which had been founded by Alain's grandfather, Pierre Bonnal, before the Second World War. It was one of the best in Paris, and was particularly well-known and highly thought of, since it specialized in Impressionist and Post-Impressionist paintings, holding a good inventory.

As she talked, Alain studied her, thinking how well she looked. It seemed to him that she had hardly aged at all. At least, as far as her appearance was concerned. Of course she was much more mature and sophisticated in her mannerisms and attitudes these days, but it would have been odd if she had not changed over the years. Her face was unlined, and she wore her pale blonde hair in the same style, long and straight, falling to her shoulders. And she was slender, had kept her lovely figure.

For a moment, he felt as though time had stood still. But it was only a fleeting thought, and then it was gone.

Their orders of white asparagus arrived, and Alain murmured, 'Aren't we lucky it's in season right now?'

Jessica nodded, and began to eat, saying, between mouthfuls, 'I hadn't realized how hungry I was.'

When the waiter arrived with the wine, Jessica agreed to have a glass, and later, once their empty plates were removed, she sat back against the banquette. A reflective look settled on her face.

After a moment or two of growing silence between them, Alain said, 'You're looking worried, Jessica.'

'Am I? Well, to tell you the truth, there's something I want to talk to you about. To do with Lucien.'

He nodded, looked at her attentively, his eyes alert.

She went on: 'Recently, I was telling a friend about Lucien's disappearance, and he presented a whole new scenario to me. I'd like to pass it by you.'

'What do you mean by a whole new scenario?' he asked, frowning, obviously puzzled.

'You and I came up with every possibility all those years ago. But we never considered one thing ... that Lucien might have disappeared of his own accord. You know, *on purpose*.'

Alain gaped at her, a look of absolute astonishment crossing his pale face. '*Mais non, non, c'est pas possible!*' he cried. He shook his head vehemently, and his eyes widened as the astonishment intensified. 'He was not that kind of man, Jessica. He would not disappear on purpose. What possible reason had he to do that?'

'He might have wanted to start a new life.'

'*Ah, non, non!* That is *ridiculous*! You and he had so many wonderful plans. And you knew him so well, he had such . . . *integrity*. He was an honourable man. No, no, he wouldn't have done anything like that.'

Jessica sat very still, staring at Alain.

It was quite obvious to her that he was startled and dismayed by her suggestion, just as she herself had been when Mark Sylvester had presented this theory to her months ago.

Ever since then, from time to time, she had wondered about Alain Bonnal, wondered if he had known more about the disappearance of Lucien Girard than he had ever admitted. Yet he had just proved to her, by his stunned reaction, that he knew only what she knew. Alain had never been very good when it came to dissembling. Only Lucien had been a good actor.

She frowned. A vague half-memory stirred at the back of her mind . . . she couldn't quite put her finger on it. It was something that had lain dormant for years. She struggled, but she could not make it come to life. She gave up, let it go.

Alain, his eyes on her, said in a concerned tone, 'What is it, Jessica? What is wrong? You have the most peculiar expression . . .' He did not finish his sentence.

Slowly, she answered, 'You know, Alain, I've always had this weird feeling, deep down inside me . . . a gut feeling . . . that Lucien is still alive. Somewhere out there. And I just can't shake it.'

Alain Bonnal had turned white, and he sat staring at her speechlessly, completely dumbfounded.

A little later, when she was back at her hotel, sorting through the samples of the fabrics she had found earlier, Jessica thought about Alain Bonnal's stunned disbelief, his total negation of the theory she had put forward.

Was it an act? *Did* Alain know more than he was saying? He had turned so white, looked so . . . *afraid*. Yes, that was it, he had suddenly looked terrified. Had she hit the nail on the head? Did he know for a fact that Lucien *had* staged his own disappearing act? Would a person need help in order to vanish without a trace? Maybe. But then again, maybe not.

'Oh for God's sake, he's dead!' she cried out loud to the empty room. Something really terrible happened to Lucien when he was in Monte Carlo, she added silently to herself. She was determined to stop dwelling on this most tragic event in her life. It was stalling her, suddenly.

Move on, she instructed herself, you've got to move on. You've got to get a life. You can't live in the past, or –

The shrill ringing of the telephone cut off her thoughts, startled her. Reaching for it, she exclaimed, 'Hello?'

'Hi, Jess, it's me. Mark Sylvester.'

'Mark, *hello*! How are you?'

'I'm great. How're you doing?'

'A bit jet-lagged, but okay. Hey, it's wonderful to hear your voice. Are you in LA? Or London?'

He laughed. 'I'm in Paris.'

He had taken her by surprise and there was a brief silence on her part. Then she said, 'Where are you staying?'

'Next door. Well, I'm not *exactly* next door, but down the corridor. I'm at the Plaza Athénée,' he answered, suddenly chuckling.

She laughed with him, but said nothing.

Mark asked, after a split second, 'How about dinner tonight? Are you free?'

'Well, yes, I am, as a matter of fact.'

'Then we've got a date. Would you like to go to Tour d'Argent?'

'I'd love it.'

'Then I'll knock on your door at eight. Is that okay with you, Jess?'

'Yes, it is. I can't wait to see you.'

CHAPTER EIGHTEEN

T hey sat together in the garden, under the ancient cherry tree, the old woman and her younger companion. The renowned teacher and her favourite former student. Anya and Alexandra.

Two peas in a pod, Nicky Sedgwick called them, because he thought they were so alike. Two women of such disparate backgrounds and upbringing, and yet, if he hadn't known otherwise, he would have said they were of the same blood, the same family. But then most people thought *he* was a blood relative of Anya's, not her great-nephew by marriage.

In a way, this was understandable, since she had worked her magic on him since the day he was born. He was her creature, just as Alexandra was.

Nicky was standing inside Anya's house, staring through the window at the two women. They were drinking their after-lunch coffee at the wrought-iron table, and chatting as animatedly as they always did. They look so comfortable with each other, he thought. Alexa was just like a young woman confiding in her grandmother.

His former assistant was as lovely-looking as ever, he noticed, although her dark hair was cut shorter. It was chic, and she was certainly smartly turned out in her tailored, grey pin-striped jacket and matching short skirt. All the better to see those gorgeous legs, he thought, his eyes sweeping over her. He liked the sleek hairstyle; it showed off her long neck and pretty ears. She wore gold earrings and a gold chain around her neck. Alexa had always had perfect style in his book.

Next to Alexandra Gordon, Anya was the *grande dame* personified, so regal in her bearing, and as good-looking as ever with her stylish blonde hair and perfect make-up. Anya was dressed in what she called her working uniform: grey flannel slacks, a white silk shirt and a navy-blue blazer. It makes her look so English, Nicky decided, but then she is very English in so many things, even though she has lived in France since her mid-twenties. When she spoke English she sounded like an upper-class English woman; once she launched into her perfect French she could easily be mistaken for a Parisienne; and, naturally, when she spoke her native language, learned at her father's knee, she was as Russian-sounding as the Prince had been. That was a special talent, being able to speak foreign languages well. His Uncle Hugo had been equally adept at them.

Glancing at his watch, realizing that the time was ticking away, Nicky now stepped out into the garden, exclaiming, 'Good afternoon, ladies!'

They both stopped talking and looked across at him. Then Alexa leapt to her feet, ran to greet him, threw her arms around his neck. After their long, smoochy embrace, he held her away. 'Well ain't you looking great, laidy,' he said in his best Cockney accent.

She laughed. He had sounded just like Jack did when he spoke Cockney.

Nicky said, 'I'm sorry I arrived a bit earlier than expected, and interrupted your time with Anya.' He now glanced across at his aunt. 'Sorry, old thing.'

'That's perfectly all right, Nicky dear, we'd more or less finished our lovely, long discussion anyway, hadn't we, Alexa?'

'I suppose so, although you know I can go on listening to you for ever,' Alexa responded, going back to her chair under the cherry tree.

Anya smiled. 'Let's listen to Nicky instead. And Nicholas darling, please do sit down. I can't stand you hovering there like an anxious waiter in a half-empty bistro nervously waiting to take an order.'

Nicky began to laugh as he strode over to one of the wrought-iron chairs arranged around the table and sat down.

Turning to face Alexandra, touching her arm with a loving hand, Anya felt it was necessary to give the young woman an explanation.

She said, 'I asked Nicky to do something for me last week, and it has to do with you, Alexa. But I do take full responsibility, I just want you to know that, to understand it was not Nicky's idea, but mine. Now I think he's here to report to me.'

Looking puzzled, Alexa frowned then glanced from Anya to Nicky, but she made no comment.

'A few weeks ago, Anya had the feeling you probably wouldn't come to her birthday party because of Tom Conners,' Nicky began. 'She felt you might be uncomfortable in Paris, because of your past with him, and how you parted. She suggested I make a few inquiries about Tom, to ascertain what he was doing, what his status was in general.'

'I see,' Alexa murmured, sounding noncommittal, but she felt herself tensing in the chair. She crossed her legs, then sat very still.

'Then almost in the same breath I told Nicky not to do it,' Anya interjected, looking at Alexa carefully. 'Because I felt that for him to poke around in Tom's life was like playing God, and in effect it was being a megalomaniac.'

'So I didn't do anything,' Nicky remarked. 'Until this past week, when Anya used her woman's prerogative and changed her mind.'

'He's still in Paris, that I do know,' Alexa announced.

She surprised them both, and they exchanged quick, knowing glances.

Alexa noticed this, and went on, 'When I received your invitation to the party, I called him at his office, on his private line, actually. Then I hung up when he answered. I guess I lost my nerve.'

'So he has been on your mind,' Anya muttered. 'I thought as much.' She felt justified for enlisting Nicky's help.

'Yes, Anya, he has. You see, I want to get rid of this unfinished business of mine. Then perhaps I can move on with my life.'

'Good girl!' Anya exclaimed, beaming at her in approval. 'Well, I suppose we've done your leg work for you. Or Nicky has, at any rate. He's probably saved you some time, actually.'

Alexa nodded. She was now eager to hear what he had to say.

'I made a few calls, spoke to several people I know who know him,' Nicky began, leaning forward slightly, giving Alexa a direct look. 'Basically, nothing's changed in Tom's life, Alex. He's not married, nor is he seeing anyone special, as far as I've been able to ascertain. Although I do hear there are a few women circling him, so to speak. But that's normal, under the circumstances. He's very good-looking, charming, successful, and a bachelor. It's to be expected. He's still with the same law firm, but then you already know that. I guess I have to say that everything seems to be the same.' Nicky sat back in the chair, and then turned his head, glanced at Anya.

'And that's all you found out?' Anya asked with a frown. 'Nothing more, Nick?'

He shook his head. 'Not very much, really. Tom even lives in the same apartment. But one of the chaps I know at Clee Donovan's photo news agency is an old buddy of Tom's and –'

'That's got to be Charles Dugdale,' Alexa swiftly cut in, 'they're good friends.'

'Correct.' Nicky gave her a faint smile, and added, 'Charlie told me that Tom inherited money from a relative recently, and that he's bought a property in Provence. A farm or an estate, I'm not sure.'

Anya's face lit up. 'Oh really, how very interesting! I wonder if he's anywhere near me?'

Nicky burst out laughing. 'Anya, you're incorrigible! Always looking for dinner and luncheon guests, eh, old thing? Always wanting interesting company.'

'And whyever not? Interesting company's much better than the bores, wouldn't you agree?'

Nicky smiled at her lovingly. 'You'll be happy to know then that Tom's place *is* near your house. He's just outside Aix-en-Provence.'

'Lovely,' Anya replied, her eyes sparkling with pleasure.

'Does this mean Tom is leaving Paris? Leaving the law firm?' Alexa ventured.

'I don't know,' Nicky answered her. 'Charlie wasn't sure about that. I'm afraid you have the sum total of everything I found out, Alex, except that he's fit and well and, according to my friend Angelique, he's still as good-looking as ever.' He grinned at her. 'A taller version of the other Tom.'

Anya frowned and repeated, 'The other Tom? Of whom are you speaking, Nicky?'

'Cruise. Tom Cruise.'

'Oh Nicky, you are such a pest with all of these eternal film references of yours!' Anya mildly chastised. 'Half the time I never know who you're talking about.' Reaching out, she now took hold of Alexa's hand, and went on softly, 'Well, darling, you now know which way the land lies. Why don't you call Tom this weekend? But this time, if a machine answers, please leave a message, for heaven's sake, otherwise we'll get nowhere very fast.'

Alexa laughed, suddenly feeling lighter than she had in

ages, as if a weight had been lifted off her shoulders. 'Thanks for doing the leg work, Nicky. I owe you one. And in the meantime, when are we going to get together to discuss the movie? Later today?'

'I'm afraid not,' Nicky exclaimed, and glanced at his watch. 'I'm sorry, Alexa, but I have to leave. My apologies, Anya, for this hit-and-run visit, but I have to go home to change. I have a special dinner date tonight.' Rising, he went over to Anya, bent over his aunt and kissed her cheek. 'I'm taking Maria to dinner, you'll be glad to hear.'

'I am indeed very pleased, she's a lovely young woman,' Anya responded, and patted his hand resting on her shoulder.

Moving around the table, he went to Alexa and kissed her. 'We can lunch tomorrow, if you're free,' he said.

'I am, Nicky, that'll be great. Where shall we meet?'

'I'll take you to the Relais at the Plaza Athénée. I know you like it there. Let's meet at one. Okay?'

'That's perfect,' Alexa answered.

Anya got up, tucked her arm through his and walked back to the house with him. 'Thank you so much, Nicky, for finding out about Tom. I do appreciate it.'

'I think Alexa does too,' he murmured in a low, confiding voice. 'Don't you think she looks tremendously relieved? Probably to know he's still single.'

'Perhaps,' Anya replied, not quite sure if this was the case or not. In her long years as a teacher she had learned one thing: young women could be very tricky.

CHAPTER NINETEEN

'I'm so glad you don't think I'm a meddlesome old woman,' Anya said to Alexa, after she had ushered Nicky out and returned to the table under the cherry tree. She sat down, sighing lightly as she did. 'Some people might, darling girl, and it would truly upset me if *you* did.'

'First, I never think of you as *old*, and second, you were not meddling. I suspect you wanted to find out what was happening with Tom, in order to protect me,' Alexandra asserted. 'Forewarned is forearmed. I can just hear you thinking that. Am I correct?'

'*Absolutely.*'

'I'm very surprised I didn't get a lecture from Nicky,' Alexa suddenly blurted out, and added, 'He was also protective of me years ago, and he and Larry kept cautioning me about Tom. They both said he would only cause me grief.'

'I know Nicky can be a pain in the neck at times, but he's

a good person, and very devoted to *you*. Anyway, let's face it, Alex, in this instance he wasn't far off the mark, was he? And neither was Larry.'

'You're right, as usual.' Alexa gave Anya a concentrated stare, and asked pointedly, 'A few minutes ago, was Nicky referring to Maria *Franconi*? Is that who he meant?'

'I do believe he did.' Anya sat back, eyed Alexa, averted her face for a moment, trying to stifle the laughter bubbling in her throat. Alexa had obviously been taken aback by Nicky's announcement about his dinner date. Her expression was one of such horror it was actually comical. Also, she knew that Alexa and Maria had locked horns at one point, just before their graduation, and there was no love lost there. She's appalled at the idea of Nicky being with Maria, Anya decided.

'I can't believe it! And certainly I don't get it. He's married. To Connie Aykroyd.' Alexa shook her head; her expression one of puzzlement mixed with annoyance.

'Not any more, at least not for much longer. Seemingly that marriage is over, except for the shouting. And the legalities, of course. Nicky moved out a long, long time ago, and I suppose he feels he can date other women if he wishes. And if the woman is willing.'

'And obviously Maria Franconi is . . . oh my God, Anya, what a weird *mix*!'

'Oh, I don't know about that. I rather think you're wrong, darling. Actually, Nicky's quite taken with her.'

'*Really?* How amazing. How is she, anyway?'

'Maria appears to be very well. And pleased that she managed to lose forty-eight pounds.'

'Maria got *fat*?' Alexa exclaimed, and then she laughed. 'Oh dear, oh dear, all that pasta, I guess.'

Anya bit back a smile. She was amused that for once in her life Alexa was being a little bitchy. She said, 'People get fat for all kinds of reasons. But at least Maria did something about her weight. She went on a very strenuous fitness regime, and seemingly it worked. Because she's so tall, she carries the remaining bit of extra weight very well. And she does have a remarkable face, you know.'

'Yes, she *is* beautiful, I'll concede that.'

Anya frowned. 'From your tone, I can tell you're still troubled by Maria, and her *treachery*. Isn't that what you called it once?'

'She *was* treacherous,' Alexa responded in a hard voice, one which brooked no argument.

'Are you still reluctant to talk to me about it, after all these years?'

'Yes, I am, Anya. It was awful, very unpleasant, and she was a bitch. She was extremely unfair to me.'

After sixty years of experience as a teacher, Anya knew better than to press the point at this moment. Instead, she said, 'Jessica is here also, and I heard from Kay Lenox the other day. She'll be arriving imminently, if she's not already here. I do sincerely hope the four of you are going to be able to bury your differences . . .' She let the sentence slide away.

Alexa looked at her quickly, at once noticing the slightly plaintive tone in Anya's voice. Reaching out, she patted her hand. 'Of course we are.' She began to laugh, and exclaimed, 'I'll beat them *all* into submission . . . they'll behave well at your party, take it from me they will!'

Anya chuckled. 'Oh, Alex, you can always make me laugh when you want to, especially when you try to be tough.'

'I am tough.'

'Not you, darling girl.'

'I hope I am. I don't want to be a cream puff. Where is that going to get me in this world? I hope I am *really tough*, because that means I'm strong and resilient. That's what tough means to me.'

'Yes, you're right, actually. Let's not mix up the words tough and hard, both have very different meanings indeed. I cannot bear hard women because they're so hardbitten, so emotionless, without feelings. What was it Hemingway once said? "I love tough dames but I can't stand hard broads." Well, anyway, it was something like that.'

Anya looked off into the distance for a few seconds, and there was a small silence. And then suddenly, unexpectedly, she said: 'I once knew a man like your Tom Conners, and it became very difficult for me in the end.'

'When was that?' Alexa asked gently. She was startled by Anya's angry voice, the odd twist to her mouth. A bitter twist, she thought.

'Oh, long ago. A few years after my darling Hugo died. I met another man, as one does if one is out in the world, living life, doing things, and not becoming a dullard, a bore, by staying at home doing nothing. He was a widower. His wife had died of cancer when she was very young. It *was* a tragedy, she was only in her twenties apparently. But, you see, he used her death constantly to prevent our relationship from going where it should have gone. His dedication to her memory, survivor guilt, all of those things got in the way.'

'What happened in the end?'

'One day I left him. It wasn't worth it to me. I couldn't understand why *I* had to be made to suffer because another woman had died too young, too soon. And I was getting awfully tired of being compared to a dead woman who had become a plaster saint in his eyes.'

'Did he . . . ever remarry, Anya?'

'Not to my knowledge.'

'And where is he now?'

'Oh goodness, how do I know! Dead probably. Or still marching around with that cross on his shoulders, feeling sorry for himself, being selfish in his continuing grief.' Anya shivered slightly, and pushed herself to her feet. 'It's growing cooler, Alexa, let's go inside. Look, the sun is already hidden by the clouds.'

Together they walked towards the lovely old house with its black-and-white façade so reminiscent of Normandy architecture. Anya led the way, and Alexandra followed her into the small library which opened off the garden.

Anya went around the room, turning on lamps, saying to Alexa, as she did, 'Darling, do me a favour, and light the fire. There's a sudden chill in the air.'

'Right away,' Alexa responded, and knelt down in front of the fireplace. There were rolled pieces of newspaper and chips of wood in the grate, and she immediately spotted the matches in the copper bucket, struck a match, brought the flame to the paper. It caught with a *whoosh*, and she knelt there until the chips also ignited, when she put on several small logs. Then she got up.

Dusting her hands together, Alexa walked over to a small

upholstered chair and sat down. Anya was already propped up against a pile of pillows on the loveseat opposite. 'Thank you, Alex.'

Then picking up the conversation where she had left off, Anya continued, 'Those sort of men are not worthy of a woman like me, or you either. So do me a favour, and yourself. Deal with Tom Conners. Don't drag it out. And if you find it necessary to walk away, then walk away. Get on with your life without him, if there's no alternative. You'll meet another man one day.' She gave Alexa a hard stare. 'In fact, I'm surprised you haven't done so already.'

'Oh but I have, Anya. Jack . . . that's his name . . . Jack Wilton . . . he's an artist, very talented and successful. He wants to marry me.'

'And you, Alex? How do you feel?'

'I like Jack a lot, I love him actually, but . . .' She shook her head. 'It's not the same as it was with Tom. As I just said, Jack wants us to get married, and we're sort of engaged, well, unofficially.'

She bit her lip, and looked away. When she finally brought her eyes back to Anya they were troubled. 'I can't marry one man while still yearning for another,' Alexa finished quietly.

'Yes, you always have been a very honourable young woman. But what is honour worth if it is honour without courage? Don't be afraid, Alex . . . don't be afraid to confront Tom, *and* Jack, if you have to . . . take your courage in both hands and be honest in your confrontations.'

'I know you're right, Anya. Honesty is the only thing that works in the end.'

'Be brave . . . it's not as hard as you think.' Anya smiled at her encouragingly, then glanced at the small desk in one corner of the room. 'There's the telephone.' She brought her gaze back to Alexa. 'Go on, call Tom now. See how he reacts to hearing from you.'

For a moment, Alexandra was thrown off balance, and she found herself shrinking back in the chair. And then she stood up, very determinedly, and walked across the room. She said to Anya, as she stood at the desk with her hand on the phone, 'What have I got to lose?'

'Nothing. Nothing at all. But you do have everything to gain, one way or another.'

Alexa picked up the receiver. She noticed her hand was shaking, but she ignored this, and dialled his private line at the office.

'Tom Conners,' he answered almost immediately, on the second ring.

She found it impossible to breathe. Just the sound of his voice had paralysed her. She was shaking inside. She leaned against the desk, swallowing; her mouth was dry.

'Tom Conners, *ici*,' he said again in a level tone of voice.

'Hello, Tom, it's –'

He cut her off. 'Alexa! Where are you calling from?'

Momentarily startled by his instant recognition of her voice, she couldn't speak. And then she said swiftly, in a rush of words, 'I'm in Paris, and I'm fine, Tom. How're you?'

'Okay, doing okay. Are you in Paris on business?'

'Sort of,' she answered, glad that she sounded normal. 'But I really came for Anya's eighty-fifth birthday.' She glanced at Anya, and saw that she was mouthing something. Leaning forward over the desk, frowning, Alexa tried to figure out what Anya was silently saying.

'Invite him if he doesn't invite you,' Anya finally said aloud in a stage whisper.

'It's hard to believe Anya's going to be eighty-five,' Tom was saying, laughing. 'I hope I look as great as she does when I'm that age.'

'So do I,' Alexa managed to agree.

'Can we get together, Alexa? Will you have time?'

She felt herself going weak with relief on hearing these words. 'Yes. I'd like to see you. When?'

'Are you available this weekend? What about lunch tomorrow?'

'I can't, I'm afraid. I'm meeting Nicky Sedgwick for lunch. I'm going to be working on a film with him later in the year, and we have quite a lot to go over. So I can't really change it.'

'That's okay. What about tomorrow night? Are you free?'

'Yes.'

'Shall we have dinner?'

'That'll be nice, Tom.'

'Where are you staying?'

'The Meurice.'

'I'll come for you around six-thirty. Is that all right with you?'

'It's fine. See you then.'

'Great,' he said and hung up.

Alexa stood clutching the phone, staring at Anya, a stunned expression on her face.

Anya began to laugh. 'You look shell-shocked, Alex. As if you can't believe it.'

'I can't,' she replied and dropped the receiver into the cradle.

Anya said, 'It wasn't so hard after all, was it?'

'Not really, but I *was* shaking. Inside and out.'

'I know. There are men who have that effect on women, and of course they are lethal.'

'I guess I *am* still in love with him,' Alexa began but her voice faltered.

'Perhaps you are. But you won't know how you truly feel until you see him tomorrow night.'

Leaning back in the chair, Alexa merely nodded, once more finding it difficult to breathe. And then she thought: Tom is lethal. He's always been lethal for me.

CHAPTER TWENTY

K ay wondered, as she walked up the Champs Elysées, how she could have stayed away from Paris all this time. Even though it was only an hour by plane from London, and not much longer from Edinburgh, she never 'hopped over' as many people did, because Ian did not like to travel, and she wanted to be with him at weekends.

Still, Paris was a city of fashion on all levels, and she was in the fashion business, and she realized now that she should have come more often than she had. There was so much to see here, and to learn, as she had rediscovered in the last few days. Silently, Kay chastised herself.

A moment later she thought of the happy years she had spent at Anya's school; Anya was another reason she should have come over, because the famed teacher had been her great mentor and her truest friend.

Everyday life intrudes, she muttered under her breath, but

that's really no excuse. How often she had wanted to confide in Anya, to ask her advice, and yet she had diligently stayed away. This, too, perplexed her. But now was not the time to analyse her behaviour, she knew that, and she pushed all such thoughts to one side. There were other situations to deal with, other problems to solve.

Taking a deep breath, Kay glanced about her. Paris *was* the most beautiful city, and she noticed that it was particularly lovely this morning. The sky was a light cerulean blue filled with sweeping white clouds, and bright sunlight washed over the ancient buildings. She remembered now that many of them had been cleaned for the Millennium celebrations, and the stone façades gleamed whitely in the clear light, looked as if they had just been newly built.

Staring ahead, Kay's eyes now fastened on the Arc de Triomphe at the top of the long avenue. Underneath that soaring arch the Tricolore fluttered in the light breeze. The sight made her catch her breath . . . there was something so poetic and moving about that simple flag flaring in the wind.

Because it symbolizes a country's courage and triumph, she reminded herself, thinking of the many history classes she had attended at Anya's school.

Anya took them, although they were not actually part of her Master Class. She was an expert in the history of the Second World War, having lived through that war, and she loved to teach about it, and what had happened on both sides of the Channel at that terrible time.

How horrible it would have been if these magnificent buildings had been blown to smithereens by the Nazi occupation forces, as Hitler had wanted. Kay easily recalled exactly what Anya had taught them in her classes. In 1944 the Allied armies were rapidly approaching Paris, and Hitler had commanded General von Choltitz to blast the historic monuments, so that the Allied forces would be greeted by smoke and debris. Dynamite had already been laid under the Arc de Triomphe, Les Invalides, the Eiffel Tower, and the Cathedral of Notre Dame, amongst others. But at the last minute, General von Choltitz had not had the heart to blow up such extraordinary edifices. When he had ultimately surrendered to General Leclerc he had handed over a city which was completely intact.

Close call that was, she thought, as she finally came to the Place Charles de Gaulle where the Arc de Triomphe stood. How dwarfed she felt by this massive structure, built on the instructions of Napoleon to celebrate his greatest victory at Austerlitz. At the time, he had promised his men they would go home through triumphal arches. And ever since this arch had been completed, long after Napoleon had lost his power, it was the starting point for national victory parades and celebrations.

She had once gone up to the top, where she had stood with Anya, Alexa, Jessica and Maria, looking out across Paris. It was then, and only then, that she had truly understood why the arch was also called the Etoile – the star. It was at the very centre of twelve avenues which radiated out to form a star. Many were named after famous generals, and had been part of the modernization of Paris by Baron Haussmann, which had begun in 1852.

As she moved through and around the arch, Kay had a sudden, unexpected thought . . . of a woman who like her had been unable to give the man she loved an heir . . . the Empress Josephine. And eventually Napoleon had had to divorce *her* in order to father a son by another woman. He had not been particularly happy with Marie-Louise, daughter of the Austrian emperor, even though she had eventually given birth to a boy. It had been a diplomatic marriage, and Napoleon had forever yearned for Josephine. At least so Anya had told them in one of her other history lessons. 'His luck changed the day he left Josephine. Unhappiness and disasters followed him to the grave,' Anya had explained dourly.

Sighing to herself, Kay wandered away from the great arch, crossed over to the other side of the Champs Elysées, began to walk down this most imposing boulevard, thinking of Monsieur François Boujon. She had gone to see him yesterday at his office on Avenue Montaigne, to discuss her own inability to conceive. She had an examination and tests, and depending on the results of the tests he had taken, she might have to spend a few days at his clinic in Barbizon, near Fountainebleau. His reputation as an expert on fertility preceded him, and after some years in California he had finally returned to practise in his native France.

Kay had made the appointment with him weeks ago, and yesterday she had been very nervous when she had sat waiting in the reception area of his offices. But within moments of meeting him she had found herself relaxing. He was the kind of doctor who immediately put a patient at ease, at least *she* felt that way.

Monsieur Boujon had asked her a lot of questions before the examination, most of which she had answered truthfully. But in some instances she had felt it necessary to lie. And now these lies troubled her, which was one of the reasons she had set out early for her appointment with Anya.

Kay knew herself, and she was well aware that if she sat in the hotel worrying she would drive herself to distraction. Better to be out and about, rather than confined within four walls, contemplating disasters that might never happen.

After a while, she came to Avenue Georges V, and she walked slowly along the street, heading towards the Place de l'Alma. In the distance, dominating the skyline, she could see the Eiffel Tower, and she remembered something Nicholas Sedgwick had once told her. That wherever she looked in Paris she would see either the Eiffel Tower or the great white domes of the Sacré-Coeur, and that was true.

She wondered how Nicky was, and the others . . . the girls who had been her companions for three years. Once they had been close friends, and it struck her now that their quarrels had been rather harsh at the end. Would they be able to enjoy Anya's party if they didn't make up? She was doubtful. For a long time she had thought of them as being bitchy and unfeeling, but perhaps she was being judgemental after all. Life was too short, wasn't it, and there were so many other things infinitely more important than female quarrels. And quarrels that had happened seven years ago, at that.

Anya had said this to her last night, when they had spoken on the phone, pointing out that they should all try to act in a mature manner. And Anya was right.

Kay found a table at a small café, on a side street just off the Place de l'Alma. She felt quite ravenous all of a sudden and needed to eat; then she remembered she had not really had breakfast, only a cup of tea, and now it was almost one.

When the waiter came, she ordered a tomato omelette, a green salad and a bottle of sparkling water. Once her order had been taken, she sat back, watching the passers-by for a moment or two, but mostly she was thinking about her life, and in particular, her husband Ian, whom she loved so much.

He, who was not at all enamoured of travelling, had been forced to fly to New York the other day, in order to deal with an unexpected business matter to do with the woollens they produced at the Scottish mills. He had gone instead of his partner, Vincent Douglas, who had broken an arm and a leg in a car accident. And how he had grumbled about going!

Poor Ian, she thought, stuck in a hotel in Manhattan. He was such a countryman at heart and in spirit, one who truly felt uncomfortable in most cities, and especially a great metropolis like New York.

He would be gone for ten days, and in that time Kay hoped to finish her tests with Monsieur Boujon; she also planned to find the perfect premises for a boutique. Her assistant, Sophie McPherson, was arriving next week, and together they would work with the estate agent who had been highly recommended.

Although Paris was one of the greatest fashion centres of the world, with haute couture houses, and top-, middle- and lower-scale manufacturers and designers, Sophie had somehow convinced her there was a need for her clothes.

But the idea of opening a boutique in this fashion-conscious and most stylish of cities had not appealed to her in the beginning; it was Sophie, young, enthusiastic, and highly committed to the running of the boutiques, who had persuaded her otherwise.

Sophie had pointed out that her clothes were selling tremendously well in Britain and the United States, and that they would find a huge market in Paris.

So be it, Kay thought, letting out a sigh. She could but try, and she hoped she would succeed. She generally tended to take Sophie's advice, trusting her judgement, knowing that her assistant seemed to have her finger on the pulse of fashion for the young woman of today.

As she sipped the sparkling water, Kay's thoughts drifted in various directions. Soon she found herself thinking of those years she had lived in Paris. Home had been a small, cosy hotel on the Left Bank, and she had loved her small room in it, and the quarter where it was located, just off the boulevard Saint Michel.

Maybe she would take a walk down the rue de la Huchette later in the day, and pop into the Hôtel Mont Blanc where she had lived for three years. She wondered if Henri, the lovely old concierge, still worked there. He had always been so kind and considerate, and concerned about her.

Kay's time in Paris had been the happiest years for her, for various reasons. She was far away from the slums of Glasgow; she was safe, *that* most of all; she was attending the famous school she had dreamed about for years, never believing she would actually become a pupil there at the age of nineteen.

At the Anya Sedgwick School of Decorative Arts, Design and Couture, Kay had studied fashion design with the renowned teachers Eliane Duvalier and Jean-Louis Pascal.

But she had also taken Anya's Master Class in classical art as well as her three history classes which dealt with eighteenth-century France, Imperial Russia, and the Second World War on both sides of the English Channel.

Kay had enjoyed every one of her classes on various subjects, and her dreams and hopes and ambitions for the future had been fuelled and strengthened here. For the first time in her life she had felt special and worthwhile, thanks to Anya's loving encouragement and belief in her. This sense of inner worth had been totally reinforced by the other teachers, who had shown their genuine belief in her and her abilities.

When her mother had first sent her away from Scotland, Alice had actually taken her to Yorkshire, to Harrogate at the edge of the Dales, where she had enrolled Kay in an old and respected school, Harrogate College. There were other girls attending the college who were boarders, as she was, and they all became good friends, and once she had settled in she found great pleasure in learning.

Being away from the bad environment in Scotland had given her a sense of enormous relief; she felt secure, not so vulnerable and exposed any more. The courses at the college were liberating, and her inbred talent soon found release. It flowered. Her potential was so apparent, so highly visible to the teachers working there that they were frequently startled by it.

She missed her mother very much, and Sandy as well, but her mother never permitted her to come back home. Whenever Alice could, she came south to Yorkshire in order to see Kay, and those times had been very special and meaningful to them both. 'Remember this, lassie,' Alice Smith would say.

'There is no such person as Jean Smith. She does not exist. You are Kay Lenox now. New name. New identity. New life. New future. There's no going back, not in any way.'

Her mother's voice seemed to echo in the inner recesses of her mind, always encouraging, always speaking about her new life and her future. In a way, her mother had sacrificed herself in order to give *her* a better life.

She made everything possible, Kay thought. And I do have so much. But I'm always afraid of losing it. I can't enjoy what I have. That is the problem.

Things are going to be all right, she now told herself firmly. They had to be.

CHAPTER TWENTY-ONE

How truly beautiful she has become, Anya thought, staring across at Kay Lenox, who had arrived at her house a few moments ago.

Because it was such a warm and sunny day, Honorine, the housekeeper, had shown her to the table in the garden which had been set for tea. But Kay had obviously immediately risen from her chair and strolled across the cobbled courtyard.

Now she waited under the cherry tree, gazing off into the distance, one hand resting on the trunk, surrounded by the double cherry blossoms of palest pink which dropped down around her. She was unaware she was being observed, and her face held a dreamy, faraway expression.

Kay is so tall, long-legged and slender she looks almost ethereal, Anya commented to herself, wishing she had a camera, so lovely was the image of Kay under the ancient, flowering tree.

Sunlight slanted through the branches laden with blossoms, and it was turning her hair into a halo of shimmering red-gold fire. She still wore it long, as she had when she had come to the school at nineteen, and from this distance Anya thought Kay did not look as if she had aged a day since then. She wore a tailored outfit of delphinium blue, composed of very narrow trousers worn with high-heeled blue court shoes and a three-quarter-length jacket styled in the manner of a maharajah's tunic. It had buttons down the front and a small, stand-up mandarin collar, and it was flattering on her.

The outfit was simplicity itself, but so beautifully made it was elegance personified, Anya decided. Well, she always was enormously talented, a little couturier even when she first came to me, she added to herself silently.

Stepping into the courtyard, Anya exclaimed, 'Kay darling, here I am! So sorry to keep you waiting.' She hurried forward, her face radiant with smiles, her joy at seeing Kay after so long reflected in her sparkling eyes.

Kay immediately swung around, then rushed forward at the sight of Anya, almost tottering on those very high heels. She embraced Anya, holding her tightly. After a moment, Kay looked into her teacher's face and her own happiness was transparent. 'It's just wonderful to see you!'

'I might well say the same thing, Kay. But come, my dear, let's go and sit at the table and have a cup of tea, like old times. I want to hear all of your news.'

Together the two women walked over to the table, where Honorine had covered the wrought-iron table with a linen cloth, and put out all the accoutrements for afternoon tea. Apart from the big silver teapot, matching milk jug and sugar bowl, there was a plate of lemon slices for the tea. On a tiered, silver stand, Honorine had arranged an assortment of the small nursery-tea sandwiches, as Anya called them, and plain biscuits. There was also a sponge cake filled with jam and whipped cream. Plus an English fruit cake, dark and rich-looking, its top decorated with blanched almonds.

Picking up the silver pot, Anya poured tea in the china cups, then sat back, staring at Kay.

The young woman was simply spectacular to look at, with her tumbling red hair, cool, polished, ivory skin and blue eyes. 'Kay, you are stunning!' Anya finally exclaimed admiringly. 'And so grown up. Very elegant.' Her eyes twinkled and she beamed at her. 'What a pleasure it is to see you looking so . . . *fantastic.*'

Kay shared her smile. 'I guess I *was* a bit awkward and gangly even when I graduated, wasn't I?'

'Never quite that,' Anya protested, dropped a slice of lemon in her tea. 'And congratulations on your extraordinary success. You've done the school proud. But then we all knew you would.'

'It's thanks to you, Madame Eliane, and Monsieur Jean-Louis, that I am where I am today. And of course my mother. Without her I would have been . . . *nothing.*'

Anya noticed the shadow that suddenly blighted Kay's eyes, fading their colour, as she spoke of Alice, dead for some time now. Mother and daughter had been very close, symbiotic, unusually devoted to each other. She was well aware that Alice had sacrificed much for Kay.

'We could only guide you, show you the way,' Anya finally remarked. 'You alone are responsible for your success, Kay.'

'I remember you used to tell us that, as individuals, we were the authors of our own lives, and that only we ourselves could accept the accolades, or take the blame if our lives went wrong.'

'But that did happen to be *your* philosophy when you enrolled at the school, Kay. I really only gave you the right words to properly express and explain what you appeared to already feel.'

Kay nodded, sipped her tea, became silent, her face instantly serious, reflecting her myriad thoughts. She fell down into the past for a few seconds, remembering so many things.

It struck Anya that there was a certain ... *regality* to Kay, that was the *only* word for it. And an inbred elegance. She was the true lady now, in every sense, in bearing and manner, as well as title. How amazing life could be for some people. Here she was, shy little Kay, who came to the school looking so undernourished, and quiet as a mouse, now a world-famous fashion designer, immensely successful, and the wife of a genuine aristocrat of breeding and wealth. Lady Andrews, wife of Ian, the Laird of Lochcraigie. Also Kay Lenox, couturier par excellence. There was a duality here but it did spell triumph, and on a grand scale.

Well, she's simply ... wondrous, Anya now thought, marvelling at her former pupil. She had not known much about Kay when she had first arrived in Paris ten years ago. Kay's personal history and background were somewhat shrouded in mystery, but her academic records from Harrogate College had told Anya a great deal. The girl was brilliant, no question about it.

BARBARA TAYLOR BRADFORD

Anya had instinctively known that Kay's early life had been poverty-stricken. There had been a sort of tenacious grimness about her mother. Alice had been pretty but a little pinched, and she was tired-looking around the eyes. Thin as a rail, she looked as if she had never had a good meal in her life. In fact, there had been an aura of genuine deprivation about Alice, Anya now recalled, and a sadness that had stabbed at her most forcibly. Alice's sorrow had been a palpable thing, and like a knife in Anya, who had empathized with her.

What Kay has made of herself, the life she has created, is quite remarkable, she thought. She was truly proud of this young woman, who was a genuine success story.

Breaking the silence, Anya said, 'I'm glad you came to Paris well before the party. It gives us a chance to talk, to catch up.' Anya chuckled and her eyes were merry again. 'The others were of the same mind as you, Kay. Alexa, Jessica and Maria are also here.'

'Oh,' was all Kay could think of to say, and she wondered how they would all feel when they finally met again after all these years.

Anya was thinking of Alexa and Jessica, who both had unfinished business to deal with. Studying Kay, she wondered about her. Did Kay also have a secret agenda tucked away?

Leaning forward slightly, she focused on the younger woman. 'Did you come early for any special reason, Kay dear?'

'Yes, actually, I did.' Kay turned to face Anya as she spoke, and continued, 'I am thinking of opening a boutique here. My other shops have been very successful, and everyone believes my clothes will sell well in Paris.'

'I'm quite certain that's true. And the idea is a marvellous one. Eliane and Jean-Louis will be most impressed and proud of you, as indeed I am.'

'Thank you. Also, I have to go to Lyon to see the textile manufacturer who produces my silks and brocades. I have some special colours I want created for my next collection.'

'You were always so clever with colour. I love this delphinium suit. It makes your eyes look bluer,' Anya murmured, then asked, 'And how is your husband?'

At the mention of Ian Kay sat up straighter. 'He's well.' She shook her head. 'Well, I hope he is. He's in New York on business, and Ian's not very fond of cities. He's probably very depressed, and itching to get home to Scotland.'

'Ah yes, the countryman, you once told me.'

'Yes.' There was a slight pause. 'So, the others are here? Have you seen them yet?'

'Maria, yes. Several times, in fact, and Alexa came to lunch yesterday.'

'Are they both married now?'

'Oh no.'

'And what about Jessica?'

'I haven't seen her, so far. But she's not married either. It appears that you are the only member of the quartet who has found the man of her dreams.'

Kay sat back in the metal chair, gaping at Anya, a look of dismay flickering on her face. Unexpectedly, alarmingly, tears gathered in her eyes, were in danger of spilling over on to her cheeks.

'Whatever's the matter?' Anya asked, her surprise and concern apparent.

Kay did not speak. The tears began to fall.

'Darling, what *is* it?' Anya leaned closer across the table, touched Kay's arm, as if to comfort.

Flicking the tears away with her fingertips, Kay said, in a hesitating voice, 'I'm so worried, Anya ... About my marriage.'

'Do you want to talk about it?'

Kay nodded. She took a deep breath, explained in a low, almost-inaudible voice, 'I haven't become pregnant, and that's what's at the root of it all.'

'Oh yes, I understand, darling. Ian wants a son and heir. The title ... the lands ... *of course*. Yes, I do see.'

Kay swallowed, cleared her throat. 'Ian is a kind person, and he doesn't talk about it. He never has. But I just know it's always there, lurking at the back of his mind. And it's a kind of ... *pressure* for me. It's always hanging over me.'

'I know what you mean.'

'I came to Paris for another reason,' Kay confided. 'To see Monsieur François Boujon. I'm sure you've heard of him.'

Anya nodded. 'Yes, he is very famous, and brilliant. And very well respected, I might add. As the world's foremost fertility expert, I am sure he will be able to help you.'

'Oh Anya, I *hope* so.'

'Have you seen him yet?'

'Yesterday. I had an examination, and tests –' Kay cut herself off, averted her head, bit her lip.

Anya watched her intently.

Kay brushed her eyes with her fingertips once more; she had begun to weep again.

'Are you all right?'

'I lied to Monsieur Boujon,' Kay blurted out, turning to Anya. Her eyes were agitated.

Startled by this announcement, Anya stared at Kay. 'I'm not sure I'm following you . . .'

'He asked me certain questions, and I didn't answer truthfully. I lied.'

'But *why*?' Anya frowned, looked more perplexed than ever. 'Whatever made you do that? It's not like you. You've always been so honest and forthright.'

Biting her lip again, Kay did not respond for a moment. Then slowly, she explained, 'I didn't want to tell him my *secrets*. I think it's better if people don't know . . . *things* . . . certain things about me.'

'Secrets? What kind of secrets?'

'Once, a long time ago, you made a comment to Alexa and me. You said you had always lived by one rule –'

'I remember that day very well,' Anya cut in. 'I said that I never show weakness, never show face, and that this had worked for me, especially in business, but also in my private life sometimes.'

'Yes, you did, and it's been *my* rule ever since. That's why I lied.'

'I see.' Anya leaned back in the chair, looking at her steadily. 'And what *exactly* are you hiding from Monsieur Boujon?'

'When he asked me if I'd ever been pregnant, I said no, I hadn't. But that's not true. I was pregnant once. Do you think he realized that when he examined me?'

'I'm not sure . . .' Anya paused, troubled. She studied Kay for a split second, then asked, 'You lost the baby?'

Kay took a deep breath. 'I had an abortion.'

'Oh, *Kay*.'

'Don't look like that, Anya. *Please*, Anya, *please*. I was abused when I was very young. When I got pregnant I was only. . . *twelve*.'

Anya closed her eyes convulsively and sat very still for a long moment. When she finally opened her eyes she thought the garden seemed just a little less sunny, as if the light had somehow dimmed. What a world we live in, what monsters some men are, she thought. Her face was no longer happy and laughing as it had been earlier, had become unusually sombre, etched with dismay. And then her eyes filled with compassion and sympathy as she quietly regarded one of her favourite pupils.

Kay exclaimed, 'It wasn't my fault, it wasn't!' and her voice was now high-pitched, almost shrill, as she grew agitated once more.

'Darling Kay, I know it wasn't your fault. I know *that*, without you having to tell me.' Anya reached out, put her hand on Kay's, her touch gentle and reassuring, she hoped.

Looking at her steadily, she saw that Kay's face was drained, whiter than usual, and she said, after a moment's reflection, 'Will it help to talk about it, do you think?'

'I've never told anybody . . . only Mam knew,' Kay whispered.

Anya squeezed her hand, then sat back, poured more tea for them both. She was silent, waiting. Waiting for Kay to feel comfortable enough to speak to her about this most painful and heartbreaking matter.

CHAPTER TWENTY-TWO

It took Kay a short while to compose herself.

She sat back in the chair, took several sips of the fresh tea Anya had just poured, and forced herself to relax. Slowly her agitation and anxiety receded.

Her gaze was level, her voice steady as she looked across at Anya and said, 'I think it's best if I start right at the beginning. My mother worked for a fashion designer in Glasgow called Allison Rawley, I was about seven when she first started as a sales woman. But after a couple of years, Mam was running the shop. You see, Anya, she was a good organizer and manager. Anyway, Allison had a close friend, a titled woman who was English. They'd been at boarding school together, and she sometimes came to stay with Allison, and of course, she bought things at the shop. This woman, who was a lovely person, offered my mother a job running her house, with Allison's approval of course.

She thought Mam was efficient and capable. I was ten at the time.'

'And your mother accepted the job?'

'Yes. How could she refuse? It sounded fantastic. The house was on the Firth of Forth, near a place called Gullane, about thirty minutes by car from Edinburgh. Her ladyship told Mam there was no problem about us – Sandy and me – that we could go with her and that we'd have our own quarters in the house. My mother saw it as an opportunity to better her position in life, earn more money, get us out of the city and into the countryside. There was a local church school in the village, and everything sounded wonderful. So she took the job as housekeeper.'

Kay paused. 'I don't think I'll ever forget that house, Anya . . . it was so beautiful, inside and out. The grounds were magnificent, and there were views of the Lammermuir Hills and that vast stretch of water . . . the Firth of Forth. It was magical. But there was a problem in that house, at least for me . . . his lordship.'

'Was he the one who molested you?' Anya asked softly.

Kay nodded. 'Not at first. And later, when he did, if his wife was at the house, he was very careful. But her ladyship travelled a lot. They had a flat in London and a country house in Gloucestershire, so she was often away. It all started when we'd been living there for about a year. I was ten and a half by then. At first it seemed almost accidental, you know; he would brush against me, squeeze my shoulder, stroke the top of my head in a fatherly sort of way. But then he began to waylay me in the grounds, in the woods. He . . . he touched me . . . you know . . . in the intimate places.'

Not wanting to break the flow of her words, Anya simply nodded.

'After a few really bad incidents, I began to struggle all the time with him, and I protested vehemently. He vowed to sack my mother, send us all away, if I didn't do what he wanted. He said he would send us into penury, and I didn't know what that meant and I was scared to death. I also knew what the job meant to Mam, to us as a family. Where would we live if we had to leave? And where was Penury? I thought it was some awful place for the longest time.'

'And you never told your mother? Or anyone else?' Anya ventured.

'I was too afraid to say anything . . . afraid of him . . . of what he might do to us. And *could* do to us if he wanted. He was a powerful man, and we were poor, vulnerable, alone. Dad had been dead for years and we only had Grandma in Glasgow and she was poor.'

'Oh Kay dear,' Anya murmured. 'How terrible it must have been for you.' Her face was bleak as she spoke, her eyes pained.

'It was horrendous, very frightening. Then, as time went on, he became bolder, more aggressive, and he went further with me. I tried to hold him off, and I never stopped protesting and shouting. But he shut me up. He was strong, and persistent, and he threatened me with dire trouble if I didn't do exactly what he wished. My only respite was when his wife returned from London occasionally.'

'Did you feel you couldn't tell her about this?'

'How could I? Anyway, who would believe me? The daughter of the housekeeper accusing the master? Certainly she wouldn't have believed a word. I would have been branded a liar. I might have even been accused of coming on to him, Anya. Think about *that*. My mother would have been dismissed. So I steeled myself to his attacks, and stuck it out, hoping and praying he would never come back whenever he went to London. He always did. When I was almost twelve he finally went, well, he went the whole way, Anya. He raped me one Saturday afternoon when my mother was in Edinburgh with Sandy.'

Kay stopped again, took a sip of tea. After a few moments, she murmured, 'That happened several times and I was in panic, very upset. Traumatized, I think, looking back. Then one day I missed my period, and I knew that what I'd feared had finally happened. I was certain I was pregnant. I was out of my mind with worry, and really terrified.'

'And so you finally told your mother?'

'I did. I had no alternative. She was wonderful with me, and appalled about what had been going on. But she didn't blame me at all. She was in a fury, and flew into a blind rage when she went to see him. Straight away, she threatened him with the law. She accused him of molesting a minor, said she was going to the police and that she would hire a solicitor in Edinburgh. She vowed to sue him. At first, he denied coming anywhere near me, but there were no other men on the estate and we were in an isolated spot. Well, there were the two gardeners, but they were old, and the rest of the staff were women.'

'So your mother went to the police.'

Kay shook her head. 'No, she didn't. She was about to do so when his lordship offered her . . . a deal of sorts. He said he would send us to a doctor he knew in Edinburgh, one who would perform an operation on me, and that he would pay for it. He offered my mother three months' severance, and told her that we must all leave. Immediately.'

'What happened? Did your mother accept, Kay?'

'No. She told him she'd think about it, and then in the end she turned it down. I suppose my mother was really quite a clever woman, even though she hadn't had a lot of education. Suddenly she understood she was holding all the cards. His lordship sat in the House of Lords, he was a businessman, and very well known socially. He moved in all of the top social circles, and so did her ladyship. It struck Mam very forcibly that the last thing he wanted was a scandal. When she realized this she made a counter-offer.'

'And what was it?' Anya asked, leaning closer.

'She made sure she had all the information about the doctor in Edinburgh, and had *him* make the appointment. Then she told him that what he offered wasn't enough for what he'd done to me . . . years of abuse, molestation as she called it, and rape. And rape over and over again, that had resulted in my pregnancy. She told him she wanted –' Kay broke off, took a deep breath. '*A million pounds.*'

Anya gaped at her. For a moment she was speechless. At last she managed to say, 'Did Alice get it? Don't tell me she actually got that much money?'

'No. She had asked for a lot because she knew she would have to bargain with him and she wanted room to manoeuvre. In the end he settled for four hundred thousand pounds.'

'Good God!'

Kay nodded, then smiled faintly. 'It *was* a lot of money,

Anya. I think even my mother was surprised. She was expecting to settle for much less . . . about a hundred thousand.'

'He must have been frightened out of his wits to pay that.'

'I believe he truly was. He was a successful man, but he didn't have the kind of money his wife did. She was heiress to a vast industrial fortune. The last thing he wanted was to be exposed, at the centre of a big scandal. Nor did he want to lose her money. Her ladyship was nice, I told you that, and if my mother had sought the help of a solicitor, gone to the police, she would have ultimately believed *us*. Not him. And she would have divorced him. I'm sure he realized that. Finally.'

'And so he paid up?'

'Oh, yes. My mother wouldn't leave until his cheques had cleared. Then we packed and went to Edinburgh where Mam found a small flat for us all.' Kay sat back, shaking her head, then she sighed, stared at Anya. Without flinching, she said, 'It was blackmail. I recognized that when I was older. My mother saw an opportunity to help me, not only then, but in the future. And so she blackmailed him.'

There was a silence.

Everything was very still in the garden. Not a leaf stirred, nor a blade of grass. Nothing moved at all. Even the birds were quiet.

But Anya's head buzzed with all that she had heard. Mostly she thought of Alice Smith, resorting to such a terrible thing as blackmail. And then she dismissed such a silly thought. What that depraved and sickening man had done to Kay was infinitely worse, and who could blame Alice Smith for demanding recompense. For that was what it really was. An eye for an eye, a tooth for a tooth, she thought. Such violence and depravity against a mere child would have caused some people to commit murder. Who could blame Alice for what she had done? The man had been monstrous, obscene.

'The money was used for your education, that's what Alice did with it. Didn't she?'

'Yes, and Sandy's. Some of it paid the rent of our little flat. And the fees for Harrogate College and your school here in Paris. Mam used it only for me, never for herself, except for the rent in the beginning. She always worked hard, and she saved. And the remainder of the money, which she'd put in a savings account at the bank, went to start my fashion business later.'

'Alice was wise, Kay, very wise. But the abortion? What happened? You haven't really spoken about it. Was it botched?'

'I'm not sure. But that's what worries me, Anya, that the doctor accidentally did something to me all those years ago. Looking back, I think he was a bit inept, he certainly looked seedy, and he smelled of alcohol. Afterwards, I bled a lot and I was in terrible pain for days. My mother almost had to take me to Emergency. At the hospital. But then I started to feel better . . .'

Kay stopped abruptly, looked away, and when she finally turned back to Anya her eyes were dark with worry. 'What if the doctor did damage me somehow?'

'I suppose he could have, but I think you would have known. Has everything . . . been all right over the years?'

'Oh yes, but I'm not sure that means anything. Do you

think . . . I mean, would Monsieur Boujon know I'd had an abortion?'

'I told you earlier, I'm not certain, Kay dear. I think he would probably soon spot internal damage if there were any.'

Kay looked at her for a long moment, her face suddenly stark, her skin stretched across the bones tautly. Tears welled; she pressed her hands to her mouth and began to cry.

Anya rose and went to her, put her arms around her, endeavouring to comfort her as best she could. Kay clung to Anya, pushed her face against her body, sobbing. Anya soothed her, stroked her head, and eventually she became quieter.

After a few moments, Anya murmured, 'He doesn't know, does he? You've never told Ian anything of this.'

'How could I?' Kay whispered. 'He knows nothing of my past. My mother created a whole new identity for me, and she had the money to back everything up. He'd die if he knew where I come from –' She paused, laughed hollowly. 'The slums of Glasgow. And of course he'd divorce me. I know *that*.'

'You can't be sure, Kay, people can be very understanding.'

'I'm not going to take such a chance, rest assured of that, Anya.'

'Words are cold comfort in so many instances,' Anya began gently, stroking Kay's hair again. 'To say I'm sorry this happened to you is just not enough. It doesn't express the pain and hurt I feel for you, darling Kay. It was horrific, and I can well understand how traumatized and scared you

THREE WEEKS IN PARIS

must have been. You were so very young, just a little girl.'
Anya's voice shook slightly with sudden emotion, and she
found she was unable to continue.

After a while, Kay pulled away, released her grip on Anya
and looked up at her. 'I lived with fear, once he'd started on
me. But I was a dreamer, you know . . . I learned to dream in
my very early childhood, and it kept me alive. I could escape
to a better place.'

'You've managed very well . . . I can't imagine what it was
like for you . . .'

'I learned one other thing, Anya.'

'What is that?'

'I learned to arm myself against the world.'

Honorine had come outside to tell Anya she had a phone
call and Anya had gone to take it. Kay was alone in the
garden.

Her tears had ceased and she sat calmly in the chair,
looking at her face in a small silver compact. There were
a few mascara smudges around her eyes, and she removed
these with a tissue, powdered the area lightly and refreshed
her lipstick. Then she put the compact and other items back
in her handbag, and relaxed.

When Anya returned she glanced at her and exclaimed,
'As good as new, my dear. Are you feeling better?'

Kay smiled. 'Yes, and thank you for listening, for being so
patient and understanding, Anya. It's helped me.' She paused,
shook her head. 'You see, I've never spoken about that part of
my childhood to anyone, except my mother. I think I buried

it all so deep it was hard to dredge up. Also, I didn't want to tell anyone my secret.'

'There's just one thing I'd like to say. When you see Monsieur Boujon again, he might ask you if you had an abortion, so be prepared for that. And frankly, Kay, I do believe you should tell him the truth.'

Kay recoiled slightly, and stared at her. 'That would be hard for me –'

'You don't have to give him any of the intimate details,' Anya interrupted. 'I mean about the childhood abuse. Just the bare facts. If you *do* have some internal problem, he must be told your medical history in order to make a judgement.'

'I suppose so,' Kay reluctantly agreed.

'Of course, it's more than likely he'll have good news for you, tell you there's nothing wrong with you, no reason why you can't conceive.' Anya peered at her. 'Then you'll have to try to relax about getting pregnant. I suppose it goes without saying that adoption is out of the question?'

Kay nodded.

Anya went on, 'So often, when a couple adopt a child, the wife immediately gets pregnant. The pressure is off, and I think that's what does it, helps a woman to conceive.'

'Ian would want only a biological child to inherit the title.'

Anya sat back, thinking Kay was probably right about this, but on the other hand, you never really knew about people. Also, it might not be Kay at all. There was the distinct possibility that Ian might be to blame; he could be sterile, or deficient in some way. She wondered if she dare suggest that he, too, should be tested, and then decided she had better not.

Instead, she reached across the table and took hold of Kay's hand. 'You've been very brave and strong all of your life, Kay, and I'm so proud of you. And I want you to know I am always here for you, whatever you might need.'

Kay was touched, and she responded, 'Thank you for those words, Anya, and for being my friend, my one *true* friend.'

This remark made Anya frown, and she exclaimed, 'I hope I'm not your only friend, my dear.'

'Well, sort of . . . I'm close to my assistant Sophie, and also Fiona, Ian's sister, but, well, yes, you are my only really intimate friend.'

How sad that is, Anya thought. She said, 'It's such a pity your little quartet fell apart. You were all *so close* for three years, and then *puff*! Suddenly, everything went up in smoke. I've never witnessed anything like it. And I do sincerely hope the four of you are going to come to terms with the situation, make an effort to set aside your differences and be friends again.' Anya gave Kay a long and pointed look, and finished, 'Take it from an old lady, life is too short to bear grudges, to carry animosity inside, so that it gnaws away like a canker.'

'I agree,' Kay answered, thinking that of the four of them she was the least to blame. It was the others who had created the problems, not her.

CHAPTER TWENTY-THREE

Alexa looked at her watch as the phone began to ring. It was exactly six-thirty. Snatching up the receiver, she said, 'Hello?' in a tight voice that didn't sound like her own, clutching the phone so hard her knuckles shone whitely in the lamplight.

'It's Tom. I'm in the lobby.'

'I'll be right down,' she managed to answer, dropped the phone into the cradle, picked up her bag and shawl from a chair, and left the room.

As she waited for the lift she glanced at herself in a nearby mirror. Her hair was sleek, her make-up perfect; she wore a tailored, black linen dress that would go anywhere, her only jewellery her watch and pearl earrings.

She took a deep breath as she stepped into the lift. She was taut, so anxious to see him she could hardly wait. She saw him immediately, the moment she stepped out. He stood off to one side, near the entrance to the Jardin d'Hiver, but something had obviously distracted him and he was looking towards the main lobby and the concierges' desk.

Stupidly, ridiculously, she found she was unable to move. She stood, rooted to the spot, staring at him, shaking inside.

His face was in profile, but she saw at once that he was as handsome as ever, and immaculately dressed. He wore a dark blue blazer, grey trousers and a blue shirt. His tie was silk, a blue-and-silver-grey stripe; his brown loafers gleamed.

She swallowed, trying to get a grip on herself, and then started in surprise as he suddenly turned his head abruptly and saw her.

His face was serious, unsmiling, as he walked towards her, his step and his demeanour full of confidence. But then he smiled suddenly, showing his perfect white teeth. His eyes were very blue. She saw too that his hair was now grey at the sides.

'Alexa,' he said, taking hold of her arm, leaning towards her, kissing her cheek.

She pulled away, almost at once, afraid he would hear the pounding of her heart. Swallowing, her mouth dry, she said, 'Hello, Tom.'

His vivid blue eyes searched her face for a split second, and he frowned. Taking hold of her arm, he said, 'Let's have a drink, shall we?' He didn't wait for her answer, and in command, as he always was, he led her forward. They went into the Bar Fontainebleau that faced out through bay windows on to the Rivoli arches, positioned in front of the hotel's main entrance.

He guided her to a small table near a window in a corner, where they both sat down. A waiter was with them in an instant.

Tom looked across at her and raised a dark brow. 'The usual?'

She nodded.

'*Deux flûtes, s'il vous plait.*'

As the waiter disappeared in the direction of the long mahogany bar on the other side of the room, Tom looked at her intently, nodding his head, obviously in approval. 'You haven't changed. You look exactly the same, except for your hair.'

'I cut it.'

'I can see that. It suits you. *Très chic.*'

She said nothing.

After a slight pause, Tom went on, 'I've read a lot about you, Alex. In the show business trades. You've been having a great success with your theatrical sets.'

'Yes, but I've been lucky in many ways.'

'I would say it has much more to do with talent.'

She smiled at him weakly, wishing her heart would stop clattering in the way it was. She also wished she didn't have the overwhelming urge to clutch his hand resting on the small table between them. It took all of her self-control not to touch him.

The waiter was back at the table, depositing the two flutes of champagne in front of them.

Once they were alone, Tom picked up his glass and clinked it to hers. '*Santé.*'

'*Santé,*' she said, and gave him a wide smile.

He put down his drink. 'At last,' he murmured. 'I thought that grim look was never going to disappear.'

'I didn't know I was looking grim.'

'Take it from me, you were.' He leaned across the table, the expression in his eyes more intense than ever. 'I'm glad you called . . . I'm glad to see you, Alexa.' When she remained silent, he asked, 'Aren't you glad to see me?'

'Yes.'

He laughed. 'Such a poor little *yes*. So timid.'

'Not at all. I *am* happy to see you, Tom. I wanted to see you, otherwise I wouldn't have called.'

He reached out, took hold of her hand, held it tightly in his, scrutinizing her carefully. Then he glanced down at her hands. 'Not married or engaged or otherwise taken?'

Alexa shook her head, not trusting herself to speak.

'There must be someone,' he probed. 'Or is every man blind where you live?'

She began to laugh – he had always managed to make her do that – and she shared his sense of humour. She was about to tell him there was no one special, but changed her mind. Instead, she said, 'I have one friend. An artist. He's very nice. English.' The words came out in a staccato delivery.

'Is it serious?'

'I – I – don't know,' she began, and hesitated. 'Well, perhaps he is serious.'

'And what about you?'

'I'm . . . uncertain.'

'I know what you mean.'

'Is there someone special in your life?'

'No,' he answered laconically.

'I can't imagine you haven't had, don't have, a girlfriend around.'

'Of course. But make that plural. And none of them mean anything to me.'

She experienced such a surge of relief her whole body went slack. She hoped he hadn't noticed this, said quickly, 'I saw Nicky Sedgwick at Anya's the other day. He mentioned in passing that you'd bought a place in Provence. At least, that's what he'd heard.'

'It is true. My French grandmother died. She left me a little money. I bought a small farm outside Aix-en-Provence, an olive farm.'

'How great! Is it actually operating?'

'Limping.' He grinned at her. 'But I'm going to put a bit of money into it, hire extra help for the manager who runs it for me. But it will be a hobby, nothing more serious, *naturellement*.'

'So you're not giving up your law practice? Or leaving the city permanently?'

'Now, who could leave Paris? Certainly not I. And surely you know I'm not cut out to be a country boy.'

'I do.'

He took a sip of his champagne, and continued, 'I booked a table at L'Ambroisie. In the Place des Vosges. But first I thought we could take a drive around Paris. It's such a beautiful evening, and you haven't been here for a long time. Three years.'

A short while later he was leading her down the front steps of the hotel, his hand under her elbow, guiding her. As they moved along the pavement, he raised a hand, signalling to a driver a little farther along who was standing next to a car.

Tom helped her into the back seat of a maroon Mercedes and climbed in after her. Alexa slid along the seat, positioned herself in the corner; Tom took the other corner, and she placed her shawl and bag in between them, as if building a barrier.

She noticed him glance down at them, saw his mouth twitch as he attempted to swallow a smile. She suddenly felt slightly foolish, and racked her brain for some kind of suitable small talk, but without success. Once more she was shaking inside and felt as though she couldn't breathe. But this was not unusual. He had always had an extraordinary effect on her, right from the beginning.

He was talking to the driver in rapid French, explaining where he should drive them ... around the Place de la Concorde, up the Champs Elysées, back down to the Seine, over to the Left Bank. She knew the latter was one of Tom's favourite parts of the city, an area where he had often driven her himself in the old days.

Once he had finished giving the driver these detailed instructions he settled back in the corner, looked at her and began to talk in an easy and effortless manner. 'So how is Nicky? I haven't run into him for a long time.'

'He looks great, and he and Larry are more successful than ever.'

'So I hear. And you're going to be working with them? Or is it just with Nick?'

'Nicky only. We had our first meeting today over lunch.

And, of course, he always loves to rope me in when it's a costume picture . . . he knows I don't mind the historical research involved.'

'And what's the movie?'

'It's about Mary, Queen of Scots.'

'To be made in France?'

'Well, yes, and in England and Ireland.' Alexa broke off, exclaimed, 'Oh Tom, how beautiful the Place de la Concorde looks tonight . . . under this perfect sky.'

He glanced out of the window, and murmured, 'Yes, it *is* a perfect sky, and there is such a marvellous clarity of light this evening. The city looks magnificent at this hour.'

'A little bit later than the Magic Hour, but nothing to complain about,' she said.

'You and your Magic Hour! Dreamed up when you were a child.' Tom laughed.

'You remember?'

'I remember everything.'

He reached for her hand, but she quickly put it on her lap, glanced out of the window again, pretending she had not realized he wanted to hold hers in his. She knew if he touched her she would fall apart or leap on him. She didn't want to do either, and certainly nothing foolish.

'So, tell me more about your movie,' he suddenly said, turning towards her.

'Well, as you know, Mary grew up here at the French court, under the patronage of her Guise uncles –'

'Ah yes, those somewhat ambitious princes of the blood,' he cut in.

'Then she married the Dauphin, became Queen of France

when his father died, and then was widowed rather soon when very young.'

'And then she was sent back to Scotland to be their rightful queen. How much of her life does the movie cover, Alex?'

'From what Nicky said, the early years . . . her time at the French court, marriage, becoming the French Queen, and then her move to Scotland, marriage to Lord Darnley and her love affair and marriage with the Earl of Bothwell. I believe the script ends when they have to part.'

'A romantic story in many ways.'

'Yes.' Stay away from the subject of romance, a small voice cautioned. She went on swiftly, 'I always complain to Nicky, when he offers me a costume picture, but actually I do quite enjoy doing historicals. They're very challenging, and I admit it, I like digging into the research, coming up with some authentic houses, as well as my own sets.'

'You'll certainly find quite a few of those in the Loire Valley: as you know it's full of châteaux. And have you actually read the script yet?'

'No, but Nicky hopes to have the first draft in a few days. I have a feeling it will be quite good. Nicky says the treatment was wonderful, very well written.'

'You suddenly sound excited about the film.'

'I am, Tom. I like designing sets for plays, but there's so much more scope, so many more opportunities to be truly creative, when it comes to movies.'

'Do you know when the film starts shooting?'

'Not exactly. At the end of the summer, early September, I think. Why?'

'I like the idea of having you here in Paris.'

'Oh,' was all she could say. She was at a loss for words.

Not long after this conversation the car came to a standstill on the boulevard Saint Michel. 'Come on,' Tom said, and opened the door, reached in to help her out. To the driver he said, '*Cinq minutes*, Hubert,' slammed the car door shut, and took hold of her hand.

Striding out, he led her down the rue de la Huchette and up into the rue de la Bûcherie at a rapid pace, without saying a word. As they crossed this small square with its little cafés, going towards the Seine, Tom exclaimed, 'Look, Alexa! You always said this was your favourite view in Paris.'

He brought her to a standstill, and together they stood staring across at the Ile de la Cité, one of the small islands in the Seine, on which stood the Cathedral of Notre Dame. Alexa turned to glance up at Tom, just as he looked down at her. Their eyes met and held; she nodded, then turned to face the Notre Dame. Its imposing Gothic towers looked magnificent in the early evening light, silhouetted as they were against the deep blue sky, and the taller spire shone in the last rays of the fading sun.

She did not say anything for a few minutes, and then she glanced up at him and said, 'Yes, it does have a very special meaning for me, this view.'

'And for me, too. Do you think I don't remember that we came and stood here the first night we had a date.'

She opened her mouth to speak but no words came out. He had bent towards her and was kissing her softly. Then he pulled her into his arms, held her very tightly against him, his kisses growing more passionate.

Her arms went around him, and she clung to him.

Finally, when they drew apart, he looked deeply into her eyes, and gently stroked one side of her face with his hand. 'I said it before, but I feel I must say it again. I am very happy you phoned me.'

'Why did you bring me here, Tom?'

'So that you would know I haven't forgotten anything . . .'

'Neither have I,' she whispered, and her heart clenched as she thought of all the pain he had caused her, as well as the happiness they had shared.

At last she said, 'I don't think I could ever come to Paris without calling you.'

'And I couldn't bear it if you were here and I didn't know you were.' Placing his arm around her shoulder, he walked her back to the car, and said quietly, 'I've missed you . . . a lot.'

Alexa gave him a look through the corner of her eye. 'So have I . . . you.'

Tom took a deep breath, blew out air, glanced around him, and then after a moment, he ventured, 'Your friend. The Englishman. Does he want to make the relationship permanent?'

She was silent at first, and then she answered in a low voice: 'He's talked about it, yes.'

'That's what *you* want, isn't it? Marriage, children, a family life?'

'I did want that, with you, yes.'

'And not with him?'

Alexandra shrugged, looked up at the sky, squinted into the light, shook her head. Finally, her eyes met Tom's, and she said, 'I just don't know. Actually, I don't want to talk about it.'

'So sorry, I *am* prying . . .' His voice trailed off, and then he dropped his arm from her shoulder, took hold of her hand and led her towards the Mercedes parked just ahead.

They hardly spoke on the way to the restaurant, sat quietly in their respective corners, although the silence between them was not angry but as amicable as it usually was. They were compatible, and comfortable with each other, even when they did not want to talk.

Alexa was in a quandary. She couldn't for the world figure out why he was asking questions about her love life. After all, it had been Tom who had broken it off three years ago. Then again, he wasn't acting as if it were over. He had pulled her into his arms and kissed her with passion a few minutes ago. She was glad it was he who had made the first move and not her. He had acted suddenly, unexpectedly, and she was so taken by surprise she had fallen into the trap . . . and into his arms. And willingly so. She had clung to him and kissed him back, and her heart had been clattering as erratically as his. So it wasn't over for him either, was it? She tried to pull her swimming senses together; she knew, only too well, that it wasn't over for her, it had never been over. She doubted that it ever would be.

For his part, Tom Conners was silently chastising himself for falling prey to his emotions in the way he had. From the moment he had seen her standing in the hotel lobby tonight, he had wanted to grab her, pull her to him, kiss her long and hard. Slake the desire he had felt for her for years, fill his need. And he had spoken the truth when he said he was glad she had phoned, that he had missed her, and that he remembered everything about their time together. The problem was, he hadn't meant to say any of those words to her, nor had he meant to start a relationship with her once more. It wasn't that he didn't want to make love to her, of course he did. But he was well aware that he had nothing to offer her . . . not in the long run. And he did not want to hurt her again.

'I'd forgotten how charming the Place des Vosges was,' Alexa was saying, breaking into his thoughts, and he roused himself quickly, pushed a smile on to his face.

'It really is the most beautiful old square in Paris,' he said. 'And I think I told you once, my mother grew up in an apartment in one of the old houses at the other side of the gardens over there.'

'How is she? And your father?'

'They're both well, thanks, and yours?'

'The same, they're great.'

Hubert, the driver, was suddenly opening the door of the Mercedes, and after Tom alighted, he helped her out. They went into L'Ambroisie together, blinking slightly as they entered the dim interior. Within a split second Tom was being greeted warmly, and then they were shown to a table for two in a quiet corner of a medium-sized room.

Alexa glanced around, once they were seated, taking note of the mellow old panelling on the walls, the high ceiling, the ancient tapestries, the silver candlesticks with white candles, the big stone urns brimming to overflowing with fresh flowers.

'It has the feeling of an old house, a private home,' she murmured, leaning across the table towards Tom.

'And that's what it was, of course. There are several rooms for dining. It's very hard to get a table unless you're famous or a politician. Or a noted lawyer.' He winked at her. 'And its undeniable charm is matched only by its delicious food. The chocolate dessert is sublime, and they have one of the best *caves* in Paris.'

'You know I'm not a big drinker.'

'But you'll have a glass of champagne, won't you?'

'That'll be nice. Thanks, Tom.'

After he had ordered their drinks, Alexa said, 'You know what I've been doing lately, because of my name being in the trade papers occasionally. But you haven't told me anything about yourself. How have *you* spent these last few years?'

He leaned back in the chair, eyeing her thoughtfully, pondering.

She thought his eyes had never looked more blue; he was very handsome, debonair in his demeanour, and irresistible. No, lethal. At least to her. She corrected herself. He would be lethal to any woman.

He said, 'I still represent a number of people in the film industry. In fact, I'm now the head of the show business division of the law firm. The firm's become rather prestigious in the last two years because we've had several big, non-show business cases, which we've won. The clients are coming in a steady stream these days. And my own work has been going well.' He gave her a lopsided smile. 'But nothing special has been happening. In fact, I do lead a rather humdrum sort of life, Alex.'

'I wouldn't call it that, Tom.'

The waiter arrived with two extra-tall, crystal flutes of champagne, pale blonde in colour and sparkling, and he was saved the trouble of answering her. He wondered why they were here; he wanted her at home in his bed.

Suddenly the maître d' was standing next to the table, talking to Tom about the menu. It was obvious Tom was a favoured client.

Alexa sat back, half listening, her eyes on Tom, mesmerized by him. Humdrum life, she thought at one moment, wished she could live it with him. And then she thought of Jack and was sad.

The only man she wanted was Tom Conners.

CHAPTER TWENTY-FOUR

'I hope you don't mind, but I've ordered for both of us,' Tom said, smiling at her. He took a swallow of his champagne, before adding, 'White asparagus, a taste of the langoustine in pastry leaves, which is their speciality, to be followed by –'

'Lamb,' Alexa interrupted peremptorily. 'I think you must have forgotten I speak French.'

'No, I haven't.' He sat back in his chair, his gaze level and steady as he studied her. If only she knew what he remembered. Images of her and their time together were indelibly printed on his brain, and she existed inside him, in his heart.

Alexa said, 'And you've ordered your favourite wine, a Petrus, which you once told me should only be drunk on special occasions. Is tonight special, Tom?' She gazed at him, the expression in her light green eyes as serious as her face.

'Absolutely. We are celebrating your return to Paris.'

'I'm just visiting. And not for long.'

He threw her an odd look, frowning, and murmured, 'Don't talk about leaving, Alex, you've only just arrived. And you're coming back for the film.' His blue eyes quickened. 'How long will you be here on the movie?'

'I don't know. Nicky hasn't said. But quite a few months, I'm fairly certain of that. There's a lot of pre-production on a film like this, because of the sets and locations, and the costumes as well. Nicky and I hope to make a schedule next week.' She lifted her glass, took a sip of champagne, and asked curiously, 'You've never been to New York in the past three years?'

'No. I was in Los Angeles two years ago to meet a client.' He shook his head. 'I should have phoned you.'

'Why didn't you?'

He reached out, put his hand over hers. 'I didn't feel I had the right. I was the one who brought our relationship to an end. I was positive you had probably met someone else by then, fallen in love, made a new life. Moved on.'

Alexa gaped at him, her eyes opening wider, and she thought: *Fallen in love, moved on.* How can he possibly think that? Doesn't he know how much I loved him, with all my heart and soul, with every fibre of my being? She held herself very still in the chair. Her eyes welled with tears all of a sudden, and she wanted to look away but discovered that she couldn't. She blinked back her tears.

'I've upset you. What is it? What's wrong?' His fingers tightened on hers and he leaned closer over the table, his eyes troubled.

'I guess I'm surprised, that's all . . . that you think I could move on . . . so quickly . . .'

'It's been a long time . . . three years.'

'You haven't moved on. Or have you?'

He did not answer at first and then he admitted, 'No, Alex, I haven't.' He hesitated slightly, and then asked, 'But what about your friend? The Englishman? You must have a relationship with him, since you said he wants to make it permanent.'

'Yes, I do, but I have always been . . . uncertain, nervous about the situation. Before I came to Paris, I had a long talk with my mother about him, you, and –' Alexa broke off, gave a strange little laugh. 'Some people would think I'm crazy for telling you this . . . feeding your ego, in a way, I guess.' She paused, took a deep breath, and finished softly. 'I love you, Tom. I always have, from the first moment we met, and I suppose I always will.'

He nodded, continuing to hold her hand very tightly in his. His blue gaze fastened on hers. 'I've spent the last few years having meaningless sex with women who meant nothing at all to me. They're a blur. You see, Alex, I didn't want anyone else but you.'

She stared hard at him, her eyes narrowing. 'Why didn't you call me? Weren't you ever *tempted*?'

'Of course I was! I must have picked up the phone a hundred times. But I felt I did not have the right, as I just told you. I had ended it, and it was not for me to attempt to start a relationship with you again. I also knew I had so many problems to work out in my own head.'

'You said at the time that you had nothing to offer, and

therefore you were setting me free. But you didn't do that . . .
I've been forever bound to you, Tom.'

There was a moment of silence.

He sat looking at her, his eyes searching her face, that face
he loved. Finally, he said slowly in a low voice, 'I've waited
a long time for the call you made last night. I could hardly
believe it was you. And ever since, I've been anxious, really
on tenterhooks until I saw you standing there in the lobby.'

'Yes, I know exactly what you mean.'

He smiled; his eyes sparkled. 'Suddenly, there you were,
looking so chic and beautiful and not a day older than when
I last saw you.'

'I'll soon be thirty-one. And you'll soon be forty-three.'

'At the end of May. And don't remind me!'

'It was Anya, you know. She made me call you.'

'*Oh.*' He sat back and gave her a long, contemplative look.
'Weren't you planning to phone me?'

'I knew I would ultimately. It was all a question of getting
up my nerve.'

The waiter arrived with the white asparagus; he took a
few moments serving it and drizzling the vinaigrette dressing
before finally stepping away from the table.

Alexa ate several spears and then sat back in the chair; she
drank some of her water.

Tom looked up from his plate, and frowned. 'Is something
wrong? You're not eating.'

'I'm not really hungry.'

'I know . . . neither am I.'

They stared at each other, exchanging a look full of yearning for each other, fully aware of what they really wanted.

Tom said, 'We cannot leave now . . . not until the entire meal has been served. If we do go, I won't ever be able to come here again.' He sighed, reached for her hand. 'I'll be *persona non grata*.'

'I understand. And after all this time, what's another hour? I'll try and eat a little of each course, and you should, if you can.'

'You are right . . .' He picked up a spear of asparagus. 'And this is delicious, you know.'

Following suit, Alex also ate a few more spears, and by the time the langoustine was served they were both more relaxed, less tense with each other, at least on the surface.

At one moment, picking up his goblet of red wine, Tom toasted her. 'Here's to you, Alex. Welcome back.'

'I'm glad to be back,' she said, touching her glass to his. She wondered if he were welcoming her back to Paris or back into his life, and she was not sure. She took a sip of wine, said, 'Smooth as silk, this Petrus of yours.'

He laughed, looked pleased.

Alexa toyed with the lamb on her plate, took a forkful, ate a bite, then put the fork down. Looking across at him, she said, 'You mentioned your problems just now. Do you think . . . I mean, well, have you worked them out finally?'

'I believe I have, Alex, yes,' he replied, took a long swallow of the wine, and leaned back in the chair. His face had changed slightly in that brief moment, and the laughter of a second ago had vanished. 'It's taken me a long time to settle things in my mind,' he said in a sober tone, 'to come to terms with everything, but I now have.'

'I'm glad. It must make you feel better.'

'It does. I do have my moments, when I'm . . . sad, but for the most part I'm much better than I ever was. I slayed the demons.'

'How did you manage to do that?' she asked, and then cringed inside when she saw his face. 'I'm sorry,' she added quickly. 'I don't want to pry. I'm just glad you feel better.'

'If I can't talk to you about it, then I don't know who I can. I did it on my own, no psychiatrists, no tranquillizers to get me through. I just faced up to what had happened, and most importantly, I managed to stop feeling guilty.'

'That must have been very difficult, Tom.'

'It was, but I had enormous incentive. I wanted to be the Tom Conners I was before Juliette and Marie-Laure died. When I told you there was no future for you with me, and you left Paris, I sort of fell apart. I began drinking. A lot.' He glanced at the glass of wine on the table. 'And not that mother's milk either. Hard liquor. Vodka mostly, because it tastes of nothing. That's all I did in my free time, I sat at home and drank. For six months. But suddenly one day I hated what I had become and I stopped. I also did something else.'

'What was that?'

'I decided to do some research.'

'*Research?* About what?'

'Terrorism. My wife and child were murdered by terrorists on a warm, sunny day in Athens. Like everyone else in that square that day, they were innocent. I wanted to know *who* and *why*, and so I spent a whole year reading, talking to experts, learning about Muslim fundamentalism, the meaning of Islamic Jihad, Hezbollah and how it worked, Abu

Nidal, Carlos the Jackal, and the other terrorist groups. I was very conscientious, Alex. Actually, I filled seven notebooks with information. And about four months ago I suddenly realized I was finally free of guilt . . . it had simply fled. I hadn't killed my wife and child by being late that day. They had been blown to smithereens by those brutes who fight a guerrilla war in the name of Islam.'

Alexa was very quiet for a moment or two, and then she reached out, touched his hand. 'Did you ever find out which group blew up the bus of Americans that day?'

'I have a good idea, and so do various governments. But what good does that do?' He sighed. 'The main thing is, I managed to rid myself of guilt, and I've felt so much more like a normal person ever since.'

'I really am so happy for you, Tom, happy that you have been able to ease your pain. There were times when I didn't know how to help you, when you were in such . . . anguish –' Alexa broke off as the waiter came to the table and began to clear away their plates.

Once they were alone, Tom leaned forward and said quietly, 'I'm afraid their chocolate dessert will arrive at any moment. Can you handle more food?'

She laughed. 'I'll cut it up, and push it around my plate. That should do the trick.'

'You may find yourself eating it.'

'I doubt that.'

'There you go again, doubting what I say. Just like the bees.'

'The bees?' She wrinkled her nose, looking perplexed and then she began to laugh. 'Oh my God, yes. The *bees*.'

He chuckled with her.

'Listen to me, Tom Conners! No one else would have believed you either! What person in their right mind would believe that bees were kept on the roof of the Paris Opera House, and that their honey was put in jars and sold. No one, that's who!'

'*True.*'

'But you were so dear when you bought me the jars of honey just to prove it.'

He looked into her eyes, squeezed her hand, and asked, 'Do you want coffee? Or anything else, Alex?'

'No, thanks, Tom.'

'Will you come home with me?'

'You know I will. Where else could I possibly want to go?'

CHAPTER TWENTY-FIVE

They stood in the foyer of Tom's apartment, alone at last as they had longed to be for the last few hours, but curiously silent now as they stared at each other intently.

Although they had laughed in the restaurant, been more at ease with each other, the tension between them had returned once they were sitting on the back seat of the Mercedes, in their separate corners.

Acutely conscious of each other, they had hardly spoken a word as Hubert had driven the car through the evening traffic, heading in the direction of the Faubourg Saint-Germain where Tom lived.

Now the electricity between them was a palpable thing once more, and they both moved forward at precisely the same moment, coming together in the middle of the floor, almost stumbling into each other's arms.

Tom gathered Alexa close, and she held on to him tightly, her body instantly welded to his. He bent down, began to kiss her fervently, and she matched his ardour, responded with equal intensity and passion.

Alexa was shaking internally, her long pent-up desire for Tom flooding her entire body, and her heart clattered in unison with his. Tom slid his hand down her back and on to her buttocks, pressed her even closer, moulded her body to his, and she felt the hardness of his growing passion through her thin linen dress. Suddenly she was suffused with warmth. Her bag and her shawl fell from her hands, but she ignored them as he led her away from the foyer and into the bedroom, his arms still wrapped around her.

It was obvious he did not want to let go of her, and he pulled her down on to the bed with him, began to kiss her once more. His hand went to her breast and he stroked it, played with her nipple which began to harden under the fabric. A small groan escaped her throat; her hands went up into his thick, dark hair and she felt his scalp with her fingertips. They were lost in their raging desire for each other, wanting only to possess and be possessed.

Tom's kisses stopped abruptly, and he pushed himself up on one elbow, looked down into her face, his own congested with raw emotion. He started to say something, and then stopped, not wanting to break the spell, or cool the heat of their rampant feelings.

Gazing back at him, Alexa recognized the longing and desire in his eyes, was swamped by that vivid blue gaze, and she was as overwhelmed by him, and her feelings for him, as she had been from the first moment they met. Her

BARBARA TAYLOR BRADFORD

throat tightened. Nothing had changed, she knew that now. She felt undone, helpless, and so in love with him nothing else, no one else, mattered. Very simply, there was no other man for her. Only he made her feel like this.

Tom touched her mouth with one finger, leaned into her, said softly, 'Take your clothes off, darling.'

She slid off the bed, did as he asked, quickly shedding everything, and then moved back on to the bed again.

Tom did the same, undressed with swiftness, and she watched him in the dim light of the bedroom, shivering slightly as he came back to her. He was so tall, long-legged, broad-shouldered, the most handsome and masculine man she had ever known, and his desire for her was now apparent. She longed for Tom to take her to him.

Tom lay down next to her, covered her body with his own, held her in his arms. Against her hair, he said, 'I've never stopped wanting you, and only *you*, Alex.'

'Oh, Tom darling, Tom,' she whispered and touched his cheek with one hand. 'And it's only *you* I want –'

He stopped her words with his kisses, his mouth firm yet gentle on hers. He parted her lips, let his tongue graze hers, and then rest still. As one of his hands moved down to smooth and fondle her rounded breast, he brought his mouth to it, smothered it with kisses.

Wanting to touch and kiss every inch of her, his mouth moved on, fluttered across her stomach, her inner thigh and all of those erotic, secret parts of her. Slowly his kisses became more languorous until finally his lips settled on the feminine core of her, and lingered there.

Alexa stiffened and gasped, and went on gasping as he

made love to her in this most sensual and intimate way, as he had done from the outset of their relationship. Loving her like this gave him as much pleasure as it did her; he was pleased and gratified when he brought her to climax and she spasmed, called his name, and told him how much she loved him.

Her excitement fed his own arousal. Tom knew only too well that he had never felt like this with any other woman, not before her, or during her recent absence from his life. Suddenly, he thought he was going to explode, and unable to hold back any longer, he moved on top of her. He needed to be inside her, to possess her totally, to make her his own.

Tom pushed himself up, braced his arms on each side of her and looked down into Alexa's light green eyes. Her emotions were explicit on her face, and as his gaze lingered for a moment longer his heart clenched. He knew, all of a sudden, what she truly meant to him. He also knew what a fool he had been ever to let her go.

As he entered her, she cried his name again, and he told her finally, and with absolute certainty, that he loved her, that she was the love of his life.

They lay amidst rumpled pillows and tangled sheets, resting quietly in the soft, dim light of his bedroom.

The impact of seeing each other again had been devastating to them both, and they had fallen into their own thoughts.

For Alexa, their passionate lovemaking on this bed for the past hour and a half was merely a confirmation of what she already knew, had known deep down inside herself for the

BARBARA TAYLOR BRADFORD

last few years. She loved Tom, always had, always would, and nothing could ever change that fact.

Endeavouring to move on, because he had been unable to make a commitment to her, she had striven for a successful career, a good life, and eventually she had even enjoyed a relationship with another man . . . Jack Wilton. The thought of Jack made her heart sink. She was going to have to tell him she couldn't marry him; she hated the thought of hurting him. But even though there might not be a future with Tom, she could not marry Jack or anyone else. Her heart belonged to this man cradling her in his arms, one leg thrown over her body, his hands clasping hers, as if he were afraid she was going to escape his tenacious grip.

He loved her; she had always known he did, and he desired her sexually. They were intense in bed and out of it; they were compatible. Yet he couldn't take that final step. At least, not in the past. Now he might. He had told her he no longer felt guilt about the tragic deaths of his wife and child. And yet she wondered . . . had he really conquered it?

As far as she was concerned, marriage didn't matter any more, she just wanted to be with him. 'Living in sin', it was called. But she didn't see it that way. If you loved each other, it wasn't a sin. Marrying a man you didn't love, and spending the rest of your life with him, well, that was surely living in sin, wasn't it?

Alexa closed her eyes, imagining the child she had wanted. Correction. *His child*. But if that were not possible, it didn't really matter. Tom was all that mattered to her, and being with him for the rest of her life.

As he lay next to her, Tom was contemplating the dichotomy

274

in his nature. How he loved her, this woman in his arms, with all his heart; sexually he craved her constantly, wanted to be joined to her. They were hot together, and perfectly matched; her passion, ardour and sensuality in bed had echoed his since their first night together years ago. She truly satisfied him and he knew he satisfied her.

Yet despite all this he was afraid to make the relationship permanent, afraid he might somehow hurt her in the long run . . .

But if he lost her again, where would he be? He groaned inwardly. When he thought of all the mindless, meaningless sex he'd had in her absence he was appalled at himself.

He had told her the truth when he said he had vanquished the survivor guilt. Sixteen years he had lived with that, and he thanked God every day that he was free of it at long last.

When Tom considered the research he had done into global terrorism, and what he had found out, he inevitably shrivelled inside at the enormity of it all. The knowledge of terrorism in the future that he now possessed was a burden. He knew too much. It weighed him down, and what he had learned filled him with despair. Apprehension about the years ahead never waned. But there was nothing he could do but go about his daily life, hoping for the best, praying that goodness would outweigh evil ultimately.

Alexa moved in his arms, and he tightened his embrace, but she wriggled around so that he had to loosen his grip, and finally she was facing him.

Her cool green eyes looked deeply into his. 'I want to tell you something, Tom.' Her face was serious.

BARBARA TAYLOR BRADFORD

'Then tell me.' He held his breath, wondering what was coming.

'I want to be with you . . . and being married doesn't really matter to me any longer. Just so long as we're together, that's all that counts.'

He searched her face; his eyes, fastened on hers, were filled with love. 'And I want to be with you, I feel the same, Alex. But mostly we're so far away from each other. You're in New York, I'm here.'

'I know, but I'm coming back soon, to do the movie.'

'And after that?'

'I think we can work it out . . . if we want to.'

'I know we can, darling.' He kissed her, and they clung to each other for a few moments. And they both knew a bargain had been sealed.

After a while, he said against the hollow of her neck, 'You're my one true love, Alex.'

She moved again, so that she could see him, and stared hard at him, frowning. Then she said slowly, 'When we were making love you said I was the love of your life . . . but . . .' She left her sentence unfinished.

He returned her gaze with one equally steady. 'I know, you're thinking about Juliette, and my feelings for her. Of course I loved her deeply, but we were children together. Childhood sweethearts, Alex darling, and in many ways we were very young. I came to you as a grown man, scarred by life, and you were a mature woman. You'd lived life a little. And it's a different kind of love I feel for you . . . and so yes, you are the love of my life. Now.'

Reaching out, she touched his cheek very gently, and

276

leaned into him, kissed him lightly on the lips. 'Everything will be all right. *We're* going to be all right, Tom.'

He smiled at her, and she settled down in his arms. He rested his face against her head, ruminating again on the evening they had spent together. It had been marvellous to see her again, to look at her across a dinner table, to make love with her, to hold her here in his arms like this . . . he was lucky.

Tom relaxed, closing his eyes, and he realized then that the pain had finally ceased. That awful pain he had lived with all these long years had miraculously ceased to exist . . . and he was at peace.

'Why do you have this photograph in your album?' Tom asked, looking up at Alexa as she came out of the bathroom in her hotel room. It was Sunday morning. They had gone to the Meurice half an hour ago so that she could shed her clothes of the night before, put on something more suitable for lunch. As he waited, Tom had seen the album and picked it up, curious as always.

She glanced at the small red leather photograph album in his hands, and shook her head. 'Which one are you referring to?'

'This one,' he said, holding the album out to her.

Alexa took it from him and stared down at the photograph he was indicating. It was of Jessica and Lucien. The two of them stood on the Pont des Arts, and she had taken it just a few weeks before graduation.

'It's Jessica Pierce,' Alexa explained as she looked up at Tom. 'She was at Anya's school with me.'

'No, no, it's the man I'm talking about. I was curious why he was in your album. I didn't know you knew him. He's a neighbour of my parents.'

Alexa was gaping at Tom. She exclaimed, 'That can't be. Lucien disapp –'

'Why do you call him that?' Tom interrupted.

'That was his name . . . Lucien Girard.'

'No, no, Alex,' Tom argued, shaking his head. 'The man with Jessica is Jean Beauvais-Cresse, and he lives in the Loire Valley.'

CHAPTER TWENTY-SIX

Alexa was speechless for a split second, and she sat down heavily on the chair opposite Tom. She had been startled and shocked by his words, and it showed on her face. After looking down at the album and the photograph of Jessica and Lucien once more, she finally managed to say, 'Tom, are you sure about what you're saying?'

He leaned back on the sofa, a reflective expression crossing his face fleetingly. 'Well, they say everybody has a twin somewhere, but I'm pretty certain this *is* Jean Beauvais-Cresse. Obviously I could be wrong, but I don't think I am.' He leaned forward, held out his hand. 'Let me look at the picture again, please Alexa.'

Rising, she bent towards him, handed him the album and then sat down, crossing her legs, waiting for him to continue their conversation. She was still taken aback, her mind racing as she considered a variety of scenarios and possibilities.

Once he had carefully studied the photograph of Jessica and Lucien on the bridge, he flipped through the album again, glancing at some of the other pictures, many of himself and Alexa.

Finally placing it on the coffee table, Tom said, 'Listen to me, Alex, people don't change that much between their twenties and thirties, their looks remain pretty much the same for the most part. The man in the picture appears to be in his mid-twenties at the time. Did you take it?'

'Yes, I did.'

'When? About seven or eight years ago?'

'Yes. Not long before our graduation actually, Tom.'

'The man I know, well, I shouldn't say I know him, I'm acquainted with him, that's all. Anyway, he's in his mid-thirties now.' Tom focused his eyes on her; leaning forward slightly, his hands on his knees, he finished, 'I know it's Jean when he was much younger.'

Alexa bit her lip and shook her head, her eyes suddenly clouded over. 'Then at a certain time he led a double life. Or he led a different life as someone called Lucien Girard.'

'Tell me about him and Jessica, Alex.'

'There's not a lot to tell. Jessica and Lucien met, fell for each other and started to date. Soon they were inseparable as they became more and more involved, and in love. She told me they planned a future together, that they wanted to marry. And then one day Lucien disappeared into thin air. Without a trace. She never saw him again.'

It was Tom's turn to be startled, and he exclaimed,

'Nobody disappears just like that! Like a puff of smoke floating away! Surely he was in touch with her eventually, gave her a full explanation.'

'He wasn't. And Jessica was heartbroken. It was all something of a mystery at the time. She and a friend of Lucien's did everything they could to find him, but without success. In the end she just gave up and went back to the States.'

'And she never heard from him later?'

'I . . . we . . . well, we weren't in touch by then. We weren't speaking. But if Lucien Girard had turned up Anya would have known, because Jessica would have told her. And Anya or Nicky would have told me. Remember, I lived in Paris for almost three years after graduation, before I went back home.'

Tom nodded, settled back against the cushions on the sofa, enormously puzzled by this odd coincidence . . . that two men could look so much alike. 'What a strange and troubling story.' He frowned, then asked, 'And what was this Lucien Girard doing at the time? Was he a student also? Or was he working? Or what?'

'He wasn't a student, Tom. He was an actor. Not well known, he only had small parts, but he was quite good, from what I heard.'

'What else do you know about him?' Tom probed, the lawyer in him coming to the surface. 'I'm very intrigued, I must admit.'

'I don't really know anything else. Jessica spent a lot of time with Lucien, usually alone, except for the few occasions when we were all together.' She shrugged, suddenly at a loss for words.

Tom also was silent. He brought a hand up to his chin, rubbed it a few times as he sat pondering on the sofa. 'Well, it's none of my business,' he murmured eventually. 'Although it's quite peculiar when you think about it . . . uncanny that two men look the same. Maybe identical twins.'

'That could be it!' Alexa exclaimed. 'Perhaps this Jean fellow who lives near your parents actually has a brother. *Even a twin*, as you've just suggested.'

'Yes, that's a possibility. I don't know much about the family. But look, Alex, as I just said, it's nothing to do with us.'

Alexa nodded, rose, went to the window, stood looking out for a moment or two at the Tuileries across the street. After a short while she turned around, came back to her chair, sat down and looked across at Tom. 'But what if Lucien and Jean *are* the same person? Don't you think Jessica Pierce has a right to know . . . that he's all right, that he's alive? That way she would have *closure* finally.'

'That's true, to a certain extent. Look, Alex, think about this . . . what would be the purpose of telling her, really? Wouldn't it be opening up a lot of old wounds? Anyway, it may not matter to Jessica now. She's probably married to someone else.'

'No, she isn't. Anya told me we were all still single, except for Kay Lenox who's now married to some lord. I ought to give Jessica this information, even though we parted on bad terms. Anya wants us to be friends. Perhaps I owe it to Jessica.'

'Honestly, you must think about this carefully,' Tom cautioned. 'Might it not be rather cruel, hurtful, to tell

Jessica that I think her old boyfriend is alive and well and living in the Loire?'

'I suppose so, especially since we don't really know whether Jean *is* Lucien. But what if they are the same man? He was a bastard, wasn't he?'

Tom inclined his head, seeing the truth in what she said. He ventured, 'Could it be that Lucien wanted to break up with Jessica, and not knowing how to do it gracefully, he simply . . . *slipped away* . . . never to be seen again?'

'That's possible. Rather cowardly, though. Here's another thing, Tom. If Lucien is actually Jean Beauvais-Cresse why did he become Lucien Girard for a period of time?'

'I don't know . . . I can't even imagine why . . .'

'A mystery,' she muttered and jumped up. 'I'd better finish getting dressed. I'll only be a few minutes, then we can leave for Anya's. We mustn't be late for Sunday lunch. It's a sort of ritual with her.'

Alexa was quiet in the taxi on the way to Anya's house, and several times Tom glanced at her out of the corner of his eye. She seemed preoccupied, and so he knew it was wisest to keep silent.

Settling back against the seat, he thought about their morning together. They had awakened early, and prepared breakfast in the kitchen; later Alexa had wandered around, exclaiming about the changes he had made in the apartment since she had last been there, showing her approval. Then she had called her hotel for messages; the only one was from Anya, inviting her to Sunday lunch. He had heard her on the phone, asking if she could bring him, and then the whoop of jubilation as she had hung up the phone. 'She can't wait to see you, Tom! You're invited, too.'

On their way to lunch they had stopped off at the hotel, so Alexa could put on make-up and change. He glanced at her now, thinking that her clothes stamped her nationality on her. She could only be an American in her blue jeans, white silk shirt, and brown penny loafers worn with white wool socks. A dark blue cashmere sweater was tied around her neck, and she carried the brown Kelly bag he'd given her years ago.

He loved her looks. Well, he loved her, didn't he, and he knew she loved him. There had never been any doubt in his mind about that; he had been the one at fault in the past. A jerk, if he thought about it.

Tom knew that Alexa was going to tell Anya about the resemblance between Lucien Girard and Jean Beauvais-Cresse. He had seen Alexa put the small, red leather album into her bag before they had left the hotel suite, and he wondered what Anya would have to say. Instantly, his thoughts settled on Jessica, who looked so young, beautiful and sweet in the photograph. She must have been utterly devastated when her boyfriend had disappeared, and he asked himself again whether it was appropriate, wise, to say anything to her about Jean.

Before he could stop himself, Tom suddenly asked, 'Why did you and Jessica part on bad terms, as you put it?'

Alexa turned away from the taxi window, and looked at him. 'It wasn't just Jessica and me. You see, Tom, there were four of us, and we *all* quarrelled. It was a big bust-up.'

'What about?'

'It's too complicated to tell you now. I'll fill you in later. But I do think we'll have to meet and make up before Anya's party.'

'That might be a good idea.' Tom took hold of her hand. 'I've been thinking about Jean Beauvais-Cresse. As I told you, I've barely met him. But I could phone my father and ask him what he knows.'

Alexa's face quickened. 'Would you mind?'

'No, I'll call him after lunch. And by the way, is anyone else going to be at lunch?'

'Anya didn't say. But Nicky could be there. He's very close to her.'

'I'd like to see him again.'

'I've just thought of something, Tom. If I remember correctly, I think it was Larry Sedgwick who introduced Lucien to Jessica, not that this means anything really.' She bit her lip, staring hard at him. 'The idea that Lucien might have been playing games really bugs me. I just don't know what to do about it.'

'Nothing right now,' Tom answered swiftly, in a firm voice. 'You can't go around accusing people of once being someone else, otherwise you'll find yourself in the middle of a lawsuit.'

'I wasn't going to do that,' she said a trifle huffily and glanced out of the window. Immediately, she turned her head and said in a lighter tone, 'But you'd always defend me, wouldn't you?'

'With my life,' he answered and put his arms around her.

CHAPTER TWENTY-SEVEN

Anya Sedgwick glanced around her upstairs sitting room through appraising eyes, decided that it looked particularly warm and welcoming this morning.

Red and yellow tulips made stunning pools of vivid colour in various parts of the room, and a fire burned brightly in the hearth. Although it was another sunny May day there was a nip in the air, and earlier she had asked Honorine to make a fire. She had always liked to see one burning in this room, even in spring and summer.

Moving around, her bearing as elegant as always, her eagle eyes sought anything that might be out of place; she found little amiss, except for a crooked photograph frame on the skirted table. After straightening this, she went and sat down behind her large desk in the corner near the fireplace.

As she waited for her luncheon guests to arrive, she once

again looked at the list of acceptances for her birthday party. It had grown somewhat in the last few weeks, since almost everyone had accepted, and new people had been added as well. Nicky had told her, only the other day, that the number had reached one hundred and fifty. She couldn't wait to greet them all, spend time with them.

She put the list down and sat back in the chair, staring into space for a moment, her blue eyes as clear and bright as they had always been. She truly was looking forward to her eighty-fifth birthday party, and had carefully planned what she would wear.

Anya knew she didn't look her age, and she certainly didn't feel it; nevertheless, she was an old woman. At least numerically.

I've been on this earth eighty-five years and I've lived every one of those years to the fullest, with energy, zest and enthusiasm. I've been involved, curious, caring, loving, interested in everything and everyone. I've never been bored or jaded, and my mind has always been active, alert, filled with optimism. She smiled inwardly, as she added to herself: And I've no intention of dying just yet. No plans for that in the works. I've a lot more damage to do. Yes, I aim to be around for a long time.

The telephone rang, and she picked it up. 'Hello?'

'It's Nicky, Anya, good morning. I'm sorry, but –'

'Don't tell me you're not coming to lunch.'

'There's a problem.'

'What is it?'

'Maria. She's very nervous about coming face to face with Alexa.'

'Well, she'd better get over it, because she's going to have to do exactly that and very soon, even if she doesn't do it today. I want this mess cleaned up before the party, and the only way to do it is through confrontation. I'm determined to get to the bottom of their quarrelling, Nicky!' she exclaimed in a tough voice.

'I agree,' he answered quickly, picking up on her militant tone, which he knew brooked no argument. 'You're absolutely right.'

'I'm glad you agree. She has to come to lunch today. Actually, I was planning on having a lunch for those four later in the week, so this makes a good beginning.'

'Oh, are the other women coming today?' he asked quickly.

'No, no, just Alexa and Tom, as I told you.'

'Are they back together?'

'I don't know . . . I understand they had dinner last night.'

Nicky sighed. 'Well, I hope I can persuade her.'

'Don't sound so weak-kneed, Nicky. Be firm. Wait . . . put her on the phone, I'll speak to her myself.'

'Oh, I'm not –'

'Don't stonewall me, Nick, and don't lie. I know she's with you, either at your flat or her hotel. You can't pull the wool over my eyes . . . I know you're having an affair with Maria, and more power to the two of you. Please, put Maria on the phone. *Now*.'

'Yes, okay, and calm down, Anya.'

A moment later, Maria said meekly, 'Good morning, Anya.'

'Good morning, my dear. I expect you for lunch at one

o'clock. Please be here, Maria. It is extremely important to me that you are present today.'

'Yes, Anya. We will come. We might be a bit late.'

'Start hurrying, Maria. And please don't be *too* late.'

'No, no, we'll hurry,' Maria promised, and hung up the phone.

Anya rose, walked around the desk to the fireplace, stood with her back to it for a few moments, thinking about Nicky and Maria. She had seen them on quite a few occasions since Maria's arrival in Paris, and it was very apparent to her that they were completely absorbed in each other. Infatuated, she thought, and then amended that. No, they're in love, she corrected herself, and she just hoped Nicky would be able to sort out his problems with Constance, and as quickly as possible. It had struck her several times that Maria and Nicky were ideally suited, that they should be together on a permanent basis.

As for Alexandra and Tom Conners, there was no question that these two had connected again last night. When Alexa had returned her phone call, earlier this morning, she had asked her if this were so. Alexa had answered in the affirmative, adding, '*big time*'. Anya loved this expression, and she smiled to herself. She definitely wanted Alexa and Tom to be together 'big time', because she had always known that her favourite pupil was still in love with him, that he was undoubtedly the love of her life.

With a sudden flash of intuition, Anya knew that these two *were* going to be together for the rest of their lives, even if they didn't know that yet. She felt it in her very old bones.

*   *   *

Ten minutes later Alexa was rushing into the room, her face filled with smiles, followed closely by Tom, who was also smiling broadly.

'Good morning, Anya!' Alexa cried, hurrying over to the fireplace, hugging Anya tightly. In her ear, she whispered, 'I'm so glad you made me call him. He's been wonderful.'

'I'm happy you're here, Alexa, and you too, Tom,' Anya said as Alexa stepped away from her. She stretched out her hand to Tom, who took it, and shook it with a firm grip.

'Thanks for including me today, Anya. I must say, it's wonderful to see you again after so long.'

'You're looking well, Tom,' Anya responded, still smiling. 'Now, what would you both like to drink?' As she spoke she glanced over at a chest in the far corner, where bottles of liquor and glasses were lined up on a tray. There were also two silver buckets filled with ice, one containing a bottle of white wine, the other champagne.

'I know Alexa will have champagne, Anya, and so will I. Why don't I pour it, and what about you? What will you drink?'

'The Veuve Clicquot also, thank you, Tom, and certainly you can be bartender.'

He nodded and moved across the room. She watched him as he strode away, thinking that she had not seen such a magnificent specimen of manhood for years. It wasn't just that he had a handsome face, beautiful, in fact, if she were honest, but his physique was also extraordinary. She had forgotten how tall and long-legged Tom was, and his broad chest and shoulders gave him a truly masculine appearance.

Anya's eyes remained on him as he poured champagne

into the tall flutes which Honorine had put out earlier. He had always been well dressed, she now remembered, and today was no exception. He wore a pale blue checked shirt, navy tie, navy blazer and blue jeans, impeccably tailored. Custom-made, Anya thought, and then accepted the glass of champagne from him.

The three of them stood in front of the fireplace, and clinking their glasses, they said, 'Cheers,' in unison. Looking up at him, Anya found his eyes blinding for a split second. They were the bluest eyes she had ever seen. If only I were fifty years younger, she thought, and then smiled, amused at herself. Imagine fancying a man at my age, she thought, and looked at Alexa.

'Is Nicky coming to lunch by any chance?' Alexa asked.

'He is, as a matter of fact, and he's bringing Maria Franconi.'

'Oh no!' Alexa exclaimed before she could stop herself.

'Oh yes,' Anya shot back. 'And I think you'd better get used to it, Alexa, since you'll be working with Nicky. Those two have become . . . well, an item is the best way to put it for the moment. That aside, I am hoping you, Maria, Kay and Jessica are going to make an effort to be civil with each other. I'm planning a lunch for later in the week, so that you can all have it out with each other, if necessary. None of you have ever told me what caused you to blow your friendships apart.' Staring at Alexa she raised an eyebrow questioningly.

'It just so happens that it all started with Maria,' Alexa finally volunteered after a moment or two. 'But since she's coming for lunch we'd better not get into it now.' Moving towards the sofa, Alexa sat down, and Anya joined her.

Tom lowered himself into the armchair next to them, and put his glass on the coffee table. Turning to Anya he said, 'I think Alexa wants to talk to you about something important. Don't you, Alex?'

Taken aback for a moment, knowing he was referring to Jessica and Lucien, she could only nod. Finding her voice at last, she said, 'I think Tom ought to tell you what happened this morning, and then I'll take it up from there.' She put her glass down, reached for her Kelly bag on the floor, and opened it.

Tom said, 'I was waiting for Alexa to change at the hotel, and I happened to pick up a small photo album which was on a table. As I went through it, I saw a picture of a man who's a neighbour of my parents in the Loire. He was photographed with this beautiful blonde. Oh, and I must add, Anya, that in the photo he looked about eight years younger than he does today. I was surprised, because I didn't understand why Alex would have a picture of him in her album.'

Anya had listened attentively, and now she glanced at Alexa and said, 'Who was the blonde? Jessica, I'm assuming.'

'Correct.' Alexa handed her the album open at the photograph of Jessica with Lucien Girard.

Anya took the album, gazed at the picture for a second, then looking at Tom, she said, 'It's Lucien, as I remember him. But who do *you* think he is?'

'Jean Beauvais-Cresse, a man in his mid-thirties who lives near my parents. He's not a friend, just a neighbour, an acquaintance, and I don't know much about him. But Lucien

Girard's resemblance to him is uncanny. He looks like a younger version.'

'He could be a relative,' Anya pointed out, nodding to herself.

'Indeed he could,' Tom agreed. 'A twin, a brother, a cousin.' As he was speaking, Tom, the lawyer who relied on facts, reasoning, analysis, common sense, and evidence, realized how true his words were . . . a family resemblance between two different men was the answer. It had to be. Taking a deep breath, Tom finished, 'Alex feels she ought to talk to Jessica. What do you think, Anya?'

'Not at the moment!' Anya exclaimed. Reaching for Alexa's hand, holding it in hers, she continued, 'Jessica shouldn't be told anything about this. It would only upset her terribly.'

'Well actually, I wasn't planning to say anything to her until we'd done a bit of investigating, Anya, and Tom suggested it might be a good idea to talk to his father, ask a few questions,' Alexa explained.

Nodding, Anya said, 'That is probably a good idea, Tom.'

Alexa said, 'Anya, you might think I'm being fanciful, but I just have a really weird feeling about this photo . . . I think it *is* Jean Beauvais-Cresse when he was a young man, and that he and Lucien are the same person. I can't explain why I feel this, but I just do.'

Anya said, 'Look, I've always been a great believer in gut instinct, and you might well be right, Alexa. But we mustn't say a word to Jessica. We really do have to keep quiet.'

'That's correct!' Tom exclaimed. 'It's very flimsy, there's no hard evidence, nothing concrete to go on. However, I do think I can ask Dad a few pertinent questions, and maybe he can supply the answers we need regarding Jean and Lucien Girard –' Tom stopped as Nicky walked into the room with Maria Franconi.

'I hope we're not *very* late,' Nicky said. After kissing Anya and squeezing Alexa's shoulder, he shook Tom's hand enthusiastically. 'Tom, it's great to see you! And this is Maria Franconi, I don't think you've ever met.'

Maria smiled, shook Tom's hand, and murmured quietly, 'I am pleased to meet you.'

'It's a pleasure,' Tom replied, smiling at her.

After kissing Anya on the cheek, Maria looked towards Alexa seated on the sofa, and forced a smile. 'Hello, Alexa.'

'Hi, Maria,' Alexa responded coolly, without smiling.

'Do be a darling, Nicky, and pour Maria a glass of champagne,' Anya said.

'Oh no, Anya, thank you, but I'd prefer water,' Maria announced.

Nicky said, 'Coming right up, sweetie, but I think *I'll* have a drop of the old bubbly myself.' He busied himself at the drinks tray.

'Do sit down, Maria dear.' Anya indicated the chair next to her, and went on, 'I haven't had a chance to tell you this before, but I've studied the photographs Nicky gave me the other day. Maria, your paintings are quite extraordinary. But then you were an enormously talented artist when you were at the school.'

Maria looked extremely pleased when she spoke. 'Thank you, Anya. Hearing those words from you about my paintings is very important to me.'

Nicky carried the water to Maria, and then stood in front of the fire, regarding all of them. After a moment he took a sip of his champagne, and said, 'Cheers, everybody.'

'Cheers,' Tom answered.

'*Santé*, Nicky darling,' Anya murmured.

Alex simply raised her glass to him, and smiled, and then eyed Maria out of the corner of her eye, thinking that Anya had not exaggerated the other day. Maria Franconi was a different person than she had been at the school seven years ago. She was indeed a beautiful woman now.

Glancing across at Tom, Nicky said, 'Did I hear you mention Lucien Girard just now? Or am I dreaming?'

The room went quiet.

Tom glanced at Alexa and they exchanged pointed looks.

Anya said swiftly, 'Oh, it was nothing important, Nicky, just a casual remark on Tom's part. Now I don't want to rush you, but we mustn't linger up here too long. Honorine's daughter Yvonne came in to cook for me today, and I know she's making something very special for the first course. So drink up, Nicky.'

A short while after this, Honorine's curly grey head appeared around the sitting room door, and beaming at everyone, she announced, '*Le déjeuner est prêt, Madame,*' and disappeared as swiftly as she had materialized.

Within the next few seconds they finished their drinks, rose and trooped down the stairs, Nicky and Maria leading the way. Alexa hung back in the sitting room, touching Anya's arm as she did, whispering, 'How much did Nicky hear, do you think?'

Anya shrugged, shook her head, and murmured in an equally quiet tone, 'I don't really know ... but not very much, I'm sure.' There was a slight hesitation on her part, before she added, 'But don't forget, he and Larry knew Lucien first. It was actually Larry who introduced him to Jessica. It might be worth asking him a few questions, you know.'

'Nicky's okay, but I can't say anything to him because I don't trust Maria. She might tell Jessica, and that would be disastrous.'

'She doesn't even know where Jessica is staying,' Anya murmured.

'Where is she staying?'

'The Plaza Athénée.'

Tom looked back up the stairs, frowned, and called to them, 'Come on, Alexa, Anya. Nicky and Maria are waiting for us in the dining room.'

The two women descended the staircase, and when they were finally in the entrance foyer, Anya hurried forward, exclaiming, 'Sorry, my dears, I'm afraid I'm a little stiff today, Alexa was helping me down the stairs. Sorry I kept you waiting.'

'That's all right,' Nicky said, came forward and took hold of Anya's arm, led her into the dining room, which overlooked the cobbled courtyard and the garden. To reflect the outside, which was so visible through the windows and the French doors, Anya had used a colour scheme of light and dark greens, accented with touches of white. With its billowing white organdie curtains at the windows, dark parquet wood floor and masses of white flowering plants, the room looked fresh, airy and cool.

Pausing at the circular table, made of highly polished yew wood and surrounded by five Louis XIV chairs upholstered in a green-and-white check fabric, Anya rested one hand on a chair and said, 'Maria, come and sit at my left, and Tom, please take the chair at my right. Alexa dear, sit down next to Tom, and Nicky, you can sit between Alexa and Maria.'

Smiling broadly, she lowered herself into her chair. 'I think that works very well,' she continued, and looking across at Nicky she said, 'Would you pour the white wine for those who want it, and there's a very nice red to have with the main course.'

Nicky did as he was asked, and he had just finished filling their glasses with white wine when Honorine came into the room carrying a large tray. She was followed by her daughter Yvonne, who held a smaller tray in her hands. Yvonne nodded, murmured a quiet greeting, and followed her mother to the serving table.

Within minutes they had all been served with an individual cheese soufflé and were soon exclaiming about it, pronouncing it delicious. Nicky announced, 'It's as light as a baby's breath.' Everyone laughed at this expression, and the ice was broken a little, but Anya noticed as this first course was being eaten that Alexa and Maria carefully avoided speaking to each other. However, Tom and Nicky had lost no time in getting properly reacquainted, and they were now chatting enthusiastically about the film industry.

She herself turned to Maria and began to talk more fully about her paintings, whilst Alexa was soon drawn into Nicky's conversation with Tom. He was holding forth on the new film about Mary, Queen of Scots, and Tom was obviously fascinated, listening attentively as Nicky explained about the pre-production plans which were slowly coming together.

After the empty soufflé dishes had been cleared away, Nicky served the Mouton Rothschild to everyone except Maria, and Tom poured the mineral water. Not long after this, Honorine came back with a platter of roast leg of lamb, followed by Yvonne with a dish of steamed vegetables and roasted potatoes. When they had been served, the two women left the dining room, but a second later Honorine returned with the gravy, which she placed on the table.

Anya asked her to bring the other sauce, and then explained to them, 'I'm very English when it comes to my roast lamb . . . it's my upbringing, I suppose. I like it thinly sliced and covered in mint sauce.' She laughed. 'The French usually shudder when they see me eating it this way.'

'It's because they can't imagine why anyone would want to put a sauce made with vinegar on their meat,' Nicky pointed out, and grinned at her. 'And as you know, I eat mine exactly the same way.'

The conversation at the table was rather mundane as the main course was eaten and enjoyed, the red wine savoured, the water drunk. Looking at each of them from time to time, Anya was pleased that they were all here with her today, and that there was an air of civility at the table. She realized quite suddenly that Maria appeared slightly more ill at ease than Alexa. And it struck her that Alexa had undoubtedly spoken the truth when she had blamed Maria for the trouble in the friendships, but it had been so long ago she wished they could forget about it. As for Maria, she was such a brilliant artist it was almost criminal to let her rot in a textile company in Milan. But then Anya knew it was none of her business . . . she could only hope Nicky was going to be the girl's knight in shining armour, that he would rescue her from a terrible kind of servitude.

Once lunch was over, Anya asked everyone upstairs for coffee, and they moved en masse to the floor above.

Anya was pouring the coffee when Tom, hovering over her, asked, 'Could I use your phone, please Anya?'

'But of course,' she said, and glancing at Alexa, she went on: 'Show Tom into that little den down the corridor, Alexa please. He can use the phone in there.'

Alexa nodded, took hold of Tom's hand and accompanied him out of the room. Once they were in the corridor leading off the main landing, he pulled her into his arms, and kissed her deeply. As he released her he said, 'Let's forget about the movie we talked about seeing later. Why don't we go back to my place instead?'

Alexa smiled up at him adoringly. 'You've got a deal, Tom Conners.'

'The best one I've ever made,' he shot back.

Still smiling, Alexa pushed open the door of the den and said, 'Don't be too long.'

As she walked back to the upstairs sitting room, Alexa wondered whether to say anything to Nicky about Lucien Girard. Normally she would have done so, but Maria's presence was acting as a deterrent. Very simply, she still didn't trust her. More often than not in the old days,

Maria's mouth was open and her foot was usually in it.

How she had changed in her appearance, though. With a tendency to overeat, she had looked slightly plump all the time she had attended Anya's school. Her face had been lovely but her body too fleshy for a young woman.

Now, if she wasn't yet svelte, she was well on the way to becoming so, and her startling face and her mane of hair gave her a kind of movie star glamour. Penelope Cruz sprang to mind, and that image was instantly reinforced when Alexa walked back into the sitting room.

Maria was standing near the window, looking casually elegant in burgundy slacks, silk shirt and matching woollen jacket, the black hair streaming down her back; her face, in profile, was stunningly beautiful.

No wonder Nicky fell for her, Alexa thought, sitting down next to him on the sofa. It was obvious to Alexa that he had fallen completely under Maria's spell.

Hook, line and sinker, she thought, as she picked up her coffee cup and took a sip, then glanced at Nicky. 'I can't wait to see the script, and once I've read it, Tom will drive me down to the Loire. He feels sure there are any number of houses that would be a perfect setting for the film.'

'He's right. Maybe we'll all go down for a weekend,' Nicky suggested.

Alexa gaped at him. 'You've got to be kidding!'

Nicky exclaimed, 'Oh, I know you're angry with Maria. She's told me all about it. And frankly I think it's about time you both grew up and behaved like the mature young women you are. It's nonsense, carrying a grudge like that!'

'Hear! Hear!' Anya exclaimed. 'It's time to move on.'

Maria walked slowly towards the fireplace, looking nervous, hesitant; then she sat down on the edge of a chair, and said in a low voice, 'I'm sorry, Alexa, for causing you so much trouble. Truly sorry. But I was young, I didn't mean –'

'You betrayed me!' Alexa snapped, determined not to give an inch, as she remembered how hurt she had been all those years ago.

'I didn't mean to! It was an accident. An error on my part. I've always been . . . so very sorry, Alexa.'

Alexa glared at her. 'I was never interested in Ricardo. That was all your imagination. And you blew it into a huge . . . atomic cloud! Into something so enormous you incited Jessica to action, and she told me off in the most awful way. She took your side, believed you, and she stopped being my friend. Actually, Maria, *you* destroyed my friendship with Jessica.'

'I'm so very, very sorry, Alexa,' Maria apologized again. Her face had turned a ghastly white, and she appeared contrite, worried.

'You were jealous of our friendship, if the truth be known,' Alexa shot back. 'Jealous to death.'

'I wasn't. That's not true.' Maria now looked as if she was on the verge of tears.

'That's enough, girls,' Anya said in a strong, firm voice. 'I want you both to come over here for coffee tomorrow morning. And I'll have Jessica and Kay here as well, and we'll straighten this out once and for all. I don't want my party spoiled because you four are quarrelling. So let us shelve the matter. This is not an appropriate time.'

301

At this moment Tom walked back into the room, and from the look on his face Alexa realized his father had told him something he found interesting. She was certain he wanted to share it with her.

She said, 'It's all right, Tom, you can talk in front of Nicky and Maria.'

Surprised, he stared at her, his expression puzzled.

Alexa nodded, then spoke to Maria. 'We're going to talk about something which has to do with Lucien Girard. But you cannot breathe a word of it to Jessica. Do you understand that, Maria?'

'Yes. I wouldn't say anything to Jessica . . . or anyone.'

Nicky, intrigued, asked, 'What's all this about then, Tom?'

Tom looked at Alexa once more. She nodded her head, and he explained, first telling them how it all started with the photo in Alexa's album.

'Oh,' Maria gasped, staring at Tom. 'So Lucien's still alive?'

'We don't know,' Tom said hastily, and continued: 'The whole idea is a bit flimsy, I must admit, although a couple of things my father said intrigued me. The two men *could* be one and the same.'

Nicky sat up straighter on the sofa, frowning. 'I didn't know Lucien all that well, Tom, but I don't think he was the kind of man to . . . how should I put it? Lead a double life, play games. Anyway, who is it that so resembles him?'

'A man called Jean Beauvais-Cresse, who's in his early thirties. Earlier, I'd more or less decided that he might be related to Lucien. Perhaps Lucien was a brother using a stage name. Lucien could have been a cousin. However, my father told me that Jean's only brother died about seven years ago.'

Maria and Alexa exchanged glances but neither of them uttered a word.

'What else did your father say?' Anya asked.

'He told me that the brother was the eldest son, and that he was killed in a terrible accident. My parents didn't live in the Loire then, so this is sort of . . . local gossip, and Dad didn't have all the details. The brother's tragic, untimely death caused the father to have a stroke. Apparently he was very attached to the son who died. He was the heir to the title, the lands, the château. Jean, the younger son, was a bit of a black sheep, so my father once heard. He'd been living in Paris for a number of years, and only came back when his father was stricken, to look after him. He inherited everything when the old man died. That's all Dad could tell me.'

'But don't you think it sort of fits in with Lucien's disappearance?' Alexa asked. She was convinced it did, and she held Tom's eyes, trying to convey this to him.

He nodded. 'The time frame is certainly right,' he said cautiously.

Nicky said, 'Let's just go over it. Seven years ago, Lucien Girard disappears never to be seen again. Seven years ago Jean's elder brother dies unexpectedly, so that Jean becomes the heir. But what if Lucien, working in Paris as an actor and using a *nom de plume*, were the eldest son and met a terrible fate? As everyone has always believed Lucien did.'

'I thought of that,' Tom answered. 'But my father said the eldest son was much older than Jean. By about fifteen years, a son by another wife, the first wife.'

'So Lucien and Jean *could* be one and the same person,' Anya stated.

'Bearing in mind the extraordinary resemblance and the similarities in age, yes. *Possibly*.' Tom now sat down in a chair, and continued, 'But it's an awkward situation, at best, Anya. My father said he'd make a few discreet inquiries, and I'll talk to him tomorrow. In the meantime, no one should say a word to Jessica. It wouldn't be fair. Either to her or Jean Beauvais-Cresse.'

'What we need is someone who can verify that Jean was an actor in Paris at one point in his life, and that he used a stage name,' Alexa said. 'Then we'd have something more concrete to go on.' She let her eyes settle on Nicky.

'Oh no, not me!' he exclaimed. 'I hardly knew Lucien. And actually, Larry didn't know him well either.'

Anya settled back against the sofa, closing her eyes for a moment. Something had stirred at the back of her mind but she couldn't quite put her finger on it. And so she let it go. For the moment.

Chapter Twenty-Eight

'Let's go for a walk,' Tom said, as they left Anya's house and came out on to the street.

'Great idea,' Alexa agreed, falling into step with him. 'I love the Seventh. It's my favourite part of town.'

Tom smiled, and took hold of her hand, tucked her arm through his, and together they headed in the direction of the rue de Solférino and the quays running parallel with the River Seine.

It was warmer now and sunny, and the sky above was a clear blue arc, unblemished, without cloud, and benign on this May Sunday afternoon.

The Seventh Arrondissement where they were walking was an elegant area of the city, and Tom's apartment in the Boulevard Saint Germain was located nearby. There were too such landmarks as the French Academy, the Ecole Militaire, and the Hôtel des Invalides wherein was housed the tomb of Napoleon. But Tom and Alexa bypassed most of these historic buildings as they headed into the Quai Anatole France.

For a short while they walked along the Quai, enjoying each other, the weather, and the charming views of the Seine. Its rippling waters glittered in the sunlight, and suddenly a faint breeze blew up, rustled through the trees that grew alongside the Seine, made the leaves flutter and dance in the silvery light.

They paused for a moment looking down, and Alexa smiled at the sight of the colourful *bateaux-mouches* smoothly moving down the river, leaving frothy trails in their wake.

She had always enjoyed the trips she had taken on them, especially those in the evenings with Tom years ago. Paris at night was romantic and magical when seen from the river on a slow-moving boat, the glittering lights of the city illuminating the inky sky. There was nowhere like it in the world.

Almost as though he had read her thoughts, Tom said, 'We must take a *bateau-mouche* one night. I must admit I always enjoyed our evenings sailing along the Seine.'

'How funny, Tom, that you should say that. I was just thinking the same thing.'

Hand in hand, they walked on, heading towards the Quai Voltaire. Ahead, reaching into the sky, were the great towers of the Notre Dame, hazy now in the soft afternoon light of Paris, a light loved by artists over the centuries and so frequently captured on canvas.

To Alexa, Paris had never looked more beautiful than it did today. It was a city that forever took her by surprise.

THREE WEEKS IN PARIS

She remembered once getting caught in a thunderstorm, and hurrying through the streets drenched, looking for a taxi. And then unexpectedly she had abandoned the idea of finding a cab, suddenly enjoying walking in the pouring rain . . . and she had filled with happiness that night, glad to be in this city, the city of her dreams . . .

As they reached the Quai Malaquais, Tom said, 'Let's head down into St Germain des Prés, and have something to drink before going home. A coffee, whatever.'

Alexa nodded in agreement, and still holding hands they strolled down the rue Bonaparte, and into a huddle of quaint old cobbled streets. Here there were chic boutiques, antique shops, art galleries and picturesque cafés that gave charm and character to this Arrondissement. Several times they stopped to look in the windows of the boutiques, and paid a quick visit to one of Tom's favourite art galleries, but for the most part they did not linger, moved on at a steady pace.

By the time they reached the Place de l'Odéon, Alexa knew Tom was taking her to the Café Voltaire, once the favourite spot of the eighteenth-century French writer and philosopher.

They found a table outside and she was glad to sit down, settling into a chair under the awning, relaxing after their long walk. After ordering coffee for them both, Tom loosened his tie and opened the neck of his shirt. 'It has become quite warm,' he said, glancing at her. 'Do you want to take your sweater off?'

'Yes, I will.' She loosened the cashmere sweater tied around her neck and laid it across her knees. Turning to Tom, she added, 'If Anya invites you to her party, will you come?'

'Only if I can be your date.' He hesitated, then asked, 'Or is your English friend going to be your escort that night?'

'Of course not!' she exclaimed, looking askance, her voice rising slightly. 'Only I was invited, and I'm sure it's the same with the other women. Nicky told me the guests are mostly favoured students from past years, her rather extended Russian, English and French family, and some of her old friends.' Alexa gave him a hard stare. 'Anyway, I told you last night that I wanted to be with you, on a permanent basis, married or not. So how could you possibly think I would want to take Jack, even if I'd invited him? I would have to ask him not to come, if that was the case.'

She sounded so angry he reached out, took her hand in his, brought it to his lips and kissed it. 'Such a dear little hand, I love it so,' he murmured. 'Don't be angry with me, Alexa.'

'I'm not, not really.' She cleared her throat, changed the subject. 'Did your father tell you anything else? Were you holding anything back when we were at Anya's?'

'Not exactly. Dad didn't have much more information. But he did say that Jean Beauvais-Cresse was known to be something of a recluse, not often seen around the village or at the local church. By the way, Dad did tell me he was married, and that there was a child. But that's about it. As I said at Anya's, my parents have not lived in the Loire all that long, and much of what he knows is local gossip anyway.'

'I understand.' Alexa paused, looked off into the distance.

After a moment or two of watching her, Tom said quietly, 'Is there something wrong, Alex? You're looking pensive.'

A little sigh escaped her. 'I was just thinking about Lucien Girard. If he *is* Jean Beauvais-Cresse and he just decided to go back to his old life one day, he must be a truly cruel man. Imagine doing something like that to Jessica, or any woman. I know Jessica suffered terribly, and Anya told me she's never married. She's probably been carrying a torch for Lucien all these years.'

He frowned. 'Do you really think so?'

'Yep, I do.' She half laughed, and looked at him pointedly. 'Women tend to be like that, you know.' Me included, she thought, but refrained from saying so. 'And there's something else, Tom. Just think of her *grief*, believing that something really bad happened to him.' She sighed. 'It makes me so mad.'

'I can understand why. Obviously Nicky didn't know Lucien well, and if my father has no additional information, I think we just have to forget I ever mentioned Jean.'

'Not so easy.' Again Alexa stared ahead, her eyes narrowing slightly, and after a moment or two of thoughtful reflection, she turned to Tom, put her hand on his arm. 'I think I have the solution . . . a way to find the truth.'

'You do?' Tom sounded surprised, and just a little alarmed by the determined look which had flashed on to her face.

The waiter arrived with their cups of coffee, and once he was out of earshot, Alexa said carefully, 'Here's my plan. I think we should go to the Loire, and confront this man who so resembles Lucien Girard.'

Tom sat back, obviously flabbergasted by her suggestion. For a moment he did not speak, and then taking a deep breath, he replied, 'And I think that's asking for trouble . . . perhaps even legal trouble.'

'No, no, I didn't put it quite right,' Alexa exclaimed. 'Let me start all over again. You and I, with Jessica, should drive down to the Loire Valley one day next week, if you can spare the time. Otherwise we have to go on the weekend. Once we arrive at Jean's house, Jessica and I will remain in the car while you go to the door. If Jean answers the door you can simply tell him you have a client who wants to shoot a historical movie in the Loire, and is looking for appropriate châteaux in which to film the interior scenes. Once you get him engaged in conversation, Jessica and I will get out of the car and walk over to join you. If he *is* Lucien, you'll know, Tom, and so will we. He'll be in shock.'

Tom nodded. 'I'm following you. And if he's not Lucien, he won't recognize either of you, is that what you're trying to say?'

'Correct.'

'But Alex, Lucien was an actor. He *could* fake it, couldn't he?'

'I don't think he was that good an actor, Tom. He wasn't in the running for an Academy Award.'

Tom burst out laughing, shaking his head. 'There's just one thing, though. You will have to tell Jessica, obviously, and that could open up her old wounds.'

'It will. But look, if we finally solve a seven-year-old mystery and she gets closure *finally*, then that's a good thing, isn't it?'

Tom saw the sense in what she was saying, and told her so, adding, 'But I'd like to think it through, sleep on it, Alex, before making a final decision. Also, it would be wise to leave Jessica in the dark, for the moment anyway.'

'I agree with you,' she said.

*   *   *

'Where is your parents' house in the Loire?' Alexa asked. She and Tom had left the Café Voltaire and were walking back towards the Boulevard Saint Germain and Tom's apartment.

'They're in that beautiful bit of the Loire which is known as the Valley of Kings,' Tom answered. 'It's between Orléans and Tours, and the reason it's called the Valley of Kings is because there are so many magnificent châteaux there.'

'Yes, I learned all about the Valley of Kings in Anya's French history class,' Alexa informed him. 'Almost three hundred châteaux stand there, including some of the greatest . . . Chambord, Cheverny, Chinon, Chaumont, Amboise, Azay le Rideau, Clos-Lucé and Chenonceau. I know it's a very beautiful area.'

'Sublime,' Tom said, glanced down at her, added, 'But my parents don't have a grand château, Alex. Just a charming manor house in rather lovely grounds sitting on a bend in the River Cher. Basically it's quite a small estate, and that's one of the reasons they love it. Also, it's only about an hour and a half from Paris, so they can easily move back and forth between their apartment here and the Loire.'

'So we could go there and back in one day, couldn't we?'

'Yes. *If* we decide to go and see Jean,' he answered quietly. 'But as I said, I must think about that idea, and I must also mention it to my father. I don't want to cause any problems for my parents.'

'I understand, of course. By the way, did you tell your father the whole story? About Jessica and Lucien, I mean? Or did you just ask him about his neighbour?'

'I told him the whole story. You've met Dad, you know what he's like. He wasn't CEO of a giant American company in Paris for twenty-five years for nothing. He knew what questions to ask, how to get to the root of it all, and I must say he was very understanding, wanted to help in any way he could.'

'I knew he would. I always liked your father, he reminds me of you. Or rather, you remind me of him in so many ways.'

Tom laughed. 'I'm a chip off the old block, is that what you're saying?'

'Yep. And where is Jean's house? I suppose it must be nearby?'

'Not too far away, and it's not a house, Alex. It's one of those grand châteaux we were just talking about. Very old. Been in the Beauvais-Cresse family for centuries. I think it was built in the 1600s, or thereabouts. It's quite magnificent. It's an agricultural estate; a lot of farming goes on there.'

'At Anya's you mentioned something about a title.'

'That's right. Jean is the Marquis de Beauvais-Cresse, to give him his accurate name.'

'I see.' She sighed. 'It's such a peculiar story, isn't it? The way Lucien just disappeared overnight . . .'

'There are thousands of cases of missing persons,' Tom told her. '*Hundreds of thousands*, if we consider all the countries in the world. People do disappear, and just like that.' As he spoke he snapped his thumb and finger together, and continued, 'Some are the victims of foul play and their bodies are never found. Others do suffer an injury which results in amnesia. And then there are those who disappear because they want to.'

'I know, that's the problem.'

Noticing the disconsolate expression on her face, the sudden weariness in her tone, Tom changed the subject, said, 'Have you ever been to Chenonceau?'

'No, I haven't.'

'I want to take you there. But that won't be possible if and when we go with Jessica to the Loire. So perhaps you'd come another weekend. We could stay with my parents and I'd drive you over there, it's not very far. You see, this is the thing . . . Chenonceau has a connection to Mary Stuart . . . the *petite Reinette d'Ecosse*, as she was called in France in those days.'

'What connection?'

'The château was once the home of Henri II, who gifted it to his mistress, Diane de Poitiers, but Henri and his son Francis II, and *his* wife Mary, Queen of Scots, all spent a lot of time there.'

'How interesting. I'd like to see it, Tom, and some of the other châteaux as well. There might be one or two people, owners of châteaux, who would let us film there for a fee.'

'I've no doubt.'

They walked on in silence for a while. At one moment Tom stopped, took hold of Alexa's arm and turned her to face him. Looking deeply into her eyes, he said, 'Quarrel or no quarrel, you really are being a good friend to Jessica. I admire you for that.'

'When Lucien disappeared her life changed radically,' Alex replied. 'Never to be the same again, that I surely know. Because his body was never found, there has been no closure. I'm sure that's why Jessica hasn't been able to settle down with another man. In my opinion, that is. And if I have a chance to help her, as I now think I do, why wouldn't I?'

Tom searched her face, then brought her into the circle of his arms. Against her dark head he said softly, 'I see into your heart, my sweet Alex . . . and you are truly a good person.' She did not answer, and he held her tightly for a moment longer. And then he thought: she fills the empty places in my heart, she makes me whole.

CHAPTER TWENTY-NINE

'I'm so glad you could come early, darling,' Anya said, smiling across at Alexa. 'I just want to go over a couple of things, before the others arrive.'

'And I have something to tell you,' Alexa responded, settling in the chair opposite Anya. The two women were sitting in the small library which opened on to the gardens. It was another beautiful day, and the French doors were wide open to reveal a view of the cobbled courtyard and the cherry tree.

'What is it you wish to tell me?' Anya probed.

Alexa shook her head. 'Tell me first why you wanted me to come earlier than the others, and then I'll explain something to you, an idea I've had.'

'All right.' Anya sat up a little straighter in the chair, and continued, 'I want everything ironed out between the four of you today, Alexa. This feud is beginning to be ridiculous, and

I'm looking to *you* to create harmony amongst you.'

'I'll do my best, and I agree with you actually. After yesterday's confrontation with Maria, I don't like the thought of any more of them. They're too upsetting. Let's face it, we're all around thirty and we should know better by now.'

Anya nodded. 'I'm glad you feel like being conciliatory. That's the way to go, and once you've talked it through I'm going to take you all out to lunch.'

'Oh, that'll be nice!' Alexa exclaimed. 'But you should let *us* take *you*. To somewhere chic and expensive. We can all afford it now.'

Laughing, Anya said, 'There's something else I want to mention. I would like Nicky to invite Tom to my party. Would he come, do you think?'

'I'm sure he would.' Alexa flashed her a wide smile.

'That's what I thought. I'll tell Nicky to send him an invitation. I'm also going to tell Kay to invite her husband, and naturally Maria will be accompanying Nicky. But I don't know what to do about Jessica. I've no idea if she's in Paris alone or with someone. In any case, I think she ought to have an escort.'

'You still haven't seen her yet?'

'No, darling girl, I haven't. I asked her several times to come and have a drink, or lunch, but she's hiding behind her work. I say *hiding* because I think she's staying away on purpose.'

'But why?'

Anya made a *moue* with her mouth, and then explained, 'Jessica identifies me with the past, in particular the last few months she was here in Paris, when Lucien went missing. I think deep down she's a little bit afraid to see me, for fear of the memories it will evoke. Memories of Lucien, the pain she suffered, her anxiety and fear . . . those sort of things. Remember, Jessica hasn't seen me since you all graduated. It's been *seven years*. And she links that time to him.'

'I know. But I'm sure she'll open up today, and we can find out if she's here alone or not. I'll do everything I can to make her feel at ease, and Kay too.'

'And Maria. Don't forget Maria, Alexa. She was awfully nervous yesterday. Afraid of you, I do believe.'

'I suppose I was a bit fierce,' Alexa admitted, looking shamefaced. 'I'll be nice, I promise.'

'Now, what is the idea you said you had? An idea for what exactly?'

'Finding the truth. Remember what you would tell us . . . *the truth sets you free*, you used to say.' Alexa took a deep breath, and shifted her body in the chair. 'I think Jessica and I, along with Tom, should go down to the Loire, seek out this Jean fellow, and confront him.'

'You could be on dangerous ground here, Alexa,' Anya warned. 'As I'm sure Tom has told you.'

'Yes, he has. But I wasn't suggesting a real confrontation, during which we ask him if he was once using another name and working as an actor in Paris. I just want him to *see* us, Jessica in particular. If he is shocked, we'll know immediately his alias was Lucien.'

When Anya was silent, Alexa stared at her, and asked, 'Well, what do you think?'

Anya ruminated for a few seconds, then posed her own question. 'What does Tom think?'

'He's cautious.'

'So am I.'

'Why, Anya?'

'Alexa darling, you can't go rushing around the country-side accusing people of leading a double life.'

'I didn't say we'd be doing that . . . I said we'd go over to his house on a pretext, just to see him, let him see us. Get his reaction or non-reaction.'

'I think I'd like to hear what Tom has to say.'

A moment later Anya was standing up, walking across to the door, a huge smile illuminating her face.

'Hello, Jessica,' she exclaimed. 'It's wonderful to see you.'

'And you, Anya, after so long.'

The two women embraced and then Anya stepped back, and stared at Jessica, an appraising look in her light blue eyes.

What a lovely woman Jessica had become, elegant in her well-tailored black suit and white silk shirt, her long, pale blonde hair falling around her tanned face. She was still the all-American girl, tall, long-legged, slender, and as pretty as she was seven years ago. But there was a sadness in her eyes, a wistfulness in her smile, and Anya was sure she knew the reason why. Lucien Girard.

Anya also knew she had been right all along about Jessica's reluctance to come and see her. In Jessica's mind she was part of the past, part of another life, one which Jessica had buried so deep within her psyche she did not want to resurrect it. Could not, perhaps. At the same time, Anya was certain

Jessica had not really moved on, that deep within her soul she still yearned for Lucien. She was thirty-one and still not married. Anya had immediately noticed there were no rings on her fingers. It seemed to her that Jessica needed closure. Maybe Alexa was right about going to the Loire to discover the truth. Might it not set Jessica free?

'Come in, come in, don't let's stand here in the doorway!' Anya exclaimed, taking Jessica's arm, leading her into the room. 'Here's Alexa. And the others should be here any moment.'

Alexa had risen and she stepped forward, her hand outstretched. 'Hello, Jessica, it's been a long time,' she said, striving for genuine cordiality.

Jessica inclined her head, rather curtly Alexa thought, and took her hand, shook it. 'Hello, Alexa.'

Alexa recoiled slightly; there was such coldness in Jessica's voice and her manner was icy. Fasten your seat belt, kid, she told herself. We're in for a rocky ride.

Anya had noticed Jessica's extreme coldness and she instantly filled with dismay and just a little trepidation. She had been foolish to think everything would go smoothly; there was obviously enormous animosity between the women. She had been aware of that at lunch yesterday when Maria and Alexa had flown at each other so fiercely, both of them sounding bitter, angry, and ready to continue the estrangement.

Anya said, 'Jessica, do sit down,' and taking her own advice she lowered herself on to the sofa.

Jessica did as she asked, glanced around, and then said in a softer tone, 'I'd forgotten how lovely the library is, Anya. It's just charming, the way you've redecorated it.'

'And I must tell you how proud I am of *you*, Jessica, and

your work. The houses and apartments you've designed are simply superb. I've loved seeing them in the magazines over the years. Congratulations, my dear.'

'Thanks, Anya. Everything I know I learned at your school.'

'The school can't teach anyone taste and style, you know, and you have an inbred sense of style, enormous taste, Jessica. I always told you that.'

'Yes, you did, and you helped to make my dreams come true, professionally. You and the other teachers were just extraordinary. I'm so lucky, I had the best training in the world, and what's stood me in great stead is my knowledge of history, English, French and European furniture through the centuries, antique fabrics, and classical architecture. You taught me so much, Anya.'

'Thank you again for those kind words.' Anya settled back against the cushions, and asked, 'Are you by any chance in Paris alone, Jessica?'

'I'm alone, yes.'

'I see. The reason I ask is that I thought you may wish to bring someone with you to my party, be escorted by a friend that evening. And if that *is* the case, I will have Nicky send him an invitation.'

Jessica blinked, and her brows furrowed together, then she nodded in a positive manner, her face softening. 'I think I *would* like to bring a friend, have an escort that night. One of my clients happens to be in Paris. His name is Mark Sylvester, and he's a movie producer from Hollywood. But he's working on a picture, shooting here and in London. He told me the other day that he'll be back and forth between the two cities for the next month or so. I'm sure Mark would love to come.'

'I'm delighted. May I ask where he's staying, my dear?'

'The Plaza Athénée, and I'll tell him to expect the invitation. Thanks so much for being so considerate, Anya.'

Suddenly, Maria was gliding into the room looking stunning, beautiful in an ankle-length black skirt and a matching jacket, long and sleekly tailored. It slimmed her down even more, and underneath the jacket she wore a low-cut black silk blouse. Her long neck was enhanced by a gold necklace composed of ancient medallions, with matching earrings. Her black shoes had very high heels, and she almost looked willowy this morning, Anya thought.

But when Maria spotted Jessica seated on a chair near the fireplace, she came to a sudden halt, looked hesitant. Maria appeared uncertain whether to enter the room or not.

Anya, detecting this at once, pushed herself to her feet and hurried to her, embraced her. 'You're looking wonderful,' she said, wanting to imbue confidence in her. 'Here's Jessica and Alexa, and we're just waiting for Kay.'

The words had hardly left Anya's mouth when Kay came walking in from the front portico, exclaiming, 'Oh dear, Anya, am I late? So sorry.'

Swinging around, Anya smiled at Kay and shook her head. 'No you're not late at all. But now that you are here, my dear, I would like to get down to business.' Escorting Maria and Kay into the room, Anya continued, 'The business being solving your problems with each other.'

*   *   *

Anya threw Alexa a pointed look as she returned to her seat on the sofa.

Understanding exactly what was expected of her, Alexa rose, walked over to the fireplace and stood in front of it. She glanced at Maria and Kay, whom she had not yet greeted, and said, 'Hi, Maria, hi, Kay.'

Both women acknowledged her, although neither sounded very friendly.

Alexa said, 'Anya asked me to speak to you about our falling out with each other seven years ago, just before our graduation. Her birthday party's on June the second, and, understandably, she doesn't want any bad feelings between us on that very special occasion. She thinks we should sort out our differences. In order to do that I think we must all speak about our feelings, get things off our chests, so to speak.'

'I want the air cleared,' Anya murmured and settled back against the cushions, hoping they would be friends by the time she took them to lunch.

Alexa unbuttoned the jacket of her suit, pushed her hands in her pockets, and went on, 'Yesterday Maria and I did begin to sort out our differences, so I'm going to let Maria explain how she and I fell out. Then perhaps Jessica could speak.'

Maria was totally taken aback, and she appeared to be startled as she sat up straighter in the chair and looked around at everyone. After a moment, she cleared her throat, and said haltingly, 'Alexa blamed *me* yesterday. She said I told Jessica lies about her. But that's not correct –'

'Yes, it is!' Alexa cut in peremptorily, and then took a step back. 'I'm sorry for interrupting, Maria. Please continue.'

Looking at Jessica, Maria said, 'I didn't tell you any lies. Truly I did not. I told you what I believed to be the truth . . . that Alexa had been flirting with Ricardo Martinelli, my boyfriend at the time, and that she was trying to steal him from me.'

Alexa had to bite off another exclamation, this time of denial. She was infuriated with Maria once again. She forced herself to remain calm, clenching her hands in her trouser pockets.

Jessica was nodding. 'Yes, I remember that. You explained that you were worried Ricardo was going to become involved with Alexa. Because of *her* behaviour. That you thought she was after him. You cried a lot. And yes, I *did* believe you.' Jessica glanced at Alexa. 'And I did take Maria's side, there's no question about that.'

'But it wasn't true!' Alexa protested. 'And don't you think you owed me the benefit of the doubt, plus a chance to defend myself? You condemned me without a trial.'

Jessica bit her lip. 'I guess that's true.' She narrowed her eyes, and a thoughtful expression crossed her face. 'But I did see you flirting with Ricardo at the party Angelique's mother gave. You were draped all over him when you were dancing, clinging to him. That's what clinched it for me.'

Alexa felt bright colour flame in her face, and she cried, 'I *was* dancing with him, and quite intimately, I suppose. I admit that. But we were *only* dancing. And *I* wasn't flirting with him. *He* was flirting with me. He had a tendency to do that, as you well know, Jessica. And *you* also know it, Maria.' Alexa gave Kay a very direct look and added, 'I saw Ricardo Martinelli flirting with *you*, Kay, the Sunday night we all went to the Deux Magots for coffee. After your birthday dinner.'

Kay sighed. 'Yes, that's perfectly correct, Alexa.' Kay turned to Maria. 'He did flirt with me. And with everyone, if you want the absolute truth. Ricardo couldn't help himself. He was after all of us. I wasn't interested in him, though, and in all honesty I don't think Alexa was either. I have to take her side in that.'

'Listen to me, Maria,' Alexa cried. 'Your self-esteem was at an all-time low, you were a very troubled young woman. Not at all happy with yourself or your relationship with Ricardo. So you dreamed up this idea of me trying to steal him, when all along *he* was at fault, not I. You just couldn't help yourself, I suppose. But you behaved very badly. You took it out on me, and that was not fair play.'

'I didn't –'

'Yes, you did! You went running off to Jessica, because you were jealous of our friendship, and you turned her against me, broke up *our* friendship.'

Maria was stunned and she stared at Alexa. But she said nothing.

Alexa continued: '*Why?* Why didn't you come to me? Have it out with me, for heaven's sake. You were really sneaky, and you genuinely hurt me. I was heartbroken about losing Jessica's friendship.'

Maria seemed about to burst into tears, and did not respond. She threw Jessica a helpless look, said in a plaintive voice, 'I know I accused Alexa, Jess, but I did *believe* she was trying to steal Ricardo from me, and I was so in love with him. Now I realize accusing her was wrong, and I apologized to

Alexa yesterday. I said I was sorry, and I do say that to you, too.'

'Maria *was* jealous of our friendship,' Alexa announced to Jessica, staring hard at her.

Jessica exclaimed, 'Oh I don't know about that –'

Maria interrupted, when she admitted, 'I think I was jealous – no, perhaps that is the wrong word. I believe I was envious of your relationship. You seemed to have so much in common. You laughed a lot. At the same things. Sometimes I felt shut out . . .'

'But we're both Americans!' Jessica cried. 'Of course we had a lot in common . . . like growing up with the same values in the same country, for one thing. And liking the same movies, music and books . . . and hamburgers and hot dogs and Dr. Pepper's and banana splits . . . And the same clothes and make-up . . . well, the list is endless, Maria. But I truly never thought we were excluding you. Or Kay.'

'But you were!' Kay shot back, her voice suddenly and unexpectedly shrill. 'And you did it a lot.'

'Let's finish with Maria and Jessica,' Alexa instructed firmly, giving Kay a warning look.

Jessica shook her head, blew out air. 'Gee whiz, to coin an American phrase! I guess I did the wrong thing, seven years ago, Alexa. I listened to Maria, a very tearful Maria, I might add, and I made a judgement. A flawed judgement, as it turns out. I guess I should have talked it out with you.'

'Yes, you should have, but you didn't want to,' Alexa snapped. 'You were caught up with Lucien's disappearance. I realized that then, and I acknowledge it now. However, you weren't fair to me. Just because you had serious personal problems should not have stopped you from being straight and open with me. You just stopped speaking to me . . .'

'I did, yes, and that was wrong. My only excuse is that I *was* extremely upset about Lucien, heartbroken. And I would like to point out that you weren't very helpful or sympathetic at the time.' She gave Alexa a hard stare. 'I expected more from you, of all people, under the circumstances.'

'You expected sympathy, and I gave it to you! But you weren't receptive. And you didn't make it easy. You were far too busy *condemning* me for being a man-snatcher, as you put it, and so you never even heard my sympathy. Or my offers to help you in any way I could. You didn't want my help, only Alain Bonnal's.'

Jessica sat back; her face had turned pale under her tan. She looked suddenly haggard, and her eyes filled with tears. 'I think you might have a point,' she admitted finally.

Alexa nodded, and then looked at Maria, and said, 'And thank you, Maria, for being honest yesterday, and again today.'

Anya said, 'Yes, it certainly does help to clear the air. And what about you, Kay? Do you have anything to add to this?'

'I . . . Well, I don't know. I don't think so.'

'Why not?' Jessica suddenly demanded a little harshly, sitting up in the chair, determinedly brushing away her tears. She glared at Kay, who sat opposite her. 'You certainly had enough to say about *us* when we were at school here, and usually it was behind our backs! You gossiped about us.'

'I certainly did not!' Kay cried, her voice once more rising an octave or two. Trying to get a grip on her anger, reminding herself she was now Lady Andrews, she took several deep breaths, striving for dignity. Then she said, 'I never talked about any of you behind your backs.'

'You're a *liar*, Kay. You did bad-mouth us – Alexa, Maria and me,' Jessica accused in an icy voice.

'How dare you call me a liar!' Kay looked at Alexa. '*She* is lying. Not *I*.'

Jessica half rose, and then sat back down in the chair. 'You did talk about us, I was told of everything you said, and by a very good source. You said Alexa was superior and a snob, that she was always snubbing you. That Maria was a *rich* snob and treated you like a servant, and that I was a la-di-da southern belle, forever taunting you, teasing you, putting you down. You called us the three bitches. Not very nice, *Lady* Andrews.'

A bright scarlet flush rose from Kay's pale neck to suffuse her face; she blinked back the tears that suddenly filled her eyes. Her hand went up to her throat, and then a moment later she fumbled in her bag for a handkerchief.

Wanting to give Kay a moment or two to compose herself, Alexa turned to Jessica and said, 'If you want the truth about how I felt, I was heartbroken, Jessica. Your friendship was – very important to me. We were two American girls alone in Paris, and we had clicked right from the beginning, and then one day you simply dumped me without a proper explanation. And all along I thought we had such a good friendship.'

Jessica stared at her, said nothing, simply twisted her gold bracelet on her wrist. Her eyes were suddenly anguished. She knew, deep within herself, that she had wronged Alexa, and she was upset. She had listened to Maria, and acted stupidly, without thinking it through. What a fool she had been.

'I felt truly betrayed,' Alexa murmured, sighing. 'I hope you understand that now.'

'I do. I'm –' Jessica cut herself off, took a deep breath. 'I'm so very sorry. I have no excuse. Except to say that I was crazy at the time, off the wall with worry because of Lucien Girard's disappearance.'

'I know. And I *did* try to help. You just didn't want to hear me, I suppose because of Maria's story, and perhaps because you were just a little jealous of me.'

'Me? Jealous of you? Come on, Alexa. I'm not the jealous type,' Jessica responded heatedly, shifting in the chair, glaring.

'That's true, to a certain extent. But you were jealous of my success at the school, and my relationship with Anya,' Alexa pointed out very softly, her anger now suddenly dissipated.

Anya sat up alertly, her eyes roaming over the four women, studying them. She remained absolutely silent, and she felt suddenly regretful that she might have played favourites at different times in the past.

'I don't believe this,' Jessica exclaimed. 'Alexa, how can you say such a stupid thing?'

'It's not stupid. It's true. You and I were in many of the same classes, and I knew then you were jealous and envious, because I received such a lot of accolades and won most of the prizes. But you were silly to be jealous. I was a set designer, not an interior designer . . . it's not the same. And you were the most brilliant interior designer in the class, so far above any other student. I knew you were going to be a huge success.'

Suddenly Jessica's face underwent change, her anger now replaced by a chagrined expression. After a moment or two of thought, she admitted in a low, deflated voice, 'Maybe I *was* jealous . . . yes, that's *true*. I'm . . . sorry, Alexa. I owe you an apology.'

'I accept your apology.' Alexa glanced at Maria. 'And I accept yours, too. Now Kay, let's hear from you.'

Kay's white face looked stark against her black dress and jacket, and she shook her head, momentarily unable to say a word.

There were a few seconds of quiet in the library. None of the women spoke. Anya glanced from one to the other, suddenly worried about Kay. She looked as though she were about to faint.

And then Kay finally spoke, breaking the silence. 'It's true that I did harbour a few grudges against all of you. We had been so close and happy together for three years, and then a few months before graduation you all changed towards me. I really didn't understand. I thought you didn't like me any more because I didn't have your upbringing, your family backgrounds. You all slighted me.'

Alexa stared hard at her, frowning, totally nonplussed. 'But we didn't slight you, and certainly we didn't think you were any different than we were. Did we, Jessica?'

'No.'

'Did we, Maria?'

'No, Alexa, not at all.'

'But I felt the change in you,' Kay protested.

Alexa said quietly, 'I think we changed for the reasons we've just discussed. The problems were about me, Maria and Jessica.' She let out a small sigh. 'Sadly, you just imagined we had changed towards you, but we hadn't. *Honestly.*'

'We never knew much about you, or your background, Kay,' Maria volunteered. She smiled at Kay, having now recovered her equilibrium. 'You never confided. But you had beautiful clothes, plenty of money, an air of breeding. We did not think of you as being different.'

Kay was silent.

Jessica said, 'Look, if I ever slighted you in any way, then I'm sorry. I do sincerely apologize, Kay. But I don't believe I did.'

'I agree with Jessica, and with Maria.' Alexa shook her head. 'We never thought you were different, not as good as us. We were simply caught up in our own troubles, as I just said.' She gave Kay a huge smile and finished, 'We always thought of you as one of us.'

'But I wasn't,' Kay said slowly. '*I was different.*' She stopped, looked across at Anya.

Anya nodded, encouraging her to continue.

'I was a poor girl from the Glasgow slums,' Kay confided in a fading voice. 'But my mother worked hard to give me an education at a good boarding school in England. And then she sent me here to Anya's school.'

'We didn't know,' Jessica said. 'And we really wouldn't have cared. We loved you for being *you*, Kay, and for your talent and caring ways.'

Kay nodded. 'I'm sorry,' she said in a regretful tone. 'But I was so hurt. I felt you'd cut me out, that's why I said the things I did.' She groped again for the handkerchief and wiped her eyes.

The four women sat quietly, saying nothing to each other, every one of them lost in her own thoughts for a few minutes.

Anya had listened to their words attentively, and she understood that Alexa had told the truth. It *had* all started with Maria, but Jessica had not helped the situation. In a sense, Alexa had been a victim of Maria's jealousy and muddled thinking, and Jessica's readiness to condemn her. As for Kay, she had allowed her insecurity and sense of inferiority to get the better of her. What a loss of true friendship, she thought, filled with an aching sorrow. Such a waste of those years when they could have given each other moral support, helped in other ways. What a shame they hadn't been able to communicate better, more explicitly, when they were here at the school.

Alexa broke into her thoughts, when she said, 'Let's bury this . . . *garbage*! Seven years have passed. We've all grown up. We're healthy, successful, and yes, we're truly lucky women. Let's be . . . friends again.'

Alexa offered her hand to Maria, who took hold of it and joined her near the fireplace. Jessica then stood up and came over to them. The three women put their arms around each other and looked across at Kay.

'Come on!' Jessica exclaimed, smiling at her. 'Make the quartet complete again.'

Kay pushed herself to her feet and rushed into their arms. The four of them stood in a huddle, half laughing, half crying. Then breaking the circle they made, Jessica said,

'We're missing one ... come on Anya. You belong here with us. For what would we be without you?'

Anya took them to Le Grand Véfour for lunch.

The ancient restaurant, dating back to before the French Revolution, was beneath the arches of the Palais-Royal, a historic landmark.

Now the five of them sat at one of the best tables, sipping champagne, surrounded by the distinctive decor of the eighteenth and nineteenth centuries.

Red velvet banquettes were balanced by simple, clean-lined *Directoire* chairs in black and gold and a richly patterned black and gold carpet, also in the *Directoire* style. Scarred antique mirrors in old, gold frames were affixed to the ceiling and to some of the walls; on other walls were neoclassical paintings of nymphs entwined with flowers and vines, set under glass.

'What a fabulous place this is,' Jessica said, her keen eyes taking in every detail of the decor. 'I just love the paintings, they look as if they come from ancient Rome.'

'I noticed a brass plaque on one of the banquettes bearing the name of Victor Hugo,' Alexa said. 'And another one with Colette's name. She must have been a regular client too.'

Anya nodded. 'A lot of writers came here, and also politicians. Why, even Napoleon used to bring Josephine here to dine.'

'*Really*,' Kay exclaimed, her ears pricking up. 'I hadn't realized the place was that old.'

'Oh yes, it dates back to 1784, but at that time it was called the Café de Chartres. Anyway, I must admit, I never tire of its charm and refined elegance,' Anya said. 'It's had a sort of rebirth lately,' she went on. 'For many, many years it was owned by the famous chef, Raymond Oliver. But he decided to sell it in 1984, because he was getting very old. It went through a transitional period, but under Guy Martin, the new chef, it's gone back to being one of the top restaurants in Paris. I know you're going to enjoy your food as much as you're enjoying the ambiance.'

Glancing at Maria, Anya added, 'They make a very nice sole, my dear, so you don't have to worry about your diet.'

'You're always so considerate, Anya,' she answered, and took a sip of her mineral water.

Anya now engaged Maria in a conversation about her paintings, and the two became very quickly engrossed.

Kay spoke to Jessica and Alexa about the premises she had found for her boutique, and then she tentatively asked Jessica if she would come and look at them later in the week. 'Maybe you'll be interested in designing the boutique for me,' she explained.

Soon the maître d' was hovering next to the table, telling them about the specialities of the house, and handing around the menus. After studying them for a while, they all settled for sole except Anya, who had decided to indulge herself. 'I'm going to have the pigeon stuffed with foie gras,' she announced with a wide smile. 'And no one is going to make me feel guilty.'

It was a warm and happy lunch. All of the women were at ease with each other once again; as Anya studied them from time to time she realized the quarrel might never have happened. They were as sweet and loving with each other as they had been in their early years at the school. And this pleased her . . . it was the best birthday gift she could ever have.

Before they knew it, the lunch was over and they were trooping out into the street. Alexa began to chastise Anya, complaining that she should not have signed the bill, that they had wanted to take her to lunch. 'It should have been our treat,' she insisted.

'Don't be silly, darling. It was my pleasure to have you all together again, and so *tranquil*, too. I'm very happy the quarrel is behind us.'

As they waited for Anya's car and driver, Alexa drew Jessica under the arches at one moment, and said to her quietly, 'I need to talk to you about something really important, Jessica. Can you spare me half an hour?'

Jessica looked at her swiftly, then nodded, glanced at her watch. 'Let's find a cab. We can talk on the way to the Bonnal Gallery. I have an appointment there with Alain, about a painting for a client.'

Alexa was staring at her intently.

Jessica frowned. 'You remember him don't you? He was a friend of Lucien's.'

'Oh yes, I remember him,' Alexa answered.

CHAPTER THIRTY

A week later, very early on a warm Saturday morning, they drove to the Loire Valley.

Tom was at the wheel of his large Mercedes, with Mark Sylvester sitting next to him in the front. On the back seat were Alexa, Jessica and Alain Bonnal.

Tom peered ahead as they finally left the environs of Paris and headed out towards the main motorway which would take them to Orléans.

Although it was balmy weather, the sun was hidden by dark clouds which floated across the horizon; they seemed threatening, hinted of an imminent downpour. Tom hoped it would not rain, wanting a fast run down to his parents' house near Tours.

Once they arrived there they planned to freshen up and have breakfast before heading over to Montcresse, the château which was the family home of Jean Beauvais-Cresse.

Only Tom, the two women and Alain would go there; this had been decided over dinner last night, when the five of them had gone to Le Relais Plaza for a meal. They had agreed that Mark would remain with Tom's parents. As soon as the meeting with Jean had taken place, the other four would return for lunch and then head back to Paris in mid-afternoon.

Because it was so early in the morning, it seemed to Tom that no one wanted to talk, and perhaps it was best that they didn't, he decided. He slipped a disc into the player on the dashboard, and turned the volume down to low. Soon the car was filled with the background themes from great Hollywood movies, and it was soothing, not at all intrusive.

Jessica's eyes were closed, but she was not dozing. She was wide awake, simply feigning sleep in order to sink down into her thoughts.

She had been determined to come and see this man in the Loire who looked so much like Lucien, but now she felt a bit queasy about it.

On the other hand, Alain was with them, and this helped. In fact, he had insisted on accompanying them, and she felt she owed it to him. After all, he had helped her so much when Lucien had disappeared. Alain knew Lucien as well as she did, and if she were at all uncertain about the man's true identity, she had Alain to turn to for a proper assessment.

Could it be Lucien? Was he alive and well and living in the Loire? Perhaps. Certainly she had sometimes had a weird feeling that Lucien was alive somewhere out there. She had even said that to Alain on the day they had lunched together at Chez André, when she had first arrived in Paris. That day she had been quite positive that Alain knew no more than she did, and he had proved that once again when she had gone to the Bonnal Gallery last Monday.

In the taxi from Le Grand Véfour, Alexa had told her about the photograph album, Tom's reaction to the photograph of her and Lucien standing at the edge of the Pont des Arts. And although she had been momentarily startled, it had not come as a great shock. In one sense, she had half expected to hear something like this over the years. Then again, Mark had put the idea into her head in February, when he had suggested that Lucien might have vanished on purpose.

Alain had pooh-poohed that over lunch, and then again at the Gallery, when Alexa had told him about Jean Beauvais-Cresse. It was apparent he had never heard of the man, that he did not know him, and he was very dismissive when Alexa said Jean could be Lucien. But when he heard they were planning a trip to the Loire he had pleaded to be included, and Jessica had agreed, knowing she owed him this because of the past and his friendship to her.

The past, she thought now. Seven years ago. I was twenty-four and so innocent at that time, even more naïve when I met Lucien when I was twenty-two, just a country girl from Texas. But Lucien had not been overly sophisticated, simply a good-looking, pleasant young man who loved being an actor. He had had a great zest for life, and they had been so compatible. And he had made her feel good about herself, their relationship, life in general and the future they planned ... California here we come, they used to say in unison. That had been their aim. An interior design business for her, Hollywood movies for him ...

It just wasn't meant to be, she thought. He had vanished

one day and her life had been turned upside down, and she had never really been the same, if she were honest with herself.

Alexa had been wonderful to her last Monday, so kind and compassionate, understanding of her sudden dilemma: to go and confront this man, or not to go. Alexa had been very determined, had opted for going down there, pointing out she really had no alternative. Jessica had at once seen the sense in making the trip.

She wanted – no, needed – to close this chapter in her life . . . she could do that only by going to Château Montcresse. If the man who lived there with his wife and child was not Lucien, then no harm had been done, and perhaps she could close the book anyway.

But if it was Lucien, then she would finally have the answers to some very pertinent questions, the most important one being *WHY?*

She had voiced all this to Mark yesterday, before they had gone to meet the others at Le Relais Plaza for dinner. He had encouraged the trip, and agreed with her. He had also asked her to allow him to come along. 'I care about you, Jessica,' he had said. 'And I'd like to be there for you, in case you need me. I'm your friend, you know.' She had smiled and squeezed his arm, and said she would be relieved if he went with them, genuinely meaning it.

Not long after he had left the motorway at the exit to Tours, Tom quickly circumvented the town, drove past Amboise and took a secondary road going towards Loches. 'We'll soon be there,' he said at one moment, and everyone sat up, looking out of the car windows eagerly.

Fifteen minutes later Tom was slowing down and turning into a driveway through iron gates which stood open and welcoming. At the end of a short drive stood a lovely old manor house, typical of the area, made of local Loire stone which was renowned for turning white as it aged over the years. The manor looked pale and elegant set against a backdrop of dark green trees with an azure sky above.

As Tom pulled up and braked outside the front door, it opened and his father came hurrying down the steps.

After embracing his son, who was a younger version of himself, Paul Conners hugged Alexa with great affection, and then Tom made the introductions all around.

'Come on, let's go inside and have breakfast,' Paul said, leading the way into the circular front hall with a terra-cotta tiled floor and white stone walls hung with antique tapestries.

Christiane Conners, Tom's mother, appeared at this moment, and once she had kissed Tom and Alexa, her son introduced their companions.

'Perhaps you would like to freshen up,' Christiane said, turning to Alexa and Jessica, and then heading towards the staircase, beckoning to them. 'And Paul and Tom, I'll leave you to look after Mark and Alain.'

Christiane led the way up the curving staircase to the floor above, and showed them both into a pretty guest room decorated with a pale blue *toile de Jouy* used throughout. It covered the walls, the bed, and was hanging at the windows as draperies.

Jessica noticed it immediately and thought the room looked so fresh and airy, but she made no comment. She was pre-occupied, nervous now that they had arrived in the area.

'You will find everything you need here, Alexa,' Christiane said, waving her hand around the room and then indicating the bathroom.

'Thank you, Christiane.' Alexa turned to Jessica. 'Why don't you tidy up first, Jess, I want to talk to Tom's mother for a moment.'

'Thanks,' Jessica replied and disappeared into the bath-room.

Once they were alone, Christiane rushed over to Alexa and hugged her. Alexa had always liked Tom's parents, and she knew this feeling was mutual. They had made her feel welcome, had always been loving.

Finally releasing her, Christiane looked into her face and said softly, 'I was so happy when I heard you were in Paris, *ma petite*, and that you and Tom were back together.' A beautifully arched blonde brow lifted, and she quickly asked, 'You are, are you not?'

'Yes, we are,' Alexa answered. 'We're meant to be together, and I think Tom knows that now.'

'I hope so, *chérie*. You are important for him, good for him. I know this . . . ah *les hommes* . . . sometimes they can be . . . stupid.' She shook her head. 'But what would we do without them?'

When Jessica came out of the bathroom, Christiane looked at her intently, said, 'Tom wished me to tell you about Jean Beauvais-Cresse, but there is not much to tell, Jessica.'

'He's the mystery man, according to Tom,' Jessica replied,

sitting down on the chair opposite Christiane while they waited for Alexa.

'Mystery man?' Tom's mother repeated, and shook her head. '*Non, non.*' She thought for a moment, before continuing. 'I think of him as a *recluse*. We do not see much of him in public. Nor his wife. They keep . . . to themselves.'

'Perhaps that's an indication of *something* peculiar,' Alexa said as she came out of the bathroom. 'I think so, anyway.'

'I hope we'll soon have some answers,' Jessica muttered.

Christiane nodded. 'Let us go downstairs and have a little refreshment. I am sure you are anxious to be on your way to Montcresse.' She now hurried out of the blue guest room, and the two young women followed hard on her heels.

Despite her preoccupation, the designer in Jessica surfaced a couple of times as she followed Tom's mother and Alexa down the stairs, across the entrance hall and into an unusual circular room. This was at the back of the house, and had many windows; these looked out on to lawns, gardens and a stand of trees. Beyond she could see a stretch of the river.

'How beautiful!' she exclaimed as she glanced around, noting the tasteful decorations, the mellow antiques, the displays of porcelain plates on the walls.

'This is the summer dining room,' Christiane explained, ushering them towards the circular table in the middle of the room.

They sat down just as Tom, his father and the other two men came into the room. 'Sit anywhere you wish,' Paul said. He took a seat next to Alexa, grasped her hand in his and squeezed it.

Alexa squeezed back, smiled into his face. She thought:

How handsome he is. Tom will look like this when he is sixty-five. *I've got to be with Tom. Always. I want to share my life with him.*

Paul said, 'Penny for your thoughts, Alex?'

She laughed. 'I couldn't possibly tell you.'

'Then I'll tell you,' he said with a small, knowing smile. Leaning closer he whispered in her ear, 'You want to be with him for the rest of your life.'

Alexa stared at Paul Conners, squinting in the sunlight streaming in through the windows. 'How did you know?'

'It's written all over your face, honey.'

Christiane was pouring coffee, and Tom was offering a basket of bread to everyone, moving around the table slowly.

'What would you like, Alexa?' he asked when he finally stopped next to her chair.

'You,' she mouthed silently, as she looked upon him and took a croissant.

Tom kissed the top of her head, made no comment.

Paul looked at Alain, and said, 'Tom explained to me that you used to know Lucien Girard when Jessica did. At the time he lived in Paris.'

'*Oui, oui,*' Alain said, nodding.

'And he was a nice guy then?'

'*Ah bien sûr,*' Alain exclaimed. 'A man of integrity. I find it hard to accept this theory that he . . . disappeared on purpose.'

Mark interjected, 'It wouldn't be the first time a man has done that. Or a woman, for that matter.'

Paul nodded in agreement. 'And there's usually a helluva

good reason when this happens. I can't imagine what his family suffered, quite aside from Jessica's grief, of course.'

'He told me he was an orphan, that his parents were dead,' Jessica volunteered.

Alain added, 'And he told me the same thing. No parents, no siblings.'

'And seemingly no past,' Mark remarked, staring at Paul pointedly.

'If you're intent on leading a double life it's always best to keep the story and the details very simple. That way you can't make too many mistakes,' Paul responded.

'That is true,' Christiane murmured.

Alexa, studying Tom's mother, thought how lovely she looked, but then she usually had in the past. Christiane Conners was one of those well-groomed French women who could manage to look chic in a plain cotton shirt and trousers, which is what Christiane was wearing this morning. She admired her for looking the way she did at her age, and she was glad Tom's mother was her ally.

Jessica had been listening to them all, quietly sipping her coffee, saying nothing very much. But once she thought everyone had finished, she said, 'Do you think we can drive over there, Tom? I'm awfully nervous, and as long as I sit here I'm prolonging the agony . . .'

Tom and Alexa both leapt to their feet, and Tom said, 'Of course we can go.' Taking hold of Alexa's hand, he moved away from the table, telling his parents he would see them later. Alain did the same, then ushered Jessica out of the dining room.

Mark pushed back his chair, excused himself, and hurried

out after Jessica. He caught up with her on the front steps, took hold of her arm, drew her towards him. Looking down into her face, he said, 'Whatever happens over there doesn't really matter, Jess darling. One way or another, you'll finally have *closure*.'

Jessica tried to smile but it faltered. 'You're right, Mark, I know that. I'm just nervous, queasy.'

He brought her into his arms, held her close, and said against her hair, 'You're going to be all right, Jessica. I'm going to make damned sure of that.'

CHAPTER THIRTY-ONE

Tom and Alain sat in the front of the Mercedes; Alexa and Jessica took the back seat. No one spoke on the way to Montcresse, but at one moment Alexa reached out, grabbed Jessica's hand and held it tightly in hers, wanting to comfort and reassure her.

Jessica sat very still on the back seat, holding her breath, anxious to get to the château. Already she was wishing the confrontation were over, and that they were on their way back to Paris. *Confrontation*, she said to herself. Who knew if there would even be one. Jean Beauvais-Cresse was more than likely a very nice man leading a quiet life with his family, who simply happened to bear a resemblance to Lucien Girard. An innocent bystander, in other words.

Tom broke the silence in the car when he said, 'That's Montcresse straight ahead of us.'

Jessica and Alexa strained to get a better glimpse.

What they saw was a truly grand château, standing proudly on a rise not far from the River Indre, another tributary of the Loire. Its white stone walls gleamed in the bright morning sunlight, while the black, bell-shaped roofs atop the numerous circular towers gave the massive edifice a fanciful air.

As Tom drove up the rise, Jessica noticed the well-kept grassy lawns edging the sand-coloured gravel driveway, and behind the château there was a dense wood of tall, dark trees. Two more circular towers with bell-shaped roofs and thin spires flanked the drawbridge leading into the interior courtyard.

Tom slowed down as he rolled over the drawbridge, went under the arch and into the yard, heading towards the front door.

Jessica felt her stomach lurch, and for a second she thought she could not go through with this encounter. She almost told Tom to turn around and leave; she looked at Alexa, opened her mouth to speak but no words came out.

At once, Alexa saw the expression of anxiety mingled with fear on Jessica's pale face, and she tightened her grip on Jessica's hand, murmured, 'It'll be fine.'

Still unable to say anything, Jessica merely nodded.

Tom parked close to the château's walls, a short distance away from the huge front door. Half turning in his seat, he said to the two women: 'One of the staff might answer the door, and in that case I'd be invited inside. Should that happen, wait five minutes and then come looking for me. You'll be allowed inside if you say you're with me.'

Now glancing at Alain, Tom went on, 'You should take

charge if I go inside, it'll be quicker and easier for you to deal with any staff member.'

'Of course, Tom, don't worry,' Alain answered.

Alexa asked, 'But what if Jean answers the door?'

'I shall engage him in conversation for a few minutes, then I'll glance at the car, wave to you. At that moment you should come and join me . . . join us. Everything clear?'

'Yes,' Alexa said, and Jessica nodded.

Tom alighted, and walked down the cobbled courtyard, heading for the huge front door made of nail-embellished wood. When he came to a stop he saw that it stood ajar. Nevertheless, he knocked and waited. When no one came, he pushed the door slightly, peered inside and shouted, 'Hello!'

A moment later an elderly, grey-haired man wearing a striped apron over his shirt and waistcoat suddenly appeared in the entrance hall. He was carrying a silver tray, and he stepped forward when he saw Tom. He inclined his head, '*Bonjour, monsieur.*'

'*Bonjour. J'aimerais voir Monsieur le Marquis.*'

'*Oui, oui, attendez une minute, s'il vous plait.*'

These words had hardly left the man's mouth when Tom heard footsteps on the cobblestones, and he glanced down towards the stables.

Jean de Beauvais-Cresse was walking towards him. He wore black riding boots, white jodhpurs and a black turtle-necked sweater. He raised a hand, and a second later the two men were greeting each other and shaking hands.

Tom then went on, 'I apologize for intruding like this, without telephoning first, but as we passed the château my clients asked me to stop the car. They were intrigued by Montcresse. You see, they're making a movie about Mary, Queen of Scots and plan to shoot in the Loire. I've been showing them this area, since they're seeking possible locations for the upcoming film –'

'*C'est pas possible*,' Jean cut in with a small, regretful smile. 'Many people have wanted to film here in the past. But it doesn't work. The château's not the best place to shoot a film, I'm afraid.'

'I see,' Tom responded, and wanting to find a way to keep him talking, he improvised. 'But what about outside? There are quite a lot of exterior scenes, and perhaps you would consider allowing them access to the property.'

Unexpectedly, Jean Beauvais-Cresse seemed to hesitate, appeared to be considering this idea. At the same time, he moved forward, stepped inside the château, stood regarding Tom from the entrance hall. 'Perhaps there might be a way to film on the estate,' he said finally.

Tom was listening attentively, but out of the corner of his eye he saw Alexa, Alain and Jessica alighting and walking towards him. Wishing to keep the other man totally engaged as they approached, Tom leaned forward slightly, and continued, 'There would be a very good fee involved, and the crew would have instructions to be extremely careful on your land. Also, the production company is insured anyway.'

'I understand. But I must think about it –' Jean broke off abruptly. Shock was registering on his narrow face, and he had paled. As if undone, he staggered slightly, leaned against the door jamb, his eyes wide with surprise and panic.

Jessica, who stood just behind Tom, now stepped forward,

staring at Jean. Immediately, she recognized him, just as he had recognized her. It *was* him. A greyer, older version of Lucien Girard. There was no doubt in her mind.

Shaking, and just as undone as Jean was, she swallowed hard. 'I often thought you must be alive somewhere out there in the world . . .' Her eyes welled with tears.

Jean stared at her, then his gaze settled on Alain and finally Alexa. His eyes acknowledged them but he said nothing.

He shook his head slowly and directed his attention on Tom. 'Your talk about filming intrigued me,' he murmured. Sighing heavily, he opened the door wider. 'You'd better come inside,' he said.

Jessica was still shaking and her legs felt weak, but she managed to hold herself together as the four of them followed Jean across the huge stone hall. It was baronial, hung with dark tapestries and stags' heads; a huge chandelier dropped down from the high ceiling. Their footsteps echoed on the stone floor.

He led the way down three steps into a long, spacious room with French windows opening on to a terrace. Jessica did not pay much attention, only vaguely noticed the dark wood pieces, the faded fabrics, the worn antique Aubusson underfoot. There was an air of shabby elegance about it.

Jean paused in the centre of the room, and waved his hand at a grouping of chairs and sofas. 'Please,' he murmured. He did not sit himself, but moved away, went and stood near the stone fireplace.

Once the others were seated, he glanced at Tom and asked, 'Did we know each other in Paris years ago?'

'Not really.'

'How did you . . . make the connection?'

'My friend Alexa has a photograph of Jessica with you. When I mentioned your name, she said the man in the picture was someone called Lucien Girard. Then she told me the story . . . of your disappearance.'

'I see.' He shifted on his feet, blinked several times.

No longer able to contain herself, Jessica leaned forward slightly, and asked in a tight voice, '*Why?* Why did you do it? Vanish the way you did, without a trace?'

He did not respond.

No one else spoke. The room was very quiet.

Outside, a light wind rustled through the trees and in the distance a bird trilled. Through the open French windows the scent of roses and other flowers floated inside, filling the air with sweetness. There was a sense of tranquillity in this long, narrow library, an air of timelessness, of gentleness.

But emotions were high.

Jessica exclaimed, 'I think you owe me an explanation. And Alain. We tried so hard to find you, and when we couldn't, we thought you were dead. We grieved for you!' She shook her head, and tears gathered in her eyes. 'I think I've been grieving for you right until this very moment.' Her voice broke and she could not continue.

'I think you should tell Jessica why you disappeared, Lucien. You owe that to Jessica, if not to me,' Alain said.

'Yes, it is true. I do owe you both an explanation.' He sat down on a chair near the fireplace and took a deep breath.

After a moment, he looked over at Jessica, and slowly began to speak.

'I said I was going to Monte Carlo to work because I couldn't tell you the truth, Jessica.'

'And what was the truth?' she asked, still tearful.

'That I was not really Lucien Girard. This name was my *nom de plume* . . . I was, I am, Jean de Beauvais-Cresse. But twelve years ago I left this house and went to live and work in Paris, after a bad quarrel with my father. He disapproved of my desire to be an actor, and washed his hands of me. In any case, my older brother Philippe was his favourite, and, of course, he was the heir to the title and the lands. Seven years ago, just before you graduated, Philippe was tragically killed in an accident. He was flying on a private plane to Corsica, to join his fiancée and her family, when the plane went down in a bad thunderstorm. Everyone on board was killed.

'When he received the terrible news of Philippe's death, my father had a stroke. My mother, who was an invalid, summoned me to return to Montcresse. I was needed here. I had a funeral to arrange, and other matters to attend to, as well as my mother and father to care for.'

'But why didn't you tell me?' Jessica demanded. 'I could have come with you, helped you.'

'It was far too complicated. I did not have time for long explanations. I was suddenly needed immediately. Urgently. Anyway, I believed I would be here in the Loire for only a week, at the most.' Jean paused, leaned back in his chair, took a deep breath.

Scrutinizing him intently, Jessica thought he looked older than thirty-five. His narrow face was lined and his fair hair was meagre. He had always been slender, but now he was really thin. To her, he seemed undernourished, and it struck her that he had lost his looks. And, not unnaturally, he was very nervous. Beads of sweat lined his upper lip and his forehead. It was not overly warm in this room, and she suddenly understood the extent of his unease with them – with her, in particular.

For his part, Jean Beauvais-Cresse was fully aware of her fixed scrutiny, and he flinched under it. His discomfort was profound. Seeing her again had sent shock waves through him. She had never looked more beautiful, and her allure for him was as potent as ever. He still loved her deeply. He had never stopped loving her. He would always love her until the day he died. She had been, still was, the love of his life. But it was not meant to be, could not be. Not any more.

Jean filled with regret. A deep sense of loss overwhelmed him, and his emotions ran high. And he had to steady himself, take hold of his swimming senses. For one awful moment he thought he was going to weep. Breathing deeply, taking hold of himself with steely determination, not wishing to break down in front of them, he rose, moved to the fireplace once more, took up a stance there.

Clearing his throat, he said, 'As I was saying a moment ago, I did not think I would be staying here for very long. Perhaps a week. I truly did intend to tell you everything when I returned to Paris, Jessica. Please believe that.'

'And then what?' Jessica asked, her voice still shaking.

'I hoped we could continue as we were, make a life together. Somehow. But then something else occurred, just after the funeral of my brother.'

Alain, frowning, asked quickly, 'What happened?'

'I became ill. Extremely ill. I had been fighting what I thought was flu. A scratchy throat, aches and pains, night sweats, fever were the symptoms. I mentioned this to my father's doctor, the day after the funeral, when he came to Montcresse to see my parents. At once, he insisted I go to his office for an examination –' Jean stopped, cleared his throat, seemed for a moment hesitant to continue.

Jessica's eyes were on Jean, and she held her breath. Even before he spoke she knew he was about to tell them something quite terrible.

Jean continued, 'Doctor Bitoun did not like what he found. He sent me immediately to Orléans, to see a cancer specialist, an oncologist. I had x-rays, a CAT scan, and an MRI. The doctor also took a biopsy of a node under my arm. Everyone's worst fears were confirmed when the results of the tests came back. I had Hodgkin's Disease.'

'But you were so young, only in your mid-twenties!' Jessica cried, her eyes wide with shock.

'That is true. It usually does strike young men in their twenties, sometimes even in their teen years,' Jean answered, and went on to explain, 'Hodgkin's Disease is cancer of the lymphatic system, and once I was diagnosed, the oncologist at the clinic in Orléans hospitalized me at once, and started radiation treatment.'

'But why didn't you call me?' Jessica interrupted heatedly. 'I would have come to you at once. I loved you.'

'I know, and I love –' He coughed behind his hand before saying, 'I loved you too, Jessica. And because I loved you I decided it was better to . . . just disappear.'

'But why?' she demanded. Her eyes filled again, and the tears trickled down her cheeks. 'I loved you so much . . . with all my heart.'

'I know,' he said in a low, faltering voice. 'However, I suddenly realized I had nothing to offer you. I believed I was going to die. I truly did not believe the treatments would work. Then again, I had an invalid mother, a stricken father, and the responsibility of running the estate . . . if I lived. It seemed . . . all too much to burden you with at the time. You were so young. And, as I just said, I did not think I would live for very long.'

'But you did live,' Alain said, staring hard at Jean.

Jean nodded. 'I did, yes. After a number of agonizing treatments, I went into remission after about eight months. Even so, the prognosis was not encouraging. The oncologist warned me the cancer could come back, in fact, he led me to believe it would do so.' He looked across at Jessica. 'Marriage was no longer a possibility.'

'But you *did* marry. And you have a child,' she responded quietly, hurting inside.

'That is true, yes. I married three years ago. I had a child-hood friend living nearby, and once I came out of the hospital she came here to Montcresse to help me handle things. Then my father suddenly died, and I inherited. My responsibilities increased. Sadly, my mother died a few months after my father. I was totally overwhelmed. Annick, my dear old friend, was my rock at the time. Slowly, we became involved, but I had no plans to marry.'

'Then why did you marry her?' Jessica asked. 'And not me? I would have come here. I, too, could have been your rock.'

'Because to my utter surprise Annick became pregnant,' Jean answered. 'I had not thought this possible, because often the treatment for cancer renders a man . . . sterile. But Annick was pregnant, all of a sudden. I cared for her. She loved me, wanted to marry me, and so I did the correct thing. Also, she was going to give me an heir to the title and the lands, someone to follow me when I died. She knew that I would probably not live to see the boy grow up, but she and I accepted that.'

'How old is the child?' Alexa said, speaking for the first time.

Jean looked at her, a faint smile flickering on his mouth. 'Three.'

'And you are in remission now, are you?' Alain asked.

'No. I'm undergoing treatment again. Chemotherapy this time.'

'I'm sorry,' Alain responded. 'I'm sorry it has come back.'

Jessica, staring at him, her eyes still moist, said slowly, 'I would have understood all this, I would have come to you, Lucien, I would, I really would. You were . . . my life.'

Jean's light, bluish-grey eyes filled with tears. He opened his mouth to reply, but found he could not say a word.

Jessica, always so close to him, always so understanding of his thoughts and feelings, rose and walked across the room, her step firm. When she drew closer to him, Jean reached out to her.

As she came to a standstill in front of him, Jessica saw the tears on his cheeks, grief and sorrow in his eyes.

He was aware of no one else in the room but her. He took hold of her gently, brought her into his arms. She clung to him, rested her head against his chest, her own face wet with tears. And she forgot every other question she had meant to ask him. They no longer mattered.

Against the top of her head, he said in a low voice, 'I thought I was doing the right thing. The best for you. Perhaps I was wrong.'

When she did not respond, Jean murmured, 'Forgive me, Jessica.'

'I do,' she whispered against his chest. 'I do forgive you, Lucien.' She blinked back fresh tears, trying to compose herself. 'I'll always think of you as Lucien, remember you as him.'

'I know.'

There was a sudden rustling noise, the sound of running feet, and as the two of them drew apart, a small boy came hurtling into the library through the French windows. '*Papa! Papa! Je suis là!*' he cried, and then stopped when he saw that there were other people with his father.

Jean walked over to him, took hold of his hand, and led him over to Jessica. 'This is my son . . . Lucien,' Jean told her, looking deeply into her eyes.

She gazed back at Jean, nodding, understanding. Then she hunkered down in front of the child, touched his soft, round baby cheek with one finger, and smiled at him. '*Bonjour. Je suis Jessica,*' she said.

The boy smiled back at her. '*Bonjour,*' he answered, in his high child's voice, his little pink face radiant with happiness and good health.

Swallowing her emotions, Jessica stood up, looked across at Alexa and the two men. 'I think perhaps we should go,' she said to them, and turning to Jean, she added, 'Thank you for explaining . . . everything.'

'And I believe you understand *everything*.'

'I do.'

Dropping his voice, he said, 'So you are not married, Jessica.'

'No.'

He sighed, looked at her sadly. 'I'm sorry. *C'est dommage*.'

'It's all right.'

Jean escorted them out of the library, one hand on Jessica's shoulder, the other holding his son's hand as he crossed the stone hall to the front door. When they stepped out into the courtyard, he leaned into her, kissed her cheek.

'*Au revoir*, Jessica. *Bonne chance*.'

'Goodbye.'

He inclined his head.

She walked away from him, heading for the car. She heard the others taking their leave, hurrying after her. Jessica paused at the car; turning around, she looked back.

He stood where she had left him near the door, holding the child's hand. With the other he blew a kiss to her, and then waved. So did Lucien.

She blew kisses back and waved to them, then got into the car, her heart full.

No one spoke as they drove away from Montcresse.

Alexa held Jessica's hand, and looked at her several times. But once they had left the château behind, she finally asked, 'Are you all right?'

'Oh yes, I'm fine,' Jessica replied in a fading voice. Clearing her throat, she went on speaking softly. 'Now that I know what happened to Lucien I can be at peace with myself. I have closure, as I always knew I would.'

'It was so sad,' Alexa said. 'My heart went out to him.'

'I also felt sorry for him,' Alain murmured, turning to look at them. 'What a pity the cancer has come back. But perhaps . . . Well, let us hope he will go into remission again.'

'I honestly think he truly believes he made the right choice. For you, Jessica. He thought he was protecting you,' Tom told her.

'I know he did. But he did my thinking for me. That's not really fair.' Jessica let out a deep sigh. 'All these years I have been in love with a memory. A memory of Lucien, a memory of my first love. But *he* is different now. *I* am different now. I just wish he had trusted me. Trusted our love enough to tell me the truth seven years ago, when all these terrible things were happening to him.'

'What would you have done?' Alexa ventured, looking at her intently.

'I would have gone to him immediately. There is no question in my mind about that,' Jessica asserted.

'And would it have worked, do you think?' Tom asked.

'I don't know, I really don't. But I am relieved I did finally see him again. Now I can move on at last.' But part of me will always love him, Jessica added to herself as she leaned back and closed her eyes. And part of me will always belong to him, as I know part of him belongs to me. He made that so very clear, just as he made it clear that he still loves me.

PART FOUR

Celebration

CHAPTER THIRTY-TWO

K ay sat staring at herself in the mirror, wondering if she needed just a touch more blusher. It seemed to her that her face was paler than usual, and she wanted to look her best tonight.

Leaning back in the small chair, she now scrutinized herself from a distance, her eyes narrowing slightly, her head held on one side. Picking up the brush, she delicately stroked her cheekbones with it, and finally, satisfied with the effect, she turned her attention to her hair. It fell around her face in a tumble of auburn waves and curls; she mussed it a little more with her hands, combed the front and sprayed it lightly. 'There, that's the best I can do,' she said out loud, again peering at herself in the dressing table mirror.

'You look beautiful, Kay,' Ian said from behind her, placing a hand on her bare shoulder.

'Gosh, you surprised me!' she exclaimed, craning her neck to look up at him towering above her.

Smiling, he bent down, touched her cheek with his finger, then turned her shoulders so that she was again looking at herself in the mirror.

'Close your eyes,' he instructed.

'Why?'

'Just do as I say.'

'All right.'

Once her eyes were tightly shut, Ian reached into the pocket of his robe, and pulled out a necklace. Very carefully, he placed this around Kay's long, slender neck, fastened it, then said, 'Now you can open your eyes.'

When Kay did so she gasped in surprise and delight. Around her neck her husband had placed the most beautiful diamond and topaz necklace she had ever seen. Loops of diamonds formed a lacy bib, and set along the front in the loops of the diamonds were eight large topaz stones.

'Ian, it's exquisite! I've never seen anything quite like it!' she exclaimed, gazing at him through the mirror. 'Thank you, oh, thank you so much.'

'I'm glad you like it, darling. I fell in love with it the moment I saw it, in just the same way I fell in love with you. Immediately, to be precise.'

She laughed, and then her eyes widened as he handed her a small black velvet box.

'These will add the finishing touch,' he said.

Again she gasped as she lifted the lid. Lying on the black velvet were a pair of large topaz earrings, each large stone encircled by diamonds. 'Ian, how extravagant you've been,' she cried. 'But they're so beautiful. Darling, thank you.'

A wide smile spread across his face. He knew her happiness,

excitement and pleasure were genuine, and this gratified him. He wanted to please her, to let her know in every way possible how much he loved her. 'Put them on,' he said.

'Right away, sir,' she answered and clipped an earring on each ear, staring at herself. 'They're just . . . *magnificent*,' she said.

'As is my beautiful wife.'

'Again, thank you, for the compliment and these beautiful pieces. But it's not Christmas, nor is it my birthday.'

'It doesn't have to be a special day for me to give you a present, does it?'

She laughed. 'No. And you're quite incorrigible.'

'I truly hope so.' He stroked her shoulder, then said, 'Do you remember when I went into Edinburgh, that Saturday in February? The day before Fiona's birthday?'

'Yes. Very well. You seemed a bit mysterious. Or maybe *vague* is a better word. Certainly you were rather close-mouthed when you came back.'

'I know. And actually I was trying to be mysterious. The reason being the necklace and earrings.'

'Oh!' she said, staring at him through the mirror.

'I'd asked old Barnes, the manager of Codrington's, the jewellers, to keep his eyes open for a diamond necklace. Imagine my delight when he phoned to say he had a diamond-and-topaz necklace, very rare, very old, and would I like to see it.' Ian paused, touched a strand of her auburn hair. 'You can't imagine how those topaz stones match this,' he said, and continued, 'I really went into Edinburgh to look at the necklace, although I did need to buy something for my sister.'

'And you've had those pieces all these months?'

He nodded. 'Actually, Kay, I was going to give them to you for Christmas, but suddenly I realized that now would be as good a time as any. So I brought them with me on Thursday.'

She nodded and rose, went to him, put her arms around his neck and kissed him firmly on the mouth. 'You are the most wonderful husband a girl could ever want.'

'Likewise, my pet.' As he spoke he untied the belt of her robe, slipped it off her shoulders. It fell to the floor, a pool of pale blue around her feet. He held her away from him, gazing at her. 'Look at you, Kay. So beautiful.'

Slipping off his own robe, Ian brought her into his arms, held her tightly, kissing the hollow of her neck, and then her breasts. Lifting his head he looked deeply into her eyes and said, 'Come to bed with me. I promise I won't mess your face and hair.'

She laughed lightly. 'As if I really care. I can do it all again.'

'We do have time,' he murmured as he drew her towards the bed. 'We don't have to meet Alexa and Tom until six-forty-five.'

They lay down together, clasped in each other's arms, their mouths meeting again. Kay let her tongue brush Ian's lips and then she opened her mouth slightly, tasting him, their tongues meeting. His kisses became more passionate, more intense, and his hands roamed over her delicately, touching, stroking, exploring. Her long tapering fingers went into his hair, and then moved down to stroke his back.

Kay felt him growing harder against her, and she rolled

away from him, on to her back, and pulled him on to her. Pushing himself up on his hands, he looked down into her eyes and said softly, 'I love you, Kay, with all my heart.'

'Oh Ian, Ian,' she whispered, and she arched her body towards him. 'I want you . . . I want to feel you inside me. Please, please.'

Leaning over her, he kissed her on her mouth, slowly, lingeringly, and then he lay on top of her, pushed his hands under her buttocks and brought her closer. He entered her swiftly, and she groaned; instantly the two of them fell into a rhythm they had made their own long ago. As she moved her body against him, breathing harder, clutching at his shoulders, he felt as though he were going to explode. A moment later, she spasmed convulsively, and so did he, and they were carried along on a wave of rising passion, lost in their mutual ecstasy.

At last, when they lay still, their hard breathing slowing to normal, Ian raised himself up on an elbow, gazed down at her, moving a strand of hair away from her face. 'Perhaps we just made that baby you want so badly,' he murmured, a half smile playing around his wide and generous mouth. 'But if we haven't, it doesn't matter. You do understand that now, don't you, darling?'

'Yes, I do.' She returned his smile. 'And as Doctor Boujon told me, I have to relax, and we have to just keep on trying. And as he mentioned, there are always ways he can help.'

Ian laughed. 'That won't be necessary, I'm sure of that. Don't forget, I'm a full-blooded Scotsman from the Highlands.'

*   *   *

Fifteen minutes later, Kay was sitting at the dressing table again, a make-up sponge across her face, adding a little powder and blusher. As she outlined her mouth with a lip pencil, she thought about the last five days. Ian had arrived in Paris unexpectedly, responding to her invitation to join her for Anya's birthday party tonight.

He had come a few days early, he explained, because he felt they needed a few days together, alone, away from Lochcraigie.

And on that first night, after they had made passionate love in her suite at the Meurice, she had found herself telling him about her visits to Doctor Boujon. There was nothing physically wrong with her; now that she knew this she had been able to confide her worries about not getting pregnant to her husband. The doctor had recommended that she do this, and it had been worth it.

After Ian had listened to her concerns about not conceiving, he had told her to stop worrying, that it didn't trouble him.

His kindness and understanding had given her the courage to tell him about her past . . . all the terrible things which had happened to her when she was a child. Ian had listened closely, and very quickly the expression of horror and shock on his face had turned to one of compassion mingled with love. And when she had finished at last he had taken her in his arms and held her close, wanting to nurture and protect her. After a while he had said, 'That a man could take advantage of a child in that way is horrendous, so vile it is inconceivable to me. However you coped with it I will never know, but you must have been a very brave little girl, and your mother must have been, too.'

Ian had touched her cheek gently, and kissed her forehead, then looked deeply into her eyes. 'But now you have me to look after you, Kay darling, and I'll never let anyone hurt you ever again.'

She had held on to him tightly, loving him more than ever for being such a good man. She also understood that he had never changed towards her. All of that had been in her head. And later she had wondered why she had never trusted their love enough to tell him about her past before. She had no answer for herself. But at that moment, she vowed never to doubt him or his love for her ever again.

Now, Kay rose from the dressing table, satisfied with her make-up and hair, and moved across the bedroom. Tall, slender, long-limbed and elegant. She was already wearing stockings and high heels, and she took the champagne-coloured chiffon dress from its hanger, stepped into it.

Suddenly, as if she had summoned him, Ian was standing there, hovering in the doorway, looking handsome in his dinner jacket. 'Shall I zip you up, my sweet?'

Turning, she smiled. 'Thanks, Ian.'

Once she had smoothed the dress down, she swung around. 'Do you like it?'

'It's wonderful on you, so . . . frothy and light, and the necklace and earrings are perfect with it.'

'Thank you again for those beauties . . . and now I think we'd better go down to the bar. I'm sure the others are waiting.'

Kay spotted Alexa the moment they entered the Bar Fontainebleu. She and Tom were seated at a table in a corner near the window, and she raised her hand and waved.

As Kay and Ian drew closer she saw that Alexa was also wearing a chiffon dress; it looked as if it was cut on the bias and was composed of variated greens. To Kay it was the perfect choice. The mingled greens matched Alexa's eyes, set off her dark hair.

Tom jumped up and greeted them, and, once they were seated, the waiter brought them glasses of champagne. A moment after this, Jessica arrived with Mark Sylvester. Jessica had chosen to wear a pale blue organza gown delicately patterned with trailing darker blue flowers, and like Kay's and Alexa's it was light and airy, floated gently around her as she moved.

As soon as Mark and Jessica stopped at the table, Alexa said, with a light laugh, 'Well, I see we all had the same idea about a June party in Paris, and what to wear.'

Mark, his eyes roving over them, said, 'You're going to be the belles of the ball.'

'Oh no!' Kay exclaimed, smiling, her eyes sparkling. 'That role is reserved for Anya.'

Alexa, glancing from Tom to Ian to Mark, exclaimed, 'But one thing is certain, girls, we've got the most handsome men for our escorts.'

'Thanks for the rather nice compliment, Alexa,' Ian responded. He liked Kay's girlfriends, and the men in their lives, all of whom he had met last night. Tom had taken everyone to dinner at the beautiful L'Ambroisie. It had been the kind of evening Ian had not had in a long time, and he had appreciated every moment of it.

But most of all he had enjoyed meeting Anya Sedgwick,

and had listened to her raptly as she had extolled Kay's virtues, acclaimed her talent, and confided how much she loved his wife, 'cherished her' was the way she had put it. He had been bursting with pride, and love for his wonderful Kay.

And her great-nephew Nicky had been charming, friendly, and highly amusing. Whilst the fourth member of the quartet, Maria Franconi, had been such a knock-out in her simple black dress and pearls none of the other diners had been able to take their eyes off her.

Now Ian said, 'I suppose Nicky and Maria are not coming for drinks with us. I rather got the impression they were going to collect Anya and take her to the party directly.'

'Anya didn't want to be late,' Alexa explained. 'She wanted to be there first, to greet the guests as they arrived.'

More flutes of champagne arrived at the table for Jessica and Mark, and the six of them now clinked glasses and toasted each other. And then they settled down to chat for a short while before leaving for Ledoyen.

CHAPTER THIRTY-THREE

Anya, flanked on either side by Nicky and Maria, stood in the entrance foyer of Ledoyen, glancing about her.

A look of enchantment crossed her face, brought a sparkle to her blue eyes, a glow to her face. 'Oh, Nicky, my darling boy, you've outdone yourself!' she exclaimed, turning to him, clutching his arm. 'This is simply beautiful!'

He smiled with pleasure and gratification. 'I'm glad you like it. I wanted you to feel . . . at home.'

Anya laughed her light laugh which was ageless, and took a step forward, her eyes everywhere. What Nicky had done was re-create the front façade of her black-and-white, half-timbered manor house in Paris, with its trellis and ivy growing up part of the façade. This replica was *trompe l'oeil*, the style of painting that gave an illusion of reality, like a photograph, and the giant canvas was attached to a long wall at one side of the foyer. This entire area had been designed to look like the cobbled courtyard of her house; the cherry tree in full bloom was there, with the four metal garden chairs standing underneath its laden branches. And her flower garden, enclosed within a white picket fence, took pride of place at the other side of the foyer.

Taking hold of her arm, Nicky said, 'Come along, Anya, I've more surprises for you.'

Still smiling broadly, Anya allowed herself to be propelled up the staircase. 'Where are we going?' she asked, filled with curiosity and anticipation.

'For cocktails,' Maria said, beaming at her.

Anya nodded, glanced at Maria out of the corner of her eye, thinking how marvellous she looked, slimmer than ever and elegant in a midnight-blue chiffon gown with a strapless top and a flowing skirt, her only jewellery a thin strand of tiny diamonds around her neck and diamond studs in her ears.

'Maria, you're simply exquisite,' Anya murmured, momentarily awed by the girl's staggering beauty tonight.

'It's thanks to Nicky. He chose my dress from Balmain,' Maria said.

'Oh it's not the dress I'm talking about, but you, my dear.'

Maria flushed slightly, smiled with pleasure. 'And you look wonderful in your red, Anya.'

Anya said, 'Well, you know I've always loved red. It makes me feel happy. Not that I need a colour to do that for me tonight. I'd be happy whatever colour I was wearing.'

When they reached the landing of the second floor, Nicky

took hold of Anya's hand and led her towards large double doors. He opened them, ushered her inside, and exclaimed, '*Voilà!*'

Anya gasped, truly surprised.

She stood staring at another replica, this time of the sitting room of her house in Provence, the house Hugo had bought for her years ago, and where they had spent so many happy times together. Nicky had used Provençal country furniture, many bright colours reminiscent of the real room, and in doing so had created a perfect copy. Waiters and waitresses, dressed in the local costumes of the area, stood around smiling, ready to serve drinks.

'*Nicky, oh Nicky,*' was all Anya could manage to say as he guided her through the room and into one which adjoined.

Now she found herself in a Russian dacha filled with rustic peasant furniture, and here, to make it completely authentic in mood, were waiters wearing scarlet and gold Cossack tunics, baggy pants tucked into black boots.

She stood stock still, glancing around, trying to take everything in, but Nicky would not let her linger long. He took her hand in his, moving her forward, and into a third room.

Anya was startled, amazed and touched all at the same time, and she experienced a rush of emotion. Here she stood, in the living room where she had grown up in London with her parents. Nicky had re-created it down to the last detail. Tears suddenly sprang into her eyes.

Turning to him, she asked a little tremulously, 'How on earth did you manage this?'

'With your sister's help. Aunt Ekaterina was my marvellous partner in crime, so to speak. She had some old photographs of your parents' living room, which were a great help. But most importantly, she has a photographic memory, and it's not dimmed by age at all.'

'I should hope not!' Anya exclaimed, blinking back her tears, walking around the room, noting the samovar, and the icons on velvet-skirted tables. Nicky had found so many objects similar to the things her mother had owned and loved, and all were arrayed here. There were photographs in old Fabergé frames . . . obviously borrowed from Katti . . . photographs of her parents, the Romanovs, her siblings . . . and of her when she was a young girl. And the colour scheme of pale blue and gold was the one which her mother had so loved. Even the furniture was similar to the pieces she had grown up with.

Slowly, she walked back to Nicky and embraced him. 'Thank you, thank you,' she said, her voice choked. 'Thank you for bringing so many of my very cherished memories to life tonight.'

A waiter rigged out as an English butler came forward with a tray of drinks, and the three of them took flutes of champagne. They clinked glasses and said cheers at the same time, and Nicky added, 'I want you to have the most wonderful evening, Anya.'

'I know I will. What you've done is quite extraordinary.'

He laughed. 'There are still a few surprises in store for you, Anya.'

'I can't believe you can top this! Such as what?' she probed.

'Oh, you'll just have to wait and see,' he teased. 'Now,

where do you want to greet your guests? Which room?'
Nicky asked.

'I'm not sure, darling boy, each room is so very special.'

'Perhaps we should wait in the first room, because everyone enters there,' Maria suggested.

'Good idea, my sweet,' Nicky said and together the three
of them walked back to the Provençal sitting room with its
small tables covered with the cheerful red, green and yellow
tablecloths from Provence. Brown ceramic jugs filled with
tall sunflowers stood on a long sideboard and the scent of
lavender filled the air.

As they entered, one of the waitresses wearing a Provençal
costume came over to them holding a tray, and Anya smiled
when she saw all of her favourite things. Warm piroshki, the
small Russian pastries filled with chopped meat, dollops of
caviar atop tiny baked potatoes, smoked salmon on toast,
and miniature English sausage rolls.

'Well,' she exclaimed, 'I can't resist these. I must sample
one of each.'

'I hoped you would,' Nicky said. 'I'll join you.'

And then a few minutes later the guests began to arrive.

Anya was suddenly surrounded by family.

Her sister and brother-in-law, Katti and Sacha, and all
the Lebedevs, kissing her, congratulating her. And then her
brother Vladimir and his wife Lilli, and their children, so
warm and loving. And behind them came her own children,
Olga and Dimitri, and their families, hugging her, wishing
her a happy birthday, their faces smiling and happy.

After them came the tribe of Sedgwicks, also full of love for her . . . and so many old friends from across the years followed, and the students who had passed through the school and remained close to her for over thirty years or more.

And then at last her special girls.

Her four favourites from the class of '94. Alexa, Jessica, Kay and Maria. How beautiful they all looked as they now walked towards her, escorted by the men in their lives, handsome, elegant in their dinner jackets.

Alexa, Kay and Jessica greeted her, and so did Tom, Ian, and Mark, and then with Nicky the three men stepped back so that she was left alone with the quartet.

'It goes without saying that you all look gorgeous!' Anya exclaimed, beaming at them. 'And before we go any further, I want to thank you all for your gifts. Kay, this shawl is exquisite, I couldn't resist wearing it tonight. And as you see, it's the same red as my gown. And Jessica, the icon is a prize, and it has pride of place in my sitting room. And so does your lacquered box, Alexa. The painting of St Petersburg on its lid is a little jewel. Thank you, thank you.' Anya smiled at Maria, and finished, 'As for your painting, Maria, it is absolutely extraordinary, and it is now hanging in my bedroom. I thank you so much for parting with it.'

Maria blushed and smiled but remained silent.

Anya's eyes swept over them again, and she said softly, in the most intimate of voices, 'I am so happy you all came to Paris early, so that we had time to talk and you had the chance to air your differences and make up. And I can see that you have.'

'It's like old times,' Alexa said. 'We're here for each other. For ever. Through thick and thin. Aren't we, girls?'

They all agreed with her, and Kay said, 'It doesn't seem like seven years at all, only yesterday that we were here at your school, Anya.'

'You taught us so much, brought out and nurtured our talents, helped us to realize our aspirations and our dreams,' Jessica told her. 'You helped to make us what we are, Anya. And for that we'll be forever grateful.'

Anya nodded. 'You all came to Paris for some other reasons as well, I realize that. You had unfinished business . . . each one of you had a quest. And I'm so very happy you found what you were seeking . . .' She looked at Alexa. 'You and Tom got back together . . . permanently?'

Alexa nodded, her face glowing as she showed Anya her left hand. A diamond ring sparkled on it. 'We got engaged tonight. Tom slipped the ring on my finger in the car as we were being driven over here.'

'I'm so happy for you, Alexa darling. He's always been the only man for you.'

Looking closely at Maria, Anya continued, 'And you and Nicky seem to be ideally suited . . .'

'Yes, we are, Anya, and Nicky wants us to marry. When he's free, after he is divorced. And I'm not going back to Milan. I'm going to live in Paris with Nicky, and I'm going to be an artist. No more textile designing for me,' Maria announced.

Anya clapped her hands together softly. 'Thank God for that, Maria. It would be such a waste of your talent if you kept your job at home. And congratulations to you, too. I shall give the wedding for you when you marry. It will be my great pleasure. And Kay, what about you? Everything seems to be working with you and your lovely Ian.'

'It is, Anya, and as I told you, there's nothing wrong with me physically. There's no reason why I can't have a baby.' Kay laughed lightly. 'But Ian doesn't care. He says it's me he wants.'

'And why wouldn't he feel that way? He's a lucky man to have you,' Anya replied. Her eyes rested finally on Jessica, and she noticed yet again that there was still a wistfulness to her, a sadness in her eyes.

'I'm relieved you found Lucien, and that you had a chance to see him, Jessica,' Anya began. 'I know what a shock it was for you, but now I believe you can close this chapter, my dear. Finally, after all these years.'

'Close the book, actually, Anya,' Jessica answered. 'It's not often a person gets a second chance in life . . . but I'm so very lucky because I have Mark. He thinks we have a future together, and I have a feeling he's right.'

'I know he is. And he's a lovely man. Why, they're all lovely men . . .'

A short while after this they all went downstairs to dinner.

Nicky and Maria escorted Anya, and as they led her into the dining room she was unexpectedly blinded by tears.

The room had been transformed into the most beautiful English garden she had ever seen. Masses of flowering plants were banked high around the room. Orange trees in tubs decorated corners. Stone fountains sprayed arcs of shimmering water up into the air. There were stone statues and stone sun dials in strategic places, and bowers and arches of fresh roses entwined with ivy leaves. And each table was skirted in pale pink with low bowls of pink roses in the centre, and votive candles flickered brightly . . . hundreds of tiny lights around the room that added to the magic.

'Oh Nicky,' Anya said, and was unable to say another word. She shook her head and clutched his arm as he led her forward to the main table, where she was to sit with her immediate family. 'Thank you, thank you, darling,' she whispered hoarsely, still choked, as he pulled out her chair for her.

'It was my pleasure, my very great pleasure, Anya,' he said, and moved away, holding Maria's hand as they went to join the others at their table for eight.

I'm so very lucky, a most fortunate woman, Anya thought, as she sipped her water, waiting for the table to fill up with her children and her beloved sister, Katti. What a life I've had. Eighty-five wonderful years. Love and happiness. Pain and suffering. And quite a lot of grief. But I've always come through my troubles. I've endured. Perhaps that's what life is all about. Enduring. Being a survivor.

And my four girls are survivors. After supper was over, Anya turned in her chair. The table next to hers had emptied, and its occupants were on the dance floor . . .

Maria was in Nicky's arms. He was moving her slowly around the room, whispering in her ear.

Kay's head was against Ian's shoulder, her expression dreamy, and he had a look of absolute contentment in his eyes.

Jessica was holding on to Mark very tightly, and her face was no longer quite so sad. She was looking up at him and laughing, her eyes sparkling.

Alexa and Tom were not dancing at all, merely swaying to the music. At one moment he looked down at her, and kissed her lightly on the lips. 'Let's get married as soon as possible,' he said softly. 'I can't wait for you to be my wife. I love you so much.'

'And I love you, Tom. For always,' Alexa said, and she held him closer to her. All she wanted was to share that humdrum life of his, as he called it. She smiled a small, secret smile. Humdrum indeed, she thought.

Anya, still watching them, wished she knew what they were saying to each other. And then she laughed out loud. Of course they were telling each other beautiful things, making promises, making commitments . . . just as she had done so many years ago. First with Michel Lacoste and then with Hugo Sedgwick.

Love, she thought. There's nothing like it in this world. It's the only thing that really matters in the end.